11-1-73

God Save the Commonwealth

The University of Massachusetts Press Amherst 1973

God Save the Commonwealth

An Electoral History of Massachusetts

by Alec Barbrook

Contents

1780623

Preface

British writers who try to present a picture of the American political system tend to look at it from the vantage point of Washington, D.C. From Bryce to Brogan this was especially true and only in the last few years have those of us who speak our English with an English accent dared to compete with American observers of the local political scene. During the middle decades of the twentieth century, even Americans have become more and more seduced by the belief that the states are rapidly declining as an effective unit of government within the federal system. A trend that started with the New Deal was felt to have become so well established by the time of the Great Society that there seemed to be no turning back. Magazine articles with titles like "End of Road in Sight for States" became commonplace as a reflection of a more serious and academic feeling that the federal government was eclipsing the states to such a degree that the latter would soon be little more than an aspect of local government. Had this trend been indicative of the collapse in state power then a growing interest in the role of the states would have seemed a belated and almost antiquarian gesture for local autonomy.

As we slip well into another decade, it would seem that the obituary notices were premature and that the states are likely to retain their position in the federal structure for some time to come. This is not to suggest that the clock should or could be put back to the days when federal power was relatively weak. A whole host of improvements in the quality of American life, from Social Security to the Voting Rights Act of 1965, were brought about at the result of federal rather than state power and it is evident that much of the major innovative character of American government will continue to stem from the federal, rather than state, level. It is also true that the efficiency of the Internal Revenue Service as a tax-gatherer will make for an increasing dependency of the states on Washington as a source of funds for new and existing enterprises. Yet the states are unlikely to become local outlets for the largesse of a centralized government. Even if "creative federalism" is heard less as an oft-quoted shorthand than it was a few years ago, probably because of its association with the last presidential administration, its emphasis on interdependence is not likely to be obscured.

What needs to be modified—and the initiative here rests largely with the individual states—is the received view that all that is innovative and progressive in the best sense of those terms stems from the federal government and that the states can only follow, kicking and screaming, in the wake of Washington. With fifty different states, experiment is possible, differences in approach to political demands inevitable, though, as suggested above, one would not want to stress the potential of the states as individual units as being necessarily greater than the federal whole. Many federal programs in the '60s seemed to proliferate too rapidly for convenient administration from the center and it is likely that these, at least, will need to be administered with a degree of decentralization to be effective; the states have a significant role in this context.

One must not lose sight of the fact that, even at a time when "centralization" was in the air, the states still retained their basic powers as laid down in the Constitution and still disbursed revenue (despite dated tax-gathering mechanisms) which, when combined with the expenditure of the localities, was about the same as the expenditure of the federal government. Many of the "new issues" of the late twentieth century, such as the need to preserve what there is left of a natural and amenable environment, are issues which seem to lend themselves to regional and local initiative, which means that the state will be able to play a major part in political decision-making. Each discrete culture that is an American state is going to make important decisions about, say, pollution in the future—decisions as important as those it is making about local educational facilities at the present, or those it took about bread-and-butter issues like local relief in the 1930s.

When the decision is made to study the system that is an American state, the reasons for choosing one rather than another may be quite fortuitous. In my case, the origin was a curiosity about the effects of the lingering ethnic differences in many northern states. A narrowing down of these effects to the question of voting behavior followed from attendance at an American Studies Seminar at Salzburg, Austria in the summer of 1963. The voting analyst, Louis Bean, helped me to examine presidential voting patterns in the state to the extent of the material that we had available. From this followed the granting of an American Studies Fellowship by the American Council of Learned Societies. This enabled me to spend the academic year 1964-65 at the Political Science Department of MIT, where Dr. Robert Wood, then Chairman of the Department, guided me along the path of Massachusetts state politics. Many people in Massachusetts helped me further on my way, academics, journalists, politicians, even the friends that we made in Boston and its suburbs. One name particularly stands out, that of the late Professor George Blackwood of Boston University. When Robert Wood joined the Johnson administration in 1966, George Blackwood took over the job of reading my manuscript as it rolled off the typewriter. At this stage it was being produced for a Ph.D. degree and from 1966 to 1968 he commented, or criticized, praised and generally helped to put the manuscript into shape. His death in a holiday accident in July 1968 was a great tragedy to all who knew him.

The present revisions are largely my own although my wife Patricia is always there to help with difficult syntax. I would like to thank the secretaries of Rutherford College, University of Kent who typed the manuscript from my handwritten drafts; especial thanks to my former secretary, Miss S. Jain, and the Secretarial Supervisor, Mrs. M. Waring. To our many friends and acquaintances in Massachusetts, we would like to extend thanks for help and hospitality over the years. If one sometimes seems critical of the state, it is perhaps due to a realization of its potential, to what it could, as well as to what it has, become. It is one of the most fascinating states of the Union. The "melting pot" has, happily, not eradicated the diverse characteristics of Yankee, Irishman, Italian, etc. Its capacity for dealing kindly with its citizens is at least as great as the capacity of some of its citizens for behaving in political affairs with an occasional lack of rectitude. At least, its villains have usually been charming villains! As an educated, technically well-equipped community, it has a tremendous potential for a way of life which, despite all the stresses and strains of modern America, is civilized and urbane. Many of the failures in the polital system which showed up in the early 1960s seem to have been partially or completely remedied and the body politic seems a great deal healthier than it seemed ten years ago. This is why one is prepared to echo the peroration found on many official proclamations and heard in the Courts: "God Save the Commonwealth of Massachusetts!"

God Save the Commonwealth

Chapter One
The Bay State Has a History

With a continuous history of settlement dating back to 1620, Massachusetts has a considerable heritage as a political system. Although it has its own special characteristics, it shares much of this heritage with the other five New England states. In geographical and climatic terms, there is certainly something of a unity in the region and this has been bolstered by historic ties, although argument has raged at times over the issue of whether or not to treat the six states as a natural region.[1] The early settlers found poor, rocky soil and a climate more extreme than that of the part of Europe from which they had come; the one great advantage was the lack of prior settlement apart from the indigenous Red Indian. Some of the geographical features, the indented coasts and the river valleys, were to be vital to the economic development of the colony and states in later years of sea-borne commerce and early factory industries.

Rather than the Plymouth landing, the origins of the state are more truly to be found in the establishment of the Massachusetts Bay Colony in 1630. This was the beginning of the "Puritan theocracy, a holy commonwealth . . . . governed by a small ruling class—an aristocracy of the pious."[2] Supervision from the mother country of England was difficult during the seventeenth century when the preoccupation with the constitutional struggles between Crown and Parliament added to the distance over which control had to be exercised. The nature of the theocracy was tempered by a limited form of representative government, some of whose trappings exist to the present day. The Great and General Court, for example, was not originally what it is now, a legislature elected via universal adult suffrage, but was a much closer body, first consisting only of freemen and later of deputies elected by church members.

The Puritan theocracy of the era of the Salem witches and the Mathers, effective as a weapon to create a new civilisation out of the wilderness of the American coast of the seventeenth century, soon gave way to a modified version of this society as the settlements grew larger and especially after the charter of 1691 which attempted to reassert the power of the English Crown. The most effective moderating force was probably to be the growth of commerce in the eighteenth century, a growth which turned the seaports into busy trading and business centers. The Puritan became the Yankee, an Englishman who had suffered a sea-change and whose dislike of royal government had thus been increased. The relatively small groups of non-English stock—French, Scots, Germans, Irish, Welsh—were easily assimilated to produce what Morison has termed "a new Nordic amalgam on an English Protestant base."[3]

One of the root causes of the American Revolution was the separate development of institutions on each side of the Atlantic. In New England, this included a form of "town" government unlike that known in old England. A "town" in New England was not a compact, urbanized area necessarily but could be an area of scattered settlement supporting a school and a meeting-house. In time, the state would be divided into several hundred "towns." "County" government was instituted as early as 1643 in an attempt to decentralize the central government of the colony but it has never developed as a branch of representative government as in England, before or after the Revolutionary Period. However, when the state constitution came to be written, there was no especial provision made for delegating authority to local government and, even when amendment allowed for this, the basic governmental power was reserved to the state.

New towns proliferated in eighteenth century Massachusetts as the economy of the colony flourished. This was the heyday of ports such as Marblehead and Salem, now relatively small centers of population in Eastern Massachusetts. Despite the growth of a more complex economy along the coast, class differentials were still less pronounced than in the Old World and this aided the development of the revolutionary spirit in the colony which might otherwise have flagged, or at least taken a different form. The colony is famous, or perhaps infamous in some quarters, for its role in the American Revolution, a role summarized by the occasional description of the Revolution, as the product of the Adams family of Massachusetts and Lees of Virginia.[4] American historians contrast "the debt-ridden mother country" of 1774 with the "geographically secure, politically mature, prosperous,

dynamic and self-reliant offspring along the Atlantic seaboard."[5]
The result was, in retrospect, inevitable.

Political and economic maturity, converting the colony into a
state, did not mean uniformity of view even when the Tories had
disappeared and the Revolution had triumphed. In fact, the first
polarization of forces came early in the life of the new state in the
arguments about its constitution and that of the Union to which it
belonged. Radicals and conservatives split on a number of issues,
including the desirability of a substantial property qualification
for suffrage purposes and the degree of power held by legislature
and executive respectively. Prior to the Revolutionary War itself,
the colony had been known for its radical fervor and this remained
strong among Boston artisans and rural farmers. The mercantile
middle class of the coastal towns was trying to reassert its right to
lead the polity and to reestablish its economic hegemony over the
new state. Upstate farmers feared that what they considered were
the gains of the Revolution would be lost; one result was Shays'
Rebellion of 1786, soon put down.

The victory of the Conservatives in the 1780s establishes the
pattern of political predominance in the state until well into the
nineteenth century. It also marks the beginnings of regional or
intra-state rivalry although paradoxically, it is the upstate area
which is now regarded as more conservative than the coastal area
due to the social and economic changes of the last century. The
effects of the inflation and the fear of "dear money" were two
principal causes of the agricultural unrest of the years after the
Revolution which made the upstate area restless and which
caused the first drift of farmers westwards.

The rights of property had been enshrined already in the state
constitution of 1780 which is popularly believed to have been one
of the chief models for the federal constitution. As with the later
document, the Massachusetts constitution continued provisions
ensuring the separation of powers, a bicameral legislature, a fairly
effective executive and a bill of rights. With the adoption of both
state and federal constitutions and the emergence of powerful political leaders such as Hancock, Bowdoin and Gerry, Massachusetts
moved out of the colonial period and into a future in which its
economic and political life was bound to flow into new channels.

For nearly forty years following the mid-1780s, political life
was almost dominated by the conservative, centralizing philos-

ophy of the Federalist Party in Massachusetts, "almost" because
there was in fact a two-party system for most of this time with the
Republicans, the Jeffersonian opposition to the Federalists at
national level, making a respectable showing against the dominant
party. The state gave the country its second president in John
Adams, a man who was eventually caught between the cross-
fire coming from the factional politics of these two nascent parties. The national gains made by the Jeffersonians in the early
nineteenth century were only partially reflected in Massachusetts;
the Republicans did not win the governorship until 1808 but after
victories in 1810 and 1811 the party was not again successful at
this level until 1824.[6]

By this time, the Federalists were in rapid decline even in their
comparative stronghold of Massachusetts. The War of 1812, un-
popular in New England, was opposed by the Federalists and
threw them back on the four or five states where they retained
local organizational strength, although it is sometimes argued
that the Jeffersonian Republicans came to accept the principles
of the defeated party such as centralization, support for manufacturing interests and the emphasis on a strong, national system
of government.[7] John Quincy Adams, the second Massachusetts
man to become president, was identified with the Republican
Party but, as the last of the "dynastic" presidents, he presided
over a transition to a new two-party system when the majority of
Republican supporters moved into the camp labelled "National
Republican" and, in the 1830s, "Whig." They were opposed by
the new "Democratic" party, composed of the minority of Republicans and Federalists who disliked Adams.[8] In the state, the
new two-party arrangement led to a Whig dominance but with a
healthy Democrat challenge by the mid-1830s.

In terms of population, the state grew from 378,787 (excluding
the Maine territory) at the time of the first census in 1790 to 523,
287 in 1820, a rate of growth of about five thousand people a
year, though the rate of growth of the urban population in the
same period was even faster, for it doubled from 51,202 to
119,187.[9] It remained a community framed in the Puritan mold,
its edges now softened by time, and the relatively small numbers
of a racial origin other than the Anglo-Saxon were easily absorbed. Away from the coast where the larger towns thrived and
the sea was a major economic factor, the farm remained the
norm, its occupants wresting a living from the difficult terrain.

As the anonymous writer of a monograph on Franklin County puts it:

Areas too steep for plowing were used for sheep-grazing and settlers became adept at animal-husbandry and walking up-hill.[10]

This contrasted with the great prosperity that could be garnered from a major participation in the shipping industry which had now grown into the great days of the "China trade." Ships from Boston, Salem and Newburyport brought in the varied treasures and manufactures of the greater part of the world, shipbuilding yards proliferated along the indented coastline, merchants and masters made profits that were translated into forms of gracious living. It was this "mercantile–shipping–financial interest" that threw its weight behind the Federalists and which resented the interruption to trade that the national government brought about by the war of 1812, an interruption more honored in the breach than in the observance.[11] After the period of the war and the abortive Hartford Convention, there appeared a few signs that heralded the long decline of the shipping industry and:

The center of interest in Massachusetts shifts from wharf to waterfall; by 1840 she had become predominantly a manufacturing state.[12]

Unlike the country as a whole, but like the English experience, the textile industry was the main stimulant which brought Massachusetts into the industrial period. The protective tariff, which made it more profitable to invest in industry than in shipping, and the natural advantage of the river valleys such as the Merrimack led to the establishment of textile towns, the archetype of which was the one named after Francis Cabot Lowell. At first, Lowell recruited its labor force from the daughters of the farmers of New England, especially the northern states, though from the 1840s industrial depression and increased farming migration to the West led to their gradual replacement by Irish girls.[13] Lowell and its sister town of Lawrence were model mill towns at first but eventually they became "models" of what has since been described as an "immigrant city".[14]

Other towns soon contained mills, machine shops and other diverse centers of manufacture. Springfield, Worcester and other upstate towns grew as a result of the rise of industrial enterprise. On the coast, as the waterfronts experienced a relative decline, ports turned to industry to survive. Boston not only prevented her trade from major slippage by capturing that of Salem, Plymouth and other ports, but soon boasted industries as diverse as clothing manufacture, sugar refining, glassmaking and shoemaking. When Daniel Webster, United States Senator from 1827 to 1841 and from 1845 to 1850, one of the major spokesmen for state and region, "seceded to high protection in 1828," it was one of the first signs of the shifting economic interests of the state, for Webster, depending on the support of financial interests, was moving to keep up with the times.[15]

Andrew Jackson's two terms in the White House helped to consolidate the antagonism to the Democrats felt by the major political factions in the state. Webster became the principal Whig spokesman in the Northeast after the emergence of the party in in the mid-1830s. The Massachusetts Whigs, as well as the Democrats, were opposed by radical movements based on the urban working class which emerged as a result of industrialization, but few serious inroads were made into the Whig hold on the machinery of the state and on the production of the state's electoral votes for Whig presidential candidates. Martin Van Buren, elected nationally as Jackson's successor in 1836, achieved 44.82% of the popular vote in the state against Webster's command of the remainder, but this was not to be repeated by a Democratic presidential candidate until Cleveland's 45.19% in 1892. Quite obviously, the Whigs must have attracted a good percentage of the vote of the working-men and this was undoubtedly due to the relatively good conditions in the early factories and the relatively mild nature of Whiggish conservatism.

By the time of Daniel Webster's death in 1852, the Whigs were in a state of rapid decline, aided by the splits caused by the slavery issue. Between 1848 and 1860, crucial years in the political history of the state, the parties were again in the "melting pot." The coalition between Free Soilers and Democrats after the state election of 1850 led to the election of Charles Sumner to the Senate by the General Court and, although the Whigs made something of a comeback when they defeated the new constitution of 1853, carrying off the governorship (as was customary) and reasserting their majority in the General Court, these were their last effective victories. After the brief successes of the

Know-Nothings, or nativists, the Republican Party, born in the mid-West in 1854, soon established itself in Massachusetts with presidential votes well above 60% for Fremont in 1856 and for Lincoln in 1860. The Civil War was to inaugurate a long dominance of Massachusetts politics by the Republican Party, one that would only be challenged by the culmination of trends that were barely out of their birth pangs at the time of the War between the States.

The brief dominance of the state government in the mid-1850s by the nativists was partially due to the beginning of the reaction against the increase of immigration from Ireland in the preceding few years. Instead of using the state as a stepping-stone to the frontier, the waves of Irish fleeing from the fungus which invaded the Irish potato fields in 1845 and ruined the one-crop peasant economy just managed to make the New World and:

> . . . once in Boston, they could not go elsewhere because poverty deprived them of the means and despondence of the desire.[16]

At first, the Boston conscience was pricked and an Irish Relief Society was set up which sent food and clothing to the unfortunate island.[17] Then the flood into Boston began and from the summer of 1847 to that of 1848, it is estimated that 37,000 immigrants, mostly Irish, arrived, a number equal to almost a third of those living in the city in the mid-1840s.[18] Professor Handlin estimates the Irish famine settlement in Boston by 1855 as approximately 50,000.[19] As the lowest strata of society, their living conditions were appalling; the death rate among these immigrants in 1850 was one in nineteen as compared to one in forty for the general population.[20] As they spread through the less attractive residential areas of Boston and the neighboring towns, the men taking the most menial jobs, the women often entering domestic service, a nativist dislike of the "foreigner" developed, a wedge between Yankee and Irishmen which remained for many generations.

The 1850s was an especially confusing period in the party politics of Massachusetts as in many another state of the Union. As well as the death of one party and the birth of another, the nativist reaction referred to above and the emergence of Free Soilers like Charles Sumner had made for a fluid situation where even flirtation between Democrats and the Free Soil men had briefly taken place in the early '50s until the Democratic administration in Washington managed to squash it.[21] With the rapid rise of the Republicans to power in the state, the Democrats had little opportunity to exploit the possibilities of gaining a majority position and the outbreak of war in 1861 made this impossible. Massachusetts became heavily committed to the Northern cause and even Democratic leaders found it expedient in the main to support the Union.

The Civil War is a convenient watershed for noting the shift in the position of the state vis-à-vis the continental United States. As one of the thirteen revolting colonies at the time of the American Revolution, the state, at least, almost dominates the early history of the rebellion. By the late nineteenth century, it was one of a much larger number of states, thirty-seven with the admission of Nebraska in 1867, forty-five with the admission of Utah near the end of the century (1896). In the century 1790-1890, although the total population of the state increased sixfold, it dropped as a percentage of the national population from about ten to about four percent. The "center of gravity" of the country tended to move away from New England in terms of the main communications networks and the increasing economic importance of other areas. Yet Massachusetts remained a leading manufacturing state, a center of learning and culture and, of course, a bulwark of the dominant Republican political spirit during the remainder of the century.

Some observers were beginning to note the transformation in the composition of the population of the state, which two later historians summarized as "this stupendous, if silent, conquest of Massachusetts by Babel."[22] The Irish invasion, which had helped to lift the figures of "foreign-born" in some Massachusetts towns and cities to levels such as that of Boston (62%) and Lawrence (72%) by 1855 slowed, but then a dramatic shift took place by the last decade of the century. Changing political and economic circumstances in southern and eastern Europe, together with the labor shortage endemic in the American economy, meant that new arrivals hoping to settle in the Northeast were more likely to have come from Italy, Russia and eastern Europe than the more Nordic part of the Continent. By 1915, Chelsea (bordering Boston) had a foreign-born population of 36,000 (mostly Jewish) out of a total of 43,000 and some other urban areas showed a similar pattern.[23]

From the end of the Civil War to the early years of the twentieth century, the political history of Massachusetts is still very much the history of the Yankee community with few instances of intrusion from these "newer races." The political history of the Yankee community is largely that of the Republican Party for it retained the governorship in relatively unbroken line from the time of the War until the early years of the twentieth century (1905) with the exception of the years 1874-5, 1883-4 and 1891-94. The General Court was firmly in the hands of the party, the U.S. Senate seats remained so until 1918 and the only time that the percentage of the Republican vote for their presidential candidate dipped below fifty percent before the Bull Moose election of 1912 was in 1884 when Ben Butler's Greenback candidature took 8.05% but still left the state's electoral votes in the column for Blaine.[24]

The Butler candidacy was one of the few really radical challenges that the Republican leadership, bereft of most of its early crusading zeal, met in these years. Butler was a flamboyant apostate, a Democrat before the War, not a particularly competent general during it, by which time he sided with the Republican defenders of the Union, and a second-time apostate in 1880 when he returned to the Democratic fold. He had swung from a defense of slavery before the War to a pro-Negro position during and after it; he was also one of the chief Radical Republican prosecutors of the unsuccessful impeachment of President Andrew Johnson. By the 1880s, he was "a stench in Republican nostrils," particularly in his native state.[25] He was a reforming governor in 1883, appointing the first Irish-American to judicial office.[26] Perhaps the main interest today in Benjamin Franklin Butler's career is his appeal to the growing coalition of dissident groups, chief among them being the veterans of the War, the Irish and the industrial workers.[27]

In the presidential election of 1884, when Grover Cleveland faced James Blaine, Butler considered Cleveland too respectable for the Democrats, yet at the same time that he defected from the Democrats, the Republican Independents or "Mugwumps" bolted from Blaine whom they considered to be the enemy of reform and campaigned for Cleveland whom they knew to be more sympathetic to their ideals of good government. Following this election, the Mugwumps attempted to work with the Democratic party in the state, giving it the appearance of a dichotomous body of Yankee reformers allied with the Irish work-

ing class led by "respectable" Irishmen like Patrick Collins and
Hugh O'Brien, though nonetheless hungry for patronage and
recognition. The alliance was at its height during the period when
William Russell held the governorship for the Democrats for
three years, a feat unprecedented since the War. But the gold-and
-silver controversy which came to a head again in 1896 and the
eventual nomination of Bryan at the National Convention in
Chicago split away most of the Mugwumps and destroyed the
influence of "Cleveland Democrats" for good.[28]

As a manufacturing state, Massachusetts was vitally interested
in the economic debates of the '90s, revolving chiefly around the
tariff and bimetallism. After the Democratic failure in the 1896
presidential election and the end of the "Cleveland Era," Democratic fortunes in Massachusetts slumped once more; in the
presidential years 1896 and 1900, for example, the party returned
only one of their number to the state's delegation to the U.S.
House of Representatives.[29] The Republicans now courted
groups such as the prohibitionists and the nativist American
Protective Association and, by the end of the century, were in as
strong a position as ever, one of their new senators, Henry Cabot
Lodge, occupying a position on the national scene as powerful
as Massachusetts statesmen of the past.

In 1900, the Census showed that Massachusetts was eighty-six
percent "urban," a high figure when one remembers that, even by
1960, the U.S.A. was only about seventy per cent "urban." Its
leading citizens were proud of the wave of enactments that put the
state in the vanguard of the fields of public health, labor legislation, civil service reform, and pure food laws, and in the responsibility of its legislative procedures.[30] Yet the strains and stresses
of this industrial society were far from overcome by piecemeal
legislation. As well as the strains of industrialization, the flood of
immigration from southern and eastern Europe introduced new
divisive possibilities into an already fragmented society. The
legacy left to twentieth–century Massachusetts was a complex
political culture, one that would be only slowly modified by the
social and economic changes that lay ahead. To a Yankee like
Henry Adams, writing a few years later but looking back on this
period, it must have seemed that the dangers of the collapse of
the old civilization were very real, as his gloomy summary of the
position suggests:

New power was disintegrating society, and setting up indepen-
dent centres of force to work, until money had all it could do to
hold the machine together. No one could represent it faithfully
as a whole.[31]

Massachusetts society has not disintegrated during the twentieth century although it has been under considerable stress. The
signs of the consequent political changes were there well before
the nineteenth century ended—for example, Suffolk County
(Boston plus three small neighboring towns) went Democratic
in presidential elections from 1876 onwards.[32] Although the
results of the changes of the last seventy years may have been
mixed, in many ways they have made the state a better place to
live in than it was seventy years ago.

Chapter Two
The "Melting-Pot" Boils Over

Up to the mid-1960s at least, the twentieth century has treated the United States fairly well if the comparison is made with the other major industrialized powers of the world. The increasing tension of the last few years may suggest that internal problems are intensifying, but most optimistic observers would give the country more than an even chance of pulling out of these in the foreseeable future. Looking backwards, it is true that the country has weathered the Great Depression and two World Wars plus at least two "minor" ones, if Korea and Vietnam can be said to be "minor." Yet its political system has been relatively untouched in its fundamentals by any of these experiences. At the same time, there have been many areas of underlying tension apart from those caused by the disturbances stemming from economic and international crisis. One of these was the "dilution" of Anglo-Saxon America by the newer waves of immigrants, a process slowed down by the Quota Acts, though not entirely halted.

The immigration patterns that evolved in the late nineteenth century and continued into the twentieth laid the groundwork for the emergence of "ethnic politics," significant in electoral appeals ever since. A few years ago, Daniel Patrick Moynihan could still note that:

> It is striking that in 1963, almost forty years after mass immigration from Europe to this country ended, the ethnic pattern is still so strong in New York City.[1]

Eastern Massachusetts especially, but the whole state generally1, has rivalled New York in the intensity of the effect of ethnic groups on politics. In the halcyon days of complete Republican domination, Massachusetts was imbued with what is termed the Anglo–Saxon "ethos" or "ethic."[2] This took its cue from that group of educated, prosperous Yankees who looked upon politics as a species of personal responsibility. Henry Cabot Lodge, Sr., suggested that the Brahmins had given the state "honesty, efficiency, prosperity and progress."[3] Another old-stock Yankee active in civic affairs in Boston early in the twentieth century, James Jackson Storrow, who believed that a successful banker could also be a highly useful citizen, "was ready to make the experiment of giving as much as twenty percent of his time to public service" at one stage of his career as a senior member of the finance house of Lee, Higginson and Company.[4] Whatever one may think of the policies favored by many of the Republican leaders prior to World War I there is little doubt of their belief that Yankee sobriety, honesty and application were essential commitments for a New England political system.

From a fairly early date, some of the Brahmins recognized that they preserved what was, in their eyes, a very special heritage that could be easily dissipated. Senator Hoar wrote to Cabot Lodge in 1883 that:

> *Unless we can break this compact foreign vote, we are gone and the grand chapter of the old Massachusetts history is closed.*[5]

Because of their relatively small numerical base, the Brahmins, the Yankee upper crust, could not provide recruits for all of the echelons of the Republican leadership. "Swamp Yankees" (i.e. those without any claims to colonial lineage), assimilated Anglo-Canadians, English immigrants, and Northeast Europeans generally were prominent among the minor leadership and the rank-and-file workers for the party. It was certainly not impossible for those lacking that most useful combination of wealth and family background to rise from the ranks. An East Bostonian, John L. Bates, achieved some success in opposing the leadership circa 1900, but when he was elected lieutenant governor in that year, he appears to have been "assimilated" by the leadership, moving up the so-called "escalator" to the governorship in 1903. Bates had a degree of lineage but no money or social position.[6] More typical of the Republican leaders of this period were Winthrop Murray Crane, Berkshire paper manufacturer, governor for the first three years of this century and later U.S. senator for nine years; Curtis Guild, Jr., Anglophile newspaperman, governor from 1906 to 1908; Eben S. Draper, Hopedale cotton manufacturer and governor after Guild.[7] These men shared power in the state party with Lodge; they all had the essential combination of colonial descent and money made or inherited from Massachusetts industry. Both Lodge and Crane were vari-

ously regarded as "boss" of the machine, but Lodge, aided by his
long tenure in the Senate and the seven-year presidency of his
friend Theodore Roosevelt, made more of a mark on the national scene than Crane. His cold, aloof manner could not entirely hide his political skill. Nicholas Murray Butler wrote of
him:

> . . . he was able, vain, intensely egotistical, narrow-minded,
> dogmatic and provincial. For him Pittsfield, Massachusetts
> represented the Farthest West except on the quadrennial oc-
> casions when he was willing to cross the state boundary to
> attend a Republican National Convention.[8]

This self-confident élite, though aware of the growing pressures from the immigrant groups, especially the Irish, felt that
they could offset the immigrants by making inroads among
groups like the French-Canadians.[9] In fact, this élite did not
adapt fast enough to meet either the changing ethnic makeup of
the state or the new economic needs of the unfolding century.
Periodic recoveries have been made, sometimes quite amazing
ones, but the roots of the élites' electoral decline can be seen even
in the early years of the century when a lowered majority for the
gubernatorial election of 1903 could be pinpointed by a later
commentator as the Republicans "heading for the political
toboggan."[10]

The confidence of the Republican Party in the early part of this
century was upheld by the state of the opposition, the Massachusetts Democratic Party of that period. Sporadic successes always took it by surprise, and the air of being an underdog on the
part of all Democrats in the region prompted one newspaper
correspondent to conclude that "the average New England Democrat doesn't expect his reward in this world."[11] The silver issue
gradually declined in importance, though "Bryan men" were
nominated on the state ticket in the closing years of the old century. Eventually Bryan's third defeat in 1908 took most of the
heat out of the issue. Since the northeast working men had been
affected by propaganda suggesting that "free silver" would mean
lower wages and unemployment, the gradual disappearance of
the issue tended to lead to a reassertion of support for Democratic candidates.

Bryanite George Fred Williams, the most prominent personality in the Democratic Party at the turn of the century, lost

ground along with the silver issue identified with him. Because of its lack of money and adequate organization, the Massachusetts Democratic Party of the early 1900s was susceptible to rich sponsors who would swap large injections of finance for the party nomination for high office. One of these, shoe manufacturer William Douglas, did oust the incumbent Republican Governor Bates in the 1904 election, when Bates was out of favor with the Republican leadership and support of him was therefore tepid. The pendulum swung back to its usual gubernatorial position in the following year with another Republican victory, but the beginning of ultimate long-term Democratic inroads were already there if one looked for the omens.

One would, or should, have looked at the larger towns and cities of the Commonwealth, especially Boston. Its experience was not unique but was shared by the mill towns and other industrial centers. Small towns in the Berkshires, Cape Cod and elsewhere sometimes had groups of recent immigrants, but these might be relatively small or perhaps were not especially politically conscious like the Portuguese of southeastern Massachusetts, itinerant fishermen and their descendants, with a political impact that has always been minimal. Of the mill towns, one could instance Lawrence which had an Irish Catholic "machine" as early as the 1880s run by John Breen and which, by 1912 and the I.W.W. strike which catapulted the town into the newspaper headlines, counted 74,000 of its 86,000 inhabitants as foreign-born or with foreign-born parents. Cole writes:

> . . . the Irish, once the despised shanty dwellers of 1850,
> were now in complete control of the city's politics and were
> in many ways indistinguishable from the natives.[12]

Holyoke, Massachusetts' "Paper City" was under the political control of a young Irish cigar salesman named James Connelly in the 1890s, until evidence of political corruption aroused the Yankee paper manufacturers sufficiently to ally with some of the Irish ward bosses amenable to their persuasions and a reform administration was temporarily installed. This was not long-lived, the industrialists lost interest and from about 1910 to the 1930s Holyoke was run by a group of Irish and French-Canadian politicians known as the "Gas and Electric machine" because of its patronage base in the municipally-owned Gas and Electric Company.[13]

Despite these and other examples, it is Boston that has become identified with a stereotype of Irish-American politics based on factual and fictional accounts of the city's political life in the first half of the twentieth century, a period when colorful and unscrupulous characters vied with each other for the Boston vote. In the beginning of the century, the city exercised a dominant position in state politics, not only because it was the state capital, but because it contained twenty percent of the population of Massachusetts. Today, the figure has dropped to about thirteen percent although the cities and towns of Greater Boston contain just about one half of the state's population.[14] Because of its size and its crucial position in the economic life of New England, Boston has always been highly visible in the political affairs of state and region—the "Hub"—and its brand of politics, perhaps not unique but seemingly highly individual, compresses many of the features of ethnic-flavored politics into one small sub-system.

The tension between a heavily urbanized "downstate" and a much more agrarian and, in population terms, dispersed "upstate" is evident in many states of the Union. Where, as also often happens, the diffenence in "life-style" is exacerbated by contrasts in religion and ethnic origin, then the resulting divisions make for an inevitable lack of sympathy between the two groups, rooted in mistrust and misunderstanding. Tensions can also exist in the city itself between immigrants and old-stock Americans. The Yankees of urban and rural areas found it difficult to appreciate the acculturation problems of the immigrants, particularly those from southern and eastern Europe, whose language and cultural baggage were so alien to the American way of living. Self-help, thrift and hard work had enabled earlier generations of Americans to establish themselves and eventually to prosper. It was difficult for the Yankee to appreciate the barriers that made this climb from the ethnic ghetto difficult in ways that his ancestors had not known (the analogy between white and black in present-day America is obvious here).

In a city such as Boston, the only helping hand that immigrants could turn to in a welfare-less America of the turn of the century was the so-called "machine." The immigrant was discriminated against economically and ethnically. The social stratification was evident though different to what he had known in Europe; material goals were soon absorbed but the means to obtain them were lacking.[15] To fill the vacuum, the urban machine provided a minimum of services in return for payment in terms of votes. It has been a remarkably persistent organism in twentieth-century politics, even if it is now obsolete. Robert Merton suggested the reasons for this in his famous analysis of the functions of the machine:

> *Any attempt to eliminate an existing social structure without providing adequate alternative structures for fulfilling the functions previously fulfilled by the abolished organization is doomed to failure.*[16]

The machine form of city politics has only eroded bit by bit, as the need for it disappears.

The essence of the urban machine was the combination of a personal relationship between boss and voter with the use of patronage and less attractive devices to keep the nominees of the boss in positions of political power. In Massachusetts, there have been instances of sharp practice by some political leaders going back to the early days after the Revolution, as with the profiteering by Harrison Gray Otis over the building of the State House.[17] The occasional example could have been written off as an extreme example of Yankee astuteness but the relative frequency of cycles of corruption made public in modern Massachusetts political history would not allow the more recent generations of political leaders any comparable excuse. Bryce blamed the failings of American urban government on the immigrants and the reluctance of able citizens to engage in politics and Lincoln Steffens laid the blame on businessmen.[18] Another line of explanation accentuates the cumbersome machinery of the American city with the inevitable reliance on patronage to make it run a little more smoothly.[19]

Adding all of these together, one can see that almost all of the actors and the institution of the city government itself have come under fire at one time or another. In fact, if one spreads the net a little wider, one might suspect that features common to all levels of American government at state and local levels must be conducive to the occasional wave of corruption in a particular area and probably to persistent small-scale corruption in most units of government below the federal level.

Boston politics at the turn of the century was heavily infiltrated by the styles described above, the boss and the machine working at ward level. Pat Maguire was the first of the "bosses" to create anything like a citywide hegemony but after his death control of Democratic policy, as far as any group could control it, reverted to the group known as the "Board of Strategy." Among them were both the maternal and paternal grandfathers of John Fitzgerald Kennedy: Pat Kennedy was boss of East Boston; John F. Fitzgerald, after graduating from insurance salesman to politician, controlled the North End, that area on the north tip of the Boston peninsular which had been a predominantly Irish quarter between 1850 and 1880 but which was already becoming what it is today, heavily Italian in complexion.[20]

Ranged against the power of this group was one "lone wolf" in Democratic politics, Martin Lomasney, whose base was the Hendricks Club in the West End, a club named for Thomas A. Hendricks, Cleveland's first vice-president and a man noted for his sympathy for Irish immigrants.[21] The club acted as an elite group within the ward (Eight, later redistricted first to Five and then to Three), and Lomasney could swing the vote of elite and rank-and-file in a uniform way behind any candidate he chose. His techniques included demagogy outstripping any revivalist preacher and the choice of lieutenants who represented the ethnic groups among his polyglot following. As a politician, and despite his use of all the tricks of the ward boss, he seems to have impressed a variety of people including Lincoln Steffens who admired his frank admission of the boss-client relationship, one which echoes the Merton thesis that machine politics filled a need, a function of the system, that no other structure did at that time. Lomasney is supposed to have said to Steffens:

> *I think that there's got to be in every ward somebody that any bloke can come to—no matter what he's done—and get help. Help, you understand; none of your law and justice, but help.* [22]

This seems to glorify Lomasney as some sort of secular priest, but in fact he was a tough politician. Until his death in 1933 he remained a power in his ward by use of tight organization, an awareness of his own limitations (he had no amibitons for high office himself), and a shrewd knowledge of the basic needs of his constituents—"food, clothing and shelter." His view was that:

A politician in a district such as mine sees to it that his people get these things. If he does, he hasn't got to worry about their loyalty and support.[23]

Politicians without Lomasney's shrewdness, men whose ambitions ran ahead of their abilities by greater lengths than was usual, often ended up with less real power than he had. John F. Fitzgerald did become mayor of Boston but failed to win either the governorship or a seat in the U.S. Senate, both of which he coveted. Fitzgerald is sometimes presented as a genial, or even comic, Irishman but some contemporaries saw him otherwise:

He was a bouncing, dapper man, so much so that one tended to overlook at first the narrow mouth, the eyes a little too close together, the reedy voice pitched just a little too high.[24]

As mayor, Fitzgerald did not live up to the standards of the city's first two Irish mayors, Hugh O'Brien and Patrick Collins. Elected in 1905, he was unseated by Republican George Hibbard in 1907, by which time he was under attack from the newly formed Finance Commission or "Fin. Comm." and the other new scourge for Boston mayors, The Good Government Association or "Goo Goos." In 1909, under the new charter which substituted a strong for a weak mayoral system (backed by reformers and by Fitzgerald, the latter seeing in it a way to outflank other Democratic bosses), Fitzgerald again emerged as a candidate and eventually faced the Yankee Democrat, banker J.J. Storrow, noted for his philanthropy, ability and honesty.[25] The reformers hoped that the 1909 election would produce a new-style administration which would curtail the powers of the ward bosses; Fitzgerald saw it as a means of depressing their powers but in such a way as to make him the political kingpin of Boston.

Since the election was nonpartisan, it was fought not on party lines, but on ethnic, religious and class divisions. Fitzgerald's victory was a close one, but the trend was unmistakeable and a analysis of the result has shown that there was a high correlation between the "native-born" and the Storrow vote as there was between the "foreign stock" and the Fitzgerald vote.[26] At this time, some 79% of Boston residents were either foreign-born or of foreign-born or mixed ancestry, and at least half of the residents had Irish ancestors.[27] Fitzgerald's support came especially from those wards where working-class immigrants were predominant; in one ward (Nine) where there was a high-concentration of native-stock working-class voters, Storrow received 54% of the vote.[28]

Reformers, such as Storrow and Lincoln Filene, may have been discouraged by this result, but it did mark the beginning of the end for the "ward boss." In the history of American city politics, the ward boss has often been replaced by the citywide "boss" and men like Fitzgerald and, perhaps, James Michael Curley seem to have had this as a goal. However, it has never been easy for one man to control votes in Boston, perhaps because of the mercurial, feuding nature of the Boston Irish, reluctant to be led and, when led, easily tempted by an alternative leader. This style of politics is often termed "feudal" by observers and it is, curiously, "feudal" in the sense that term was used in Ireland rather than elsewhere in Europe, that is, not hierarchical but dependent on local chieftains, self-styled "kings" who were easily toppled from power. Whether or not there are elements of folk memory in this use of the phrase, few would deny that one of the chief characteristics of Massachusetts Democratic politics in the twentieth century was a lack of identifiable and lasting hierarchy and a frequent shifting of allegiance by all but close lieutenants of the competing leaders.

Certainly, James Michael Curley came nearer to attaining the position of "boss" of Boston than any other politician, including Fitzgerald, before him and perhaps more than any since the time of his ascendancy. Even more than that, he came close to breaking out of the bounds of ethnic-based Boston politics but in the end he remained a transitional figure, one who succeeded in breaking the power of the ward bosses without putting any moderate ideological or pragmatic base to the nature of urban politics as practiced in eastern Massachusetts. His power remained personal and rarely could he transfer his support among the voters to a candidate other than himself. He represented much of the resentment of the Boston Irish faced with the closed world of the Yankees and his political success epitomized the breaking down of certain of the economic, if few of the social, barriers yet in time his political techniques came to appear uncouth in the eyes of the younger generations of Irish-Americans.

One cannot defend the graft that took place during his terms as mayor, even though both sides might rationalize their motives;

the givers, often businessmen, as a means of carrying on legitimate business under obsolete regulation; the takers, like Curley and his aides, as a means of obtaining a fair return on effort plus resources in terms of jobs and welfare to satisfy his constituents. It should have been possible for both sides to see that "good government," the needs of the underprivileged and even a healthy salary for the mayor were not incompatibilities. Curley's near contemporary, Al Smith of New York, did bridge the gap between envy and achievement in much of his career and is remembered as a more noble example of Irish aspiration than Curley. As the latter's chief biographer notes:

> *Curley had accepted the system as he found it. It was his ambition to master it, not reform it. What other ward leaders had done, he would do in a larger way, even on a magnificent scale. He had vision and inventiveness. Greater skill would come in time.*[29]

Curley's record of victories and defeats in his long political career was impressive. From city councillor to alderman, from state representative to congressman, from Mayor to Governor of Massachusetts, the line extrapolated almost to the U.S. Senate but in that instance he was defeated by Henry Cabot Lodge in 1936. He also suffered defeat twice for the governorship and no less than six times for the mayoralty (which he won on four occasions). His two terms in prison are not as ominous as they seem, for on the first occasion he impersonated a constituent at a Civil Service examination and on the second he was involved in a mail fraud in which he was more gullible than criminal.

Curley epitomized the last stage of bossism—he was not a backroom politician but an active candidate who used his office, when in power, to patronize the voter in terms of jobs, improved facilities and such personal services that would attract increased support from his natural base among the Irish and the other immigrant groups. The city was always a hive of activity when he was mayor and the money spent on construction could always be "tapped" for the amounts needed to keep the personal organization running smoothly. Boston city politics have never been quite as swashbuckling since his decline and eventual death. His immediate successors were either functionaries or pale imitations of the Curley style. At the end, he became dated and crude, a political dinosaur romanticized in fact and fiction, but lacking the finesse and skills needed in a more complex urban age.

Although the patterns of Boston-style politics seemed to dominate Massachusetts in the early part of this century, this is largely illusory since a great deal of power was wielded from outside the city, even in the Democratic Party itself. If Curley is a useful archetype of the Boston style, David Ignatius Walsh is as effective an example of the contrasting type in Democratic politics, representing as he does the edging of many Irish families into the middle class and sharing few of Curley's more intense antagonisms for the dominant Yankees. Walsh seemed highly respectable and kept aloof from the excesses of machine politics. A bachelor lawyer, free of scandal until an incident at the end of his political career, his solid presence seemed to epitomize the values being acquired by the "lace curtain Irish." From a start in the Great and General Court, he rose to achieve the double distinction of being the first Irish Catholic to occupy the governor's chair and then the first Democratic senator to be sent by Massachusetts to Congress since the Civil War. Because of his place in the state's politics in the early twentieth century, it is often suggested that a "Walsh revolution" pre-dated the "Al Smith revolution."[30]

Walsh's professional base was in Fitchburg, a paper-making and textile town near the New Hampshire border with a large foreign-born population in which French-Canadians and Finns loomed even larger than Irish. He was therefore more typical of "upstate" attitudes to politics, less radical and welfare-oriented when concerned with questions of distribution of material things and equally conservative about "moral" and foreign policy issues as the Boston Irish. This combination gave him a broader based of support than leaders of the Fitzgerald or Curley type and, in particular, allowed him that long stint in the U.S. Senate from 1919 to 1946 with only one two-year break. He often succeeded when Democratic fortunes were at a low ebb and for a brief time in the early 1930s appeared to be perhaps the most powerful politician in the state. This was a time when he worked closely with the Yankee Democrat Governor Ely. Once Roosevelt came to power, he never seemed to occupy this position again, perhaps because of his support of Al Smith in 1932.[31]

Men like Walsh, and for that matter Ely, were more acceptable

outside the Boston area because of the general suspicion that
Democrats and Republicans alike who lived out of the metropolitan area had for the city's political style. Of course, because
of the tendency for both parties to have easily discernible social
bases, this was mainly a suspicion that the predominantly rural
and small town Republicans had for the predominantly urban
Democrats. The Republicans had their urban "bosses," such as
Charles Innes in Boston, and as late as 1940 a Republican "boss"
in Boston's Ward Twenty-one was in the public eye for a conviction on charges of income tax evasion.[32] In the early years of
the century, industrial centers such as New Bedford, Brockton
and Lynn were still Republican strongholds, but this changed as
the century wore on.

Although the Democratic Party was attracting colorful, and
occasionally able, leaders in the early twentieth century, it was
still distinctly the minority party in the state. The Republican
position as the dominant party tended to make it the more likely
prey for factional offshoots as the Mugwump period showed.
Third-party movements as such have not tended to make much
headway in the state in the last hundred years. On only one
occasion did a genuine third-party movement occur which
posed a real threat to the two main parties at state level. This
was in 1912 when the progressives in the Republican Party
across the country, having become disillusioned with William
Howard Taft as President, turned to Theodore Roosevelt in
the hope that he could recapture the party and the presidency.
When the first part of that equation failed, many of them followed him into the "Bull Moose" wing which took on the trappings of the Progressive Party for a battle against Taft and
Democrat Woodrow Wilson.

In Massachusetts, progressive rumblings had been evident for
some years and had been capitalized upon by Eugene Foss,
the Democratic candidate in the gubernatorial election of 1910,
enabling him to overturn incumbent Eben S. Draper and win
the governor's chair with 52% of the total vote, even taking several
cities (Worcester, Taunton, Northampton) normally safe for the
GOP.[33] In 1911, progressive Republicans, annoyed that the
chair remained in the hands of Democrat, if ex-Republican,
Foss, looked for a candidate they could support under the banner
of a newly-formed Progressive Republican League of Massachusetts. They lighted upon Charles Sumner Bird, paternalistic

manufacturer and ex-Mugwump, but when he ran, in 1912 and 1913, he came third to the candidates of the regular parties. In the former year, not only did he trail behind Theodore Roosevelt (who attained a respectable 29% in the three-cornered fight) but he did badly in districts heavily populated by the foreign-born and fared well only in "traditional Republican areas, primarily in eastern Massachusetts."[34]

After this, Wilson took over much of the Progressive Party platform but, in Massachusetts, the Progressives drifted back into the Republican Party finding, like the Mugwumps in a slightly different context, little in common with the increasingly Irish-led Democrats. The "progressive spirit" did not entirely die at this point and its particular brand of what might be termed "patrician radicalism" has tended to reappear from time to time in the twentieth century.

The Progressives did achieve a few minor successes on their way back into the Republican fold. One was the calling of a constitutional convention (1917-1919) which they hoped would lead to a measure of direct democracy, based on such provisions as a unicameral legislature, proportional representation and compulsory voting. The Legislature, having turned a deaf ear to the call for a convention at the time of Walsh's gubernatorial term, agreed during the term of his successor, Republican Samuel W. McCall, and in part, at least, this was a move to placate the progressive wing and unite the party once more. Of the 320 delegates though, only five were Progressive Republicans while no less than 172 were regular Republicans unsympathetic to radical reform. The major results of the convention were the adoption of the devices of the "initiative" and the "referendum" as some sop to the idea of direct democracy and another amendment (drafted by Martin Lomasney) which allowed the localities to distribute "the necessaries of life at reasonable rates" in times of emergency.[35] The theorizing of the progressive elements in both major parties clashed with their prevailing cautious and backward-looking attitudes and Massachusetts once again decided to make haste slowly.

By 1919 and the end of the convention, the United States had been through its brief immersion in World War I and the tide of progressivism was rapidly ebbing, not to reappear, much altered, until the time of the "New Deal." To the Republicans of Massachusetts, the Wilson years soon seemed an aberration and few of them realized that the state would soon be dislodged from its secure place in the GOP. True, the influence of the recent waves of immigration were beginning to show themselves. One of the many reasons for Henry Cabot Lodge's opposition to Wilson over the ratification of the Versailles Treaty was to be found in the changing nature of his constituency. He could not afford to ignore the feelings of the growing Irish and Italian vote, angry with Wilson over what they considered to be his indifference to the "legitimate" aspirations of their respective homelands. Lodge now faced popular election under the seventeenth amendment to the Constitution and he had already once fought Fitzgerald in such an election in 1916, beating him but by a narrow margin (33,000 votes). The senatorial election of 1918 when Walsh, who had avoided tangling with Lodge two years previously, beat incumbent John W. Weeks by 17,000 votes was even more of a salutary warning to Lodge. Walsh was helped by the intervention of an Independent, Thomas Lawson, son-in-law to ex-Governor McCall who did not favor Weeks, and this rift in the Republican ranks caused Frank Hall, Republican State Committee chairman, to describe the defeat as "the greatest calamity that has befallen the (Republican) party in Massachusetts in its history."[37]

To some extent, Republican alarm must have been soon allayed as the post-war decade got under way. For the first time in nearly a century, Massachusetts was to provide an inhabitant for the White House, even if he did get in by the back-door of the vice-presidency. Calvin Coolidge, "the Man from Vermont," had made his political career in the Massachusetts Republican Party, ascending to the office of governor by the "escalator" system whereby election to the post of lieutenant governor virtually assured succession to the governorship a few years later (see Table One). This dour and silent man, who typified much of what Americans elsewhere in the Republic thought of as typically "Yankee," had achieved constitutional office via a succession of minor offices. He had been mayor of Northampton and had served in both houses of the legislature before the "ladder" gave way to the "escalator." This was a familiar pattern in the party which laid tacit emphasis on an orderly procession of candidates for major office, much of the decision-making on the choice of candidates remaining with the leadership and the efficient working of the party machine ensuring the necessary vote at the right time.

Coolidge might well have sunk back into the semi-obscurity enjoyed by most ex-governors if it had not been for two fortunate accidents. The first was the way in which his intervention in the Boston police strike of 1919 was inflated out of all proportion to his contribution in ending the strike. Coolidge's terse phrase, "There is no right to strike against the public safety by anybody, anywhere, anytime," took the limelight away from the mayor, Andrew J. Peters, who expended the most telling effort in ending the strike.[38] The second accident, if indeed it was one and not planned by the party leaders, was his nomination for vice-president by an Oregon delegate at the presidential nominating convention in 1920, a nomination accepted by the delegates.[39] Harding's death, in the wake of the notorious "Teapot Dome Scandal" extrapolated the "escalator" right into the White House on this occasion and the taciturn but seemingly honest Coolidge, a "Puritan in Babylon" in William Allen White's description, became the solid symbol of probity as the so-called "Jazz Age" swirled around him.[40]

The regained confidence of the Republican Party in Massachusetts appeared sealed when David Walsh failed to gain re-election in 1924. That the party was changing, though, was indicated by the rise of leaders of the business community like Coolidge's crony, William Murray Butler, a New Bedford textile manufacturer who became the party's national chairman. They tended to coexist with the Brahmins, still an important reservoir of leadership talent. Coolidge's successor as governor, Channing H. Cox, in a 1961 interview, gave a picture of the self-confident Republican Party of the early and mid-1920s, knitting together the expertise of the business community with the slightly different skills of the professional elite of the state. Cox's ascent paralleled Coolidge's, for although only the son of a New Hampshire storekeeper, he rose to be Speaker of the House, then lieutenant governor, after which the "escalator" allowed his succession to Coolidge. His phrase, "It was really considered quite an honor to go to the legislature in those days," gives a picture of a well-organized party supplying men of integrity for office, though even he faced at least one major graft scandal during his administration.[41]

Although there were signs in the early 1920s that the Republican hegemony in Massachusetts would not last, they are not evident in the gubernatorial vote or the relative strength of both parties in the legislature. The Democratic percentage of the two-party vote for governor did reach 46.5% in 1922 but dropped back again to 42.9% and 40.6% respectively in 1924 and 1926. On the other hand, the contests for U.S. senator were close in both 1922 and 1924, the Democrats reaching 49.5% and 49.2% of the two-party vote respectively in the two years, then "going over the top" again in Walsh's win (by 52.8% of the two-party vote) in 1926. [42] Many of the issues of these years were national rather than local but were designed to accentuate the ethnic divisions within the state—as for example, the restriction of future immigrants by the Quota Acts, a measure which could only be seen as favoring the Anglo-Saxon rather than the American of southern or eastern European stock.

One local issue that did grow in importance was the depression in the footwear and textile centers that made "Coolidge prosperity" seem like a sour joke to the workers in those towns. In the senatorial election of 1926, a comparison of the vote received by Walsh in Haverhill, Brockton, Fall River, Lawrence and Lowell with that received by the Democratic contender in 1922, suggests that Walsh benefitted from their resentment over economic conditions and a similar comparison in wards where "newer immigrants" were concentrated suggests that Walsh profited from their distaste for the Quota Acts and the Eighteenth Amendment which established Prohibition. [43] Primary election support was still dominated by the hard ethnic cores of each party, i.e. Yankee and Irish. Democratic Party leaders supported Joseph Ely, a Yankee from western Massachusetts, for the lieutenant governor nomination in 1926 and persuaded his opponent, Henry P. Dooley, to withdraw, though not before the latter's name was printed on the ballot paper. Though he formally declined the nomination Dooley won the primary by 6,000 votes; Ely withdrew, bruised by the rebuff, and a French-Canadian was eventually nominated. "Irish-American votes for an Irish-American, and therefore Dooley won, whether he wanted to or not." [44]

The occasional inclusion of a French-Canadian or a Jewish name on the Democratic slate at this time may be an indication of the arrival of the "newer races" to recognition in state politics, even if a rather half-hearted one. During the 1920s, it was probably easier for the Democrats to do this than for the Republicans, since a Republic nomination for constitutional office meant almost certain election, while the Democratic nomination was little more than a nominal honor. In fact, the Republicans did pick non-Yankees for appointive office from time to time: Governor Cox, in the interview mentioned earlier, was still proud of the fact that he had appointed Irish-Catholics and a Jew to judgeships and felt that "more of that should have been going on."[45] At this time, the "vote" represented by the newer waves of immigrants was not quite as weighted in favor of the Democratic Party as it was to be a few years later.

By the use of hindsight, one can see that the presidential election of 1928 was the great occasion when the immigrant waves of the previous eighty years (i.e. the Irish and those who had followed them, as distinct from the Anglo-Saxon influx which had slowly wound down in the nineteenth century) achieved "recognition" by voting for "one of their own." Differences between the Irish and the "newer races" were obliterated for a time and the division that was drawn was that between the "true" and "hyphenated" American. Al Smith, nominated by the Democratic Convention that met at Houston, Texas, was a Catholic, the descendant of Irish immigrants, a city-bred politician and a "wet" as far as the prohibition issue was concerned. His Republican opponent, Herbert Hoover, was a Quaker who would trace his ancestry back to Swiss and English forebears, country-bred and a "dry" who wished the "noble experiment" to continue.

V.O. Key considered 1928 a "critical election" in his description of that typology.[46] It was certainly that for Massachusetts; apart from neighboring Rhode Island, it was the only northern state won by Smith. Recent analysis has tended to modify the rank order of the four issues and attributes that divided the two men, though even in 1928 some observers realized that the simplified explanation of the defeat of Smith as an anti-Catholic vote essentially would not hold water. Even the *Boston Transcript* felt that "the issues of prohibition and religion cut both ways."[47] Ruth Silva has shown that the most significant correlation with Smith's strength is not Catholicism, known sentiment on the liquor issue; or even the urban factor but with the index of "foreign, white stock." Where the voters were mainly immigrants or the children of recent immigrants, the vote for Smith was high, and where there were few of these "ethnic" voters, the vote was low.[48]

In 1928 Massachusetts voters for Smith were voting "against"

all that old-stock America stood for at that time, not only Prohibition and the Quota Acts, but the "blue laws" which restricted
Sunday freedom and even the Ku Klux Klan which represented
nativism at its most sinister level. In the industrial centers, where
localized depression coincided with the high density of ethnic
groups, the percentage increase over 1924 was in excess of twenty
percent. This applied to New Bedford, Fall River and Lawrence
for example, though as Hutchmacher pointed out, Chicopee,
with many fewer economic problems, showed the largest gain
among the state's industrial centers with 23.6%. The desire for
"recognition," expressed through the French-Canadian and
Polish communities there, appears to have been the overriding
motive.[49]

David Walsh, running for a full term in 1928, won comfortably
with a lead of 124,000 over the Republican candidate, Benjamin Loring Young, compared with Smith's lead of 17,000.
Smith's percentage of the total vote in the state (50.5%) was in
fact closer to the showing that Democrat gubernatorial candidate Charles H. Cole made against Republican Frank Allen,
than to Walsh's percentage (49.4% for Cole, 54.1% for Walsh).
Table Two, which presents a county-by-county breakdown,
shows that there were a few areas where in fact Smith lagged
behind Cole but that Walsh was fairly consistently ahead of both
of his colleagues.[50]

The fact that the Smith vote followed the Cole figures more
closely than it did the Walsh vote might suggest that the
"ethnic" argument is not a very strong one since Cole was an ex-
general of the Yankee Division and not likely to have much of an
ethnic "pull." However, it is more reasonable to suggest that
Smith and Walsh pulled Cole along by their coattails and that
Walsh's good showing was based on his earlier successes and
high standing (even higher than Smith) with the immigrant
groups that were so important in this election. The economic
overtones of the election were also well hammered home by
Cole, a liberal Democrat as well as a Smith supporter, and
this was obviously a major issue in the industrial centers. For
example, in a speech of October 8th, 1928, Cole alleged that:

> *The Republican Party is responsible for the business conditions*
> *which today compel at least 3,000 mill operatives to walk the*
> *streets of Lawrence seeking employment . . .Not only are*
> *the mill and factory employees of cities like Lawrence, Lowell,*

New Bedford and Fall River being thrown out of employment, but hundreds of others whose livelihood depends on the maintenance of steady employment in the big industrial establishment. The effects are widespread.[51]

In using this election as an archetype, Key showed that 1928 established an electoral cleavage which presaged the "coalition" of the Roosevelt years, the one which made the Democrats the natural majority party in the United States for a generation or more. Even the Republican leadership in the state realized that the days of easy victories might well be over and the *Transcript* echoed this feeling:

The next few years, it is evident, must become a period of strenuous work, organization and education if the traditional margin of the Republican party is to be maintained.[52]

Unfortunately for the Republicans, the stresses which had brought about the beginning of this electoral shift did not ease up. After 1929, they became more severe and readjustment became more difficult. On the face of it, the "New Deal" period would seem to provide the opportunity for Massachusetts Democrats to widen and deepen their assault on the Republican stronghold and, as far as putting together an electoral college majority for presidential candidates, this was to hold for the next twenty years. Other strongpoints, like the Great and General Court, would take much longer to sap and the Democrats would hand opportunities to their opponents time and time again. What we can see in 1928, though, is an election which can be described as the first truly "modern" one for Massachusetts, containing as it does ingredients paramount in Massachusetts politics ever since that time.

Chapter Three
The Politics of Revenge

1780623

When the balance of power in Massachusetts was seriously under attack for the first time and the changes which were to transform the state's politics were getting under way, the country as a whole was also entering a period which was to provide great strains and stresses. In fact, America has seemed to lack the so-called "normalcy" of the '20s for over forty years. Depression, war and "cold war" affected state as well as nation, but the former had its own special problems, not the least being economic ones, and these made a contribution to the changes that took place in the political culture of the state.

There are two trends that should be singled out from the economic history of Massachusetts in the years following the 1920s. One is that unemployment, highly localized in part of New England in the 1920s, much more widespread in the 1930s and therefore affecting the state as a whole, was virtually bound to have political effects in terms of transference of votes from party to party and politician to politician. The second point of note is that the long-term changes that a new "industrial revolution" brought about, the substitution of new technologies for old, has had results that one is only beginning to evaluate in full. Old goals become less meaningful for a new generation of economic sophisticates but the new goals may not seem initially as clearly defined as the old. Whatever the change in the economic environment, the political system must adapt to take account of it. Both common sense, and contemporary theory that stresses the importance of the "intra-societal environment" would seem to support this view.[1]

Massachusetts now contains an industrial base which is, technologically speaking, one of the most advanced in the world, but the process of achieving this has not been easy. The problem facing the New England states in the inter-war years was not dissimilar to that facing "old England". According to a 1933 writer:

New England manufacturers since the war have faced a com-

petitive situation similar in many respects to that of old Eng-
land, where former world markets have been seriously im-
paired by industrial developments in India, China and
continental Europe.[2]

Within the continental United States, New England's advantages
as a trailblazer of industrial revolution began to dissipate in the
twentieth century, while at the same time its disadvantages as an
economic region asserted themselves—a comparative lack of raw
materials, distance from many of its best markets, its reputation
as a high wage area. The result of a declining competitive position
was that unemployment and factory closures followed the exodus
of many firms, especially in the textile industry, from New
England, or even within the area, from Massachusetts to Maine,
where wage rates were lower. Between 1919 and 1939, employment in the region's textile industries went down by 158,000 and
in the shoe and leather industries by 38,000, a loss only partially
offset by a growth of employment in newer durable goods industries such as airplane manufacture.[3] Even during the boom years
of the '20s when the overall increase in American employment
was over seventeen percent, the figure for New England was only
six percent and for Massachusetts just under five percent.[4]

In the state, it was the textile and the boot and shoe towns that
were affected first. In Lowell in the '20s, mills were liquidating or
moving south after a slump which started as early as 1924.[5] The
aggregate decline in manufacturing employment in Massachusetts
has been estimated at about 94,000 jobs in the decade 1919-1929.[6]
As well as the southern attraction of cheap labor, cheap power
and access to nearby raw materials, Lowell's historian suggests
that competition from the first of the synthetics—rayon—was
also hitting the textile industry.[7] The Depression only worsened
this state of affairs and 70,000 jobs are reputed to have disappeared
in the first few months after the Wall Street crash. As it was ahead
of the rest of the country in encountering the Depression years,
New England was also slowest in its recovery, and it was the war
years before the economy was on the upswing again. It is hardly
surprising that the economy and its travails were so important
in the political dialogue of the inter-war years.

If 1928 was as significant a date as was suggested in the last
chapter, one would expect to find some changes in the electoral
patterns within the few years after it. Perhaps the most interesting
erosion of Republican power during the Depression years was in

the constitutional offices. As we saw earlier, Democratic governors had occasionally appeared even before this time, in the
person, for example, of David Walsh, an Irish-American one.
The salient now came in an area where Democratic success was
virtually unknown. After the governor, five constitutional offices
have to be filled in Massachusetts. The lieutenant governor's
post had been important while the "escalator" lasted, but once
that broke down the office tended to lose some of its former
status. In fact, the relation between governor and deputy has
often been a strained one, as can be seen with Endicott Peabody
and Frank Bellotti in recent years, or Charles Hurley and the
flamboyant Frankie Kelly in the 1930s.

It is the post of attorney general that has overtaken that of
lieutenant governor in prestige. He is the senior law officer of the
state and both common law and Chapter Twelve of the General
Laws of the Commonwealth give him a wide range of duties in
law enforcement, much of which brings him into the public eye,
as for example when circumstances allow him to take a crusading
stance against crime and corruption. Both parties have produced
competent and liberal attorney generals but also some less attractive. Bushnell, Brooke and Dever can be contrasted with the anti-
labor Clarence Barnes and Frankie Kelly, when he was attorney
general. The definition of the office by Eddie McCormack as
"the second most important post in state government" is one
that would be generally accepted.[8]

The remaining elective constitutional offices in the state—
secretary of state, state treasurer and state auditor—are invariably
considered as the minor three and tend to attract either less
experienced or less well-qualified candidates. There is an order
of succession should both the governor and the lieutenant governor die or resign—secretary, attorney general, treasurer, auditor—
but it does not itself mean very much.[9] These minor constitutional
offices can be used as launching pads, but very often the launching aborts and the incumbents are glad to hang on to their posts
for as long as they can. Reverting to the "upper three", it is
worth noticing that the post of lieutenant governor was upgraded
in the '60s in the hands of men like Elliot Richardson and Francis
Sargent to be something of a real deputy governor, but this is
dependent on a good relationship between the two men in office
at any one time.

In the '30s and '40s, a turnaround took place in terms of the

junior constitutional offices and, from being Republican sine-
cures, they became virtually Democratic ones. It is true that a
Democrat did not become Secretary of State until 1948 with the
dislodging of the long-established Fred Cook who held the office
for some twenty-eight years. Since 1930, however, the Republicans
have recaptured the auditor's office only once (1938) and the treasurer's office only four times, the last occasion being 1946. On
the whole, the three junior constitutional officers do not tend to
change hands as often as the senior ones. Incumbents, if they find
it difficult to move on to one of the "senior three", tend to become entrenched and, like Cook or Democrat Thomas J. Buckley
(Auditor 1941-1964), their reelection is virtually institutionalized.
For many years, this was not possible with the post of treasurer
for there was a constitutional bar to this office being held for
more than three terms, but it has been a feature of the other two
posts in the twentieth century.

Although until comparatively recently there was a bar on lon-
gevity as far as the post of treasurer was concerned, there was
a strong connexion between this post and the curious Massachusetts custom known as "the name's the same." This is a device by which one successful candidate with a common (usually
Irish-American) name blazes a trail for his namesakes to enter
either the primary or general election and cash in on the resulting
confusion caused, by picking up votes intended for the "original".
Its prevalence has been noted by a number of observers of the
state's political idiosyncrasies.[10] The most famous is the "imper-
sonation" of John Fitzgerald Kennedy by a John F. (for Francis)
Kennedy in the 1950s, a convenient coincidence which led the
Kennedy from the Gillette Razor Company to three successive terms as state treasurer, though it failed him when he tried
to climb to the post of Governor of the Commonwealth. In the
1930s, the device was established in the state treasurer's office by
successive Hurleys (four of them, three Democrats and a Republican). Even the Communists tried to trade on this device by
putting up an Arthur R. Buckley for auditor in 1940 when
Thomas H. Buckley of Abington had been auditor for two separate terms in the previous decade. In 1940, Thomas J. Buckley
of Boston won the election on the Democratic ticket, but the
Communist candidate did pull almost double the figure of the
next highest candidate on the Communist "slate". In Massachusetts, it is not always possible to say "what's in a name?"

In fact, the new names appearing in the lists of constitutional officers in the 1930s indicate the impact of Democratic success. Irish names (like Hurley and Kelly) oust the Anglo-Saxon ones of previous decades. In the '30s and '40s there are no less than four Irish-American governors (Curley, Hurley, Tobin and Dever), compared to one (Walsh) pre-1930. Although Italian and French-Canadian names appeared occasionally on the major party tickets (Dionne, Santosuosso), it was to be the 1950s before the Italians, for example, broke through to victory, and the real triumph of the ethnics took place as distinct from the false dawn of twenty years earlier. The late V. O. Key is reported to have summed up this triumph as a succession of waves—revolution, revenge and responsibility. The '30s following closely on the election of 1928 and shot through with the effects of the Depression and its would-be remedy, the "New Deal," is distinctly a period of revolution in the sense of the spiralling of the ethnic influences in state politics up to the top, and it is followed closely by influences of the "revenge" style of ethnic politics, an attempt to redress the distributive balance away from the Anglo-Saxons and towards the ethnics (especially the ethnic politicians!), first seen on any scale in Boston city politics.

The Quota Acts led to a decline in the problems of assimilation by first-generation immigrants as their numbers dropped off, but the general ethnic affiliation for the leaders of similar origin to the voter has only slowly declined. Warner and Srole's research in the Greater Boston area in the 1930s confirms the view that a "pecking-order" of racial groups existed: the "natives" or Anglo-Saxons topped the social-class table, followed by Jews and Irish, with Russians and Poles near the bottom end.[11] Apart from the Jews, who were small in numbers, this "scale" reflects the development of participation and recognition by ethnic groups at this time. While the most fervent ethnic activity continued to take place inside the Democratic Party, the Republicans were active in appointing "newer Americans" to judicial office in particular. Much play was made by Governor Frank Allen (in office 1929-1931) of the names of judges like Pinanski, Beaudreau, and Vera (Portuguese-American) appointed at this time.[12]

A word of caution should be sounded here for one could give the impression of this "watershed" as being more abrupt than it was. In fact, the transition was party-oriented as well as ethnically-oriented, though, since the party in question is the Democratic Party of Massachusetts, the overlap between the two was high.

That the Yankees still had a place in the Massachusetts Democracy
in the immediate pre-"New Deal" period is illustrated by the
election of 1930 where the party's nominees for governor, lieutenant governor and U.S. senator were all of Anglo-Saxon origin.
Joseph Ely, to be the new Democratic governor, was from West-
field in Hampden County, had a rich legal practice and seemed
more typical of the Republican establishment in many ways than
of the eastern Massachusetts Democrats. Yet he represented a
real strand in the party, especially in this period, and was quite
close to David Walsh who had appointed him a district attorney
at the time of his governorship. Curley, representing the "gut
Irish" core that was becoming such a powerful force in the party,
called Ely the "boy from the sticks," much as Wendell Willkie
was later called by Democrats "the barefoot boy from Wall
Street," but a newspaper leader at the time of the 1930 campaign
puts up a good case for Ely as the latter faced the primary election:

> *Joseph Ely still says he ought to be nominated and has lifted
> the campaign into the rather thin air of academic discussion by
> rising under the lack of being called "a high priced lawyer" to
> ask what's the matter with being a high priced lawyer. Well, its
> a fair question. Now and then a cheap lawyer gets into office,
> and he doesn't do any better than we might expect a high priced
> one to do.*[13]

Ely won by a narrow majority 16,000 votes, and the party's
senatorial candidate by a handsome 112,000. The man who
garnered this vote was a Coolidge, no less! Marcus Coolidge was
a cousin to the more well-known Calvin and the name, on the
Democratic ticket, must have helped to amass this vote. Both
candidates were undoubtedly helped by the onset of the Depression which was beginning to drive a deeper wedge of economic
identification—haves vs. have-nots—between the two parties.
That the ethnic blocs were basically "have-nots" in this game
could only intensify their hardening identification with the Democrats.

The growth of the Democratic Party's electoral fortunes in
state and nation from the 1930 and 1932 elections onward might
make the casual observer draw parallels between the outlook of
the Roosevelt brand of "New Deal" politics and the political ethos
of Massachusetts Democrats. In fact, there was to be compara-

tively little sympathy between the dynamic and dramatic figure who entered the White House in March 1933, and the Democratic chiefs in Massachusetts. In the few years surrounding the 1932 election, the two leading figures in the Bay State were obviously Walsh and Ely, yet their ethos was essentially pre-"New Deal" and the party seemed suspicious, to say the least, of the patrician outlook of the man who was to dominate the party nationally in life and death for the next twenty years. Non-Yankees found it difficult to identify with the aristocratic attitudes that observers claimed to detect in Roosevelt, and even the Yankee element in the Democratic Party were often men who had made their own way economically and were proud of the fact. Al Smith's brand of bread-and-butter liberalism was still popular and he would have been a much more popular candidate than Roosevelt was in the Massachusetts of 1932.

The identification of the party with Smith was shown by the fact that Ely made the principal nominating speech for him at the Chicago Convention. His support for Smith was echoed in the state by almost every Democrat of note, including Walsh and Marcus Coolidge—"almost" but not quite "every Democrat," for "New England's original Roosevelt man," as he described himself, preferred Roosevelt over Smith, and James Michael Curley, no less, showed a certain vision and courage in opposing Smith who had now "wrapped himself up in du Pont cellophane and Morgan ticker tape" by his involvement in New York business deals.[14] To the surprise of the Massachusetts delegation, Curley appeared at the Convention as the chairman of the Puerto Rican delegation which cast its votes for Roosevelt. He hoped that his efforts on behalf of Roosevelt would not go unnoticed in the event of the latter becoming President and he acquiesced in efforts to bring unity to the party prior to the election. The local tide and the national were now running towards the Democrats and these benefited Ely to the tune of a 120,000 majority (77% of the total vote) on this occasion. Roosevelt's share of the vote though was only 0.4% up on Smith's and his reasonable looking majority of 63,000 is explained by what appears to be a degree of "blanking" by Republicans who deserted Hoover but could not bring themselves to vote for his opponent.

As suggested earlier, the Republicans retained hold of many of the major offices of state despite the beginning of the Democratic "tide", including the lieutenant governorship in the person of

Gaspar Bacon, one of the "new men" who were trying to trim the
party's attitudes to the new wind. His allies in this venture were
men like Henry Sparkman in the State Senate, Speaker Leverett
Saltonstall and Christian Herter in the House, Henry Cabot
Lodge, Jr., just elected to the U.S. House, and Mayor Sinclair
Weeks of Newton.[15] Given the political setting and, in particular,
the tendency to the two-party system in most (though certainly
not all) of the states, it is perhaps inevitable that a party suffering
electoral reverses will examine its appeal to the voters to see in
what ways it can increase its attraction at election time.

Many theorists, such as Anthony Downs and David Easton,
have formulated this principle in slightly more elaborate terms.
Easton, for example, uses the phrase "maximum inclusiveness"
to describe the aim of the type of party that achieves electoral
success in a democratic system.[16] Changes in the social system
should lead to adaptation in the political system and a re-emer-
gence of what Parsons, in this context, has termed the "two realistic alternatives."[17] The Republican Party, between 1932 and
1966, found it difficult to do this and often appeared as an "ex-
clusive" party with the Democrats as the "inclusive" one.[18] By
the end of the '60s there were signs that the Republicans might be
coming out of their long trough of relative unpopularity. In the
1930s, when the outlines of the new Democratic "coalition" were
so close that they were blurred, it was more natural for the Republicans to be less than sure that they should change their habits of
several generations to rebuild their electoral base. Roosevelt and
the Depression were aberrations that might be short-lived and
the Republicans could assume once more their "rightful" place
as the dominant party in all but a few areas such as the South.
For these reasons, change in the party was not easy to bring about,
as the Massachusetts "Young Turks" soon found, though it is to
their credit that the party image did shift to some degree by the
end of the decade.

An added fact that consoled the Massachusetts Republicans
at this time was their continuation of legislative dominance. 1932
saw four Senate seats lost to their opponents, giving still a 26-14
majority in their favor, while in the House, the Democrats actually
lost six seats, the 147-93 balance giving the Republicans a substantial majority. Neither did their opponents present much of a
united front at state level. The pro-Smith section of the leadership could not expect to be in favor with the Roosevelt administration but neither was Curley, who was offered nothing more

attractive than the Warsaw Embassy, rather than the Navy Department he coveted. FDR's son's description of James Michael as "the flamboyant political brawler" evidently summed up the father's wish to banish his "booster" to Eastern Europe.[19] Curley lay low temporarily, with his eye on the 1934 gubernatorial election; but Ely gravitated to a more and more critical position in his view of the "New Deal," describing the NRA as "a bureaucracy so enormous as to result in the maze of confusion, inefficiency, waste and political chicanery compared with which the prohibition experiment pales into insignificance."[20] Dineen, Curley's biographer, has argued that Ely was a "liberal, broad-minded Yankee Protestant."[21] In the context of the '20s this might have been a fair assessment, but in the following decade, his commitment to what were now the main liberal views seems very slight.

Since Ely was not a contender for renomination in the 1934 gubernatorial election, the Walsh wing, anxious to preserve the relatively broad appeal that his alliance with Ely seemed to imply, supported the candidacy of General Charles H. Cole, who had been the 1928 gubernatorial candidate. The Convention upheld this decision but Curley determined to challenge Cole in the primary, challenging in fact the whole Walsh concept of the Democratic Party as one with a potentially broad ethnic base. The Curley concept seems to have been that the party—and particularly he—could win by stressing the separation between old-stock citizens, by implication all potential Republicans, and the "newer races," all potential Democrats. In the primary, he adopted the ethnic role and thus cut Cole off from the support he received in 1928. Table Four gives an idea of the distribution of the vote in the primary and in the general election where Curley faced Gaspar Bacon. A heavily "ethnic" area like Suffolk (virtually Boston) went for Curley in the Democratic primary and in the general election. "Yankee" areas like Barnstable with fewer representatives of the recent immigrant groups would obviously be for Bacon in the general election and their registered Democrats were less militantly "ethnic" than in an area such as Boston. The intermediate counties show a less clear preference, occasionally containing a Curley-tending Democratic faction but with an overall Republican tendency (e.g. Plymouth). One does not want to push this too far but it seems reasonable to suggest that Curley did polarize the ethnic rivalry in this election in a way that a contest between Cole and Bacon would not have done.

Curley's emphasis in both sections of his campaign was on "work and wages" and his victory in both elections indicated that this was the right chord to strike, appealing as it did to the combination of class and ethnic feeling now coincident in the state. Roosevelt would have preferred to see a Democratic Party in Massachusetts free of Curley dominance as much as of Walsh, but this was wishful thinking and ignored the development of the state in the early twentieth century. 1934 was a "triumph of the ethnic" in a sense and, in the words of Francis Russell:

> *Boston had taken over Massachusetts at last. The crowd from the City Hall moved up Beacon Hill to the State House.* [22]

Well, almost all. Joseph Santosuosso failed to beat Fred Cook for the post of secretary of state: not only the "habit voting" we have described earlier intervened here but it may have been that Democratic voters were less enthusiastic about electing an Italian than an Irishman as yet. Santosuosso certainly thought that discrimination did exist and expressed this feeling when interviewed by a research student some years later. [23] After an even more resounding victory by Cook in 1936 (6% of the two-party vote as against 0.8%), political commentator John Bantry suggested that:

> *The case of Dr. Santosuosso shows that racial prejudice is just as strong in the Democratic Party as in the Republican Party. It is at its strongest right here in Boston. Various highly qualified young men of Italian blood have tried to get somewhere in politics in the city only to be swamped by Democratic votes.* [24]

This is a clear exposition of the ethnic tensions that existed at this time inside the parties as well as between them. However, the differences between the votes garnered by the members of the Democratic slate were not considerable. The highest vote-getter was Charles Hurley, the new treasurer (772,000)—helped perhaps by the fact that his opponent was French-Canadian Oscar Dionne? Santosuosso's figure (682,000) was not that much under Paul Dever's in his first victory for constitutional office—attorney general (706,000)—indicating that though this "cutting" did exist, Bantry might have made a little too much of it. [25]

Curley entered office—that short walk from City Hall to Beacon Hill—with a great deal in his favor. Republican majorities in the legislature were cut (in the Senate to two, in the House to ten) and the one-man majority in the archaic Governor's Council was reversed by Curley's appointment of two Republican councillors to attractive offices and the substitution of two Democrats for them, giving a Democratic majority in the Council for the first time. Even at county level there were setbacks for the Republicans with, for example, an Essex county commissionership falling to the Democrats, eroding this notorious Republican "ring" for the first time.

For all of this, Curley found it difficult to deliver on his "work and wages" policy. His past kept catching up with him, as the Boston Finance Commission investigated the case of the Mohawk Packing Company, allegedly used by an associate to defraud the city. But the real fault seemed to lie in the man, his limitations as an "ethnic" politician, lacking a united party in the state and the confidence of the Roosevelt administration in Washington. Massachusetts was one of the few states where federal relief projects were not funnelled through the governor but through a succession of WPA administrators.[26] As well as a dislike of the city machine, Roosevelt appeared to resent the Curley faction both for its limited base in the Boston Irish and for its suspicion of the ideological overtones, faint as they were, in the "New Deal." When Curley conceived the idea of running for the U.S. Senate in 1936, it was evident that he would not receive support from Roosevelt. Inside the state, few politicians have ever received such waves of antagonistic propaganda, countered by rebuttals from the Curley stable. He was either "James the First," a reckless demagogue, or "an outstanding leader in the current life of our state and nation." More likely, there was a little of both in the man.[27] What was certain was that his methods were dated and inadequate for the problems of the time and, as an "ethnic prisoner," his addiction to the "politics of revenge" prevented his building up enough of a united front to improve the economic situation in the state.

It was suggested earlier that the Republicans were beginning to adapt minimally to the changed conditions of the 1930s. True, this was a slow process and the *Worcester Telegram* seemed to catch a note of despair in August 1935:

> . . . *what the Massachusetts Republicans need is a party*
> . . . *there is no rallying around anyone or anything.*[28]

However, some of the younger Republican leaders were more

urbane than the manufacturing and business interests that seemed to dominate in the '20s; they reverted more to the older Republican type of concerned, well-bred Yankee. Lodge, Saltonstall, and Herter were all of this type. The first of these, Henry Cabot Lodge, Jr., was only thirty-four in 1936 when he contested the Senate seat after persuading the delegates at the Republican Convention that he was their man despite his relative lack of experience. He had served two terms in the Massachusetts House but undoubtedly his name counted more than that. During his election campaign, he was well aware that his election depended on vote-getting among the ethnics and the wage-earners threatened by the Depression:

> *He ducked meetings of Republicans he felt sure of, to concentrate on Syrian picnics, French-Canadian clambakes, and hostile CIO meetings where the great Democratic unwashed gathered together and could be won over. There he was cautious on the issues, attacking Federal spending but at the same time promising that as long as the spending was going on he would do his best to get a good slice of it for Massachusetts.*[29]

Curley did not recognize Lodge as a rival and dubbed him "Little Boy Blue." Walsh had been reelected with 61.4% of the two-party vote in 1934 and, though Curley could not hope to rival this, he felt that the tide was sufficiently in his favor for him to win. A minor candidate in the race was the Father Coughlin inspired National Union nominee Thomas O'Brien of Boston who gained 134,000 votes, just short of Lodge's majority over Curley, refuting the usual contention that minor party candidates do badly in Massachusetts but also casting doubt on Curley's own contention that O'Brien's candidacy cost him the election.[30] Roosevelt took 51.2% of the total vote despite the Union Party's entry of a presidential candidate, but Curley was less popular than the President. Lodge, a young, personable Yankee had defeated "Curleyism" and the one-to-one Republican/Democratic ratio for senators was restored. Table Five, which compares a random sample of towns and cities with a selected group of large centers of population, suggest an even pattern of allegiances over the state as a whole as far as the presidential and senatorial elections were concerned.

The Republican swallow represented by Henry Cabot Lodge's victory heralded no Republican summer in electoral terms, for

four constitutional offices remained in Democratic hands. Yet
it stayed the rot and it may have seemed to Republicans in the
state that both the country and the party were coming out of the
Depression despite Roosevelt's huge popular majority nation-
wide. In fact though, the state emerged slowly from the Depression, suffering as it did from a localized as well as a national
economic ailment. The late '30s, especially when one considers
the 1937-38 recession pattern, was still a time of adjustment
for the Massachusetts economy, a process which would only be
interrupted by the artificial stimulation of the war economy of the
1940s. A certain amount of diversification was beginning to
take place. New Bedford brought in glass-making and
electrical goods manufacture to offset the decline in textiles,
while Fall River encouraged the development of industries as
varied as garment manufacture, optical goods, mattresses and
ice cream cones. [31] Other industrial centers followed a similar
pattern as far as they could. If recovery was not yet apparent,
there were now some signs of hope on the horizon.

It would not be wise to lay too much stress on these initial
signs of recovery and their influence on political choice. Equally,
one would suggest that the fluctuating fortunes of the state's
economy, important as it is as an important element in the conditioning process, should take second place to the ethnic attitudes burgeoning earlier in the century. One cannot ignore the
interrelation of the two factors though. For example, the '30s
was a time of relatively low prices and, although the Depression
was a tragedy for those in the industrial centers who lost their
livelihood as a result, those who remained in any sort of regular
employment did benefit from low prices and interest rates. Some
"embourgeoisement" of the Irish especially among the ethnics
was undoubtedly taking place and this began to affect political
attitudes at the same time as rudimentary welfare provisions,
Social Security for example. Francis Russell commented:

> *Voters were no longer gratefully held in line by a job shovel-
> ling snow, by the odd ton of coal, by the perennial thanks-
> giving turkey and Christmas basket. Social security and the
> psychiatric social worker had taken over. The Irish were be-
> coming middle class.* [32]

By the late '30s, the sense of identification that politicians like
Curley and Fitzgerald had given to the "little people" (as

Fitzgerald's biographer terms them) was already beginning to wane and, even though the process would be a lengthy one, the implications were not lost on the men who had made their political careers on the support of these people. Cutler comments:

> *Curley could sense that the old order was changing, and his oratory lacked its customary ringing conviction. Symbol of the new order . . . was a Harvard College student, John F. Kennedy.*[33]

It is arguable just how "new" were the politics of Honey Fitz's grandson in the immediate post-war years at least, but there were signs in the late '30s that some of the Democratic voters were beginning to get a little ahead of their elected representatives. Curley's successor as governor, Charles Hurley, left little mark on the state at a critical time in its history though he was liberal in the narrow field where most Irish Democrats were liberal (minimum wage laws for instance). Frankie Kelly was his lieutenant governor, a man who has become something of a standing joke in the state because of his bizarre solutions to its problems, such as giving away electric light bulbs or running a state lottery. Kelly had the classic immigrant background—early poverty, evening law school at Suffolk University—eventually becoming the state's youngest lieutenant governor at thirty-three. For all of this, he was described a few years later by fellow Democrats as a "rabble-rousing tub-thumping breast-beating demagogue."[34] Attorney General Paul Dever was a cut above these two but less well known at this time.

In the late '30s, the Democrats seem to have missed an opportunity to broaden their base and the party battle became more and more a Yankee-Irish one, with both parties competing for the votes of Italians, Poles, Franco-Americans and the other groups outside this axis. On the whole, these groups were slow to penetrate the party organizations in anything but the occasional example already cited. Their participation was hampered by their proximity to immigrant status and the disabilities that flowed from this; for example, 39% of the North End Italian community were illiterate at the time of the 1930 Census.[35] Numbers would be important in time: voters of Italian origin in the state increased from 74,000 in 1930 to 174,000 by 1948.[36] Yet, although Edward A. Bacigalupo had broken the Hendricks Club hold in the North End to become

the first Italian representative by 1934, the Great and General
Court was still weighted towards Yankees firstly and Irish
secondly. A name count of the State Senate elected in 1936
indicates that twenty-two out of the twenty-six Republicans have
Yankee names and eight out of the fourteen Democrats have
Irish ones.[37] Yet even the Italian second generation immigrants
were spreading out from their original concentrations and would
obviously extend their political influence in time.

The weakness in the Democratic position was seen vividly in
the election of 1938 when the Republicans won five out of the
six constitutional offices (all except attorney general), and to
many it must have seemed that an interlude was over. The divi-
siveness of the Democrats was well illustrated by the bitter primary in which three Irish Democrats fought each other so well
that there was little unity left for the November election (see
Table Six). Curley's strength lay in the Connecticut River Valley
and the Boston area, but since these were areas of a high con-
centration of voters, he won. His share was only 40% compared
to Saltonstall's near 70% in the four-cornered Republican primary. This was not a good sign for the general election, though
on a long term view, the fact that the relative Democratic/
Republican primary totals were 525,000 and 469,000 respectively
showed the trend of party orientation, since corresponding figures
for ten years earlier had been 205,000 and 331,000 (all to the
nearest thousand).

With hindsight, it is not difficult to see why Curley lost this
election, though Table Six shows how badly he ran behind Paul
Dever in many areas, even in the Boston area where the primary
indication had been that he might have done well. Evidently,
"independents" ready to support Dever would not support Curley, both because he had toppled an incumbent governor and because he was Curley! Leverett Saltonstall, perhaps helped by
a "South Boston face" that Curley unconsciously helped to
publicize, felt that these were the reasons:

> . . . *the issues had grown out of some of the difficulties
> during his* [Curley's] *regime. And then there was the fact that
> he had won a popular primary against the then Governor
> Hurley so that there was a sort of split Democratic feeling and
> it gave me a feeling of confidence.*[38]

Curley's defeat was not just the fate of an old-style politician defeated by a man who seemed to represent a certain integrity. Curley had promised too much, and had produced more in the way of flamboyance than in performance. Saltonstall, though a Republican, settled for an "image" that seemed to chime not only with his own kind but even with many of the more established immigrant families. His "liberalism" was no wider and no narrower than the bulk of his constituents and, although the hard core of the ethnic vote stayed with Curley, some of the fringes must have gone to Saltonstall. The position in one of the heavily "Italian" areas of Boston was summed up by William Foote Whyte in his well-known book on "Cornerville," retitled from the North End:

Wickham [Saltonstall] *was elected governor that fall, but Murphy* [Curley] *carried Cornerville for the Democrats by almost six to one. The Republicans did poll a somewhat larger vote in Cornerville than they had in 1936, but the gain was not nearly as greet as had been expected . . .*[39]

The next few years in Massachusetts politics have somewhat of a fin-de-siècle air about them, as international affairs move into center stage and domestic policies, federal and state, gradually appear less important in comparison. The one peacetime election left, that of 1940, did provide another set of variants on the economic and ethnic themes of the 1930s. Roosevelt's attempt for a third term, though successful, did result in a drop in the national vote for the Democratic presidential candidate of nearly six points (60.8% in 1936 and 54.7% in 1940), yet in Massachusetts there was a rise in Roosevelt's percentage from 51.2% to 53.1%. The gap between the country's enthusiasm for Roosevelt and the state's support of him was dwindling almost to nothing. The state's position as an industrialized one, aided by the beginnings of American rearmament in the face of the European War, was undoubtedly a factor here. Lubell has pointed out the effects of the expansion of work in the Boston Navy Yard on the voters of Charlestown. [40]

In general, the cities and industrialized centers were for Roosevelt and the smaller towns, lacking industry, were for Wendell Willkie (see Table Seven). While the war in Europe tended to attract voters of Polish and Jewish extraction towards Roosevelt, those of Italian descent were alienated to some extent by Roosevelt's criticism of the Axis, especially in the Charlottesville,

Virginia, "stab in the back" speech given on June 10, 1940. In Boston's Ward One, Italian precincts showed a 31% drop in the Roosevelt vote over 1936; yet in the Jewish Ward Fourteen Roosevelt polled 89.3% of the vote, 34.9% more than the vote given to David Walsh on the same ballot.[41] Walsh in turn made up for this to some extent in the neighboring Irish Ward Fifteen where Roosevelt trailed him by 17%.[42] Walsh defeated Republican Henry Parkman, who campaigned on an "internationalist" platform which included support of aid to Britain and advocacy of compulsory miltary training, but his vote dropped from the 61.4% of 1934 to 56.5% in 1940. Strained relations with Roosevelt over the third term sought by the latter may have contributed to the decline in Walsh's support.

Nineteen-forty was the year in which Leverett Saltonstall's burgeoning career was nearly nipped in the bud. His victory over Paul Dever was one of the narrowest in a gubernatorial election of the state in modern times, only 5,588 votes or 0.28% of the total.[43] Dever moved up to contest the governorship after beating Frankie Kelly in the primary (there was a Francis P. Kelley in the primary for the nomination for lieutenant governor which meant that someone thought that the Kelly name was an appealing one to the electorate that year). If Dever had won, he would have been governor eight years earlier than 1948 and he might well have gone on to be U.S. senator as Saltonstall did after the relatively quiet period of the war years. In fact, Dever suffered from "split ticket" voting in many places where Roosevelt did well. Between the presidential and gubernatorial sections of the ballot, the Boston vote dropped sixteen thousand, Worcester ten thousand, while Springfield dropped five thousand and changed its allegiance from Democrat to Republican.

Once the war came in 1941, it had the effect of dampening partisan interest in politics, and the 1942 elections in particular were described in the press as "playing second fiddle to the war headlines" while wartime conditions were "held responsible for the general apathy."[44] Saltonstall, advertised as "Our Great War Governor,"[45] found the third term no more difficult to secure than had Roosevelt, and his majority against Democrat Roger L. Putnam was over nine percent of the total vote. Lodge's majority in the Senate contest with Congressman Joseph Casey was less (80,000 as against 128,000), but the contest was intriguing for its role reversals as compared to the Walsh-Parkman election of two years earlier—this time the Republican was being attacked as an isolationist. Though Lodge denied the charge, it may well have helped rather than hindered him with some of the Boston Irish, for his opponent's lead was 67,000 in the city— less than the 100,000 or so that someone like Walsh could usually rely on (it had been 113,000 for Walsh in 1940). It should be pointed out though that both Saltonstall and Attorney General Robert Bushnell were well ahead of him in the city with only 45,000 and 51,000 respectively to overcome in the rest of the state.

Saltonstall's six years as governor, endorsed in this 1942 election victory, appeared to sit easily on the state at a period when the ethnics should have been consolidating their earlier gains, but when they failed to do so, almost certainly because of the low caliber of many of their candidates. The solid but unspectacular administration of Saltonstall appealed to the independent or marginal voter, including many of the ethnics who were becoming increasingly "acculturated" to the Anglo-Saxon "ethos." By 1944, he was gaining a national reputation and, like many a successful governor, was being suggested as potential vice-presidential, or even presidential, timber.[46] In the state, he succeeded as much for his quiet style and lack of pomp and ceremony, which a Curley needed to emphasize that he and his kinsmen had arrived at the seats of power. Yet by the war years especially, a quiet and sober style was more appropriate to the times. The governor was additionally fortunate in that he was successful in his relationships with the Republican legislature and with the Boston city government under Mayor Maurice Tobin. Of Tobin, Saltonstall said:

I don't think we had any difference of opinion on important matters except once, on what is now the MTA.[47]

Although the war effort directed immediate attention from state problems, it did release ambitions for a better post-war world which would involve a degree of planning to achieve economic and social well-being and this would have been an anathema to some Republicans. Saltonstall, however, recognized its inevitability (he had set up a planning board for economic development even before Pearl Harbor) and was reconciled to the innovations of the past decade. He wrote in 1943:

The average American does not want the New Deal entirely

scuttled if that means losing what has been unquestionably gained in the past decade. There can be no thought of our turning our backs on the advances made in social security, regulation of securities exchanges, working conditions, wages and hours, and similar progressive measures. The average citizen wants only to discard government by edict, collectivism and experiments made simply for the sake of change.[48]

John Gunther quotes a saying about Saltonstall—that he had "everything except brains and top-flight intellect"—but adds that the sources of his political power rested on a combination of other and possibly more useful talents such as integrity, modesty, moderation, frugality and a lack of sophistication.[49] Despite the ingrained effects of group pressures on voting in the state, there is a counter tendency to support men rather than parties and a candidate who impresses himself on the electorate as competent, compassionate and honest can attract large numbers of so-called "independent" voters, who may lean to one or the other of the two parties but who are open to persuasion by a candidate whom they might not accept solely because of party label. This was true of Saltonstall and was especially exemplified when he ran for the U.S. Senate in 1944. Lodge had resigned to engage in active service in the European campaign and the seat was temporarily filled by Sinclair Weeks who had agreed not to challenge the Governor in the November election.

Saltonstall's victory in 1944 against Democrat John H. Corcoran by an almost two-to-one majority was the greatest Republican victory in a statewide contest for many years and upset many of the usual rule-of-thumb generalizations about the normal vote distribution between Democrat and Republican. Saltonstall carried Boston, for example, the first Republican contender for constitutional office, U.S. senator or the presidency to do so for twenty years.[50] Of the industrial centers with ethnic coloration, only Holyoke, New Bedford, Lowell and Fall River gave Corcoran majorities, only Fall River giving him a majority of reasonable size (over 5,000). The list of Saltonstall gains—Springfield, Worcester, Fitchburg, Lynn, Cambridge, Pittsfield, Somerville, Chelsea—reads like a list of Democrat strongholds in most elections since the late '20s and his overall percentage of the two-party vote (64.8%) was even better than Walsh's record vote of 1934.

Columnist Sara White indicated the appeal that Saltonstall had built up as that of the "common man," a Republican with whom many Democrats could identify:

He is a man who can be reached by a publicised telephone number at home; who walks from Back Bay, if he takes the train, or from Kenmore Square otherwise, to his office; who declines a special elevator to the State House and abolished the practice of having uniformed guards in the anteroom. He goes to movies and to hockey, football and baseball games.[51]

To many Democratic politicians, Saltonstall's style must have appeared to be that of the amateur, but he was in fact every inch the professional with a long training in legislative politics going back to 1923. His appeal to the Irish Democrats was suprising but was generally accepted as self-evident since he had the reputation of being a "decent upstanding man."[52] Entry into the Senate was a reward for good behavior as governor by an electorate, which had learned not to expect too much from some of the previous holders of that office.

In 1944 the electorate, in effect, had to make a new choice for governor for the first time in six years, instead of the "confirmation" that Saltonstall's reelection in 1942 and 1944 had represented. In an attempt to hold onto the office, the Republicans reverted to the "escalator," relying on Lieutenant Governor Horace Cahill to move up. Cahill had a career which, up to this time, had resembled that of Saltonstall—a period in the Massachusetts House culminating in the Speaker's chair, for example —but he appeared to lack the appeal that Saltonstall had for the voter.

He faced a Democratic contender of some weight in Maurice Tobin, the handsome young Mayor of Boston. A Curley protégé, he had snatched City Hall from his mentor. Tobin's background—a rise from modest beginnings as the son of a carpenter—did him little harm among his fellow Irish. As Mayor he pursued a strong line, which antagonized some interests in the city, but his popularity among Democrats in the state as a whole was considerable.[53]

It is doubtful, in retrospect, whether Tobin's political standards were any higher than those of Curley, but he impressed what the latter scathingly described as "Henry Shattuck and other well-heeled do-gooders" who helped him, so it is alleged, with money. [54] Shattuck and other Boston Yankees were often prepared to help those whom they felt were the more reputable among the political leaders of their city's Irish majority. Presumably, they reasoned that the expanding role of the Irish Democrat first in the city, and then in state politics was inevitable and that it was up to them to encourage the more able and apparently honest elements in the leadership rather than those they distracted. This meant making value judgements that could be wrong as often as they were right!

Certainly, Tobin had money in this campaign for he spent $174,000 according to the press, a goodly sum in 1944.[55] It was used especially to work on the small towns and it seems to have paid off for his vote in those towns rose, compared, say, to Dever's near successful campaign in 1940. (Tobin's vote in the small town of Deerfield in Franklin County, for example, rose from Dever's 35.8% to 47%.)[56] The traditional centers of Democratic strength held firm and his percentage of the total two-party vote (53.8%) was a comfortable one if not an overwhelming comeback for the Democrats.

Tobin supported Roosevelt for a fourth term, and the latter again took Massachusetts with only a tiny percentage drop on 1940 (0.3%). The reason for this was almost certainly a further defection on the part of certain ethnic groups, particularly the Italians, for Serino's figures show a further small drop in support in certain of the Italian Wards of Boston.[57] Taking into account the national drop in the Roosevelt vote, the Massachusetts figures indicate a hardening of the loyalty towards the Democrats in presidential contests. In Boston, the Jewish Wards Twelve and Fourteen were the most heavily Democratic in the presidential election, followed by two Irish Wards, and this tended to make up for the Italian defections, just as in 1936, Irish defectors in Boston (to Coughlin) were balanced off by rising Italo-American and Jewish votes. According to Lubell, "almost nine out of every ten voters in wards 12 and 14 favored Roosevelt" in 1944.[58]

Tobin's new lieutenant governor, Robert Bradford, was a Republican, some recompense to the GOP at the time of Cahill's eclipse. A descendant of William Bradford, second governor of the Plymouth colony over three centuries earlier, Robert Bradford had come up the political ladder via the district attorney's office in Middlesex County where he had achieved spectacular success by raising the percentage of convictions from 26 to 93 percent in one year.[59] After polling more than the combined total of the other four candidates in the Republican primary, he went on to pile up a 93,000 majority over his Democratic opponent, John Carr. Frankie Kelly, the winner of a four-way Democratic primary, failed to stop Clarence Barnes in the attorney general contest despite the opposition of organized labor to Barnes, whose legislative program they opposed. One of Barnes' bills, for example, was designed to prevent unions from making political contributions.[60] With Barnes and Bradford elected, the latter described by the press as "a new star of the first magnitude," some of the Republican chagrin at Tobin's election was almost certainly mollified.[61]

The mid-1940s is something of a nodal point in the political history of Massachusetts, since it marks a rough balance between the committed supporters of both parties. Gunther quotes the *Boston Herald*'s W. E. Mullins in fixing the "irreducible vote" at this time at 800,000 for the Republicans and 700,000 for the Democrats, but this is likely to have been too favorable towards the former. Primary turnouts tended to be higher in 1944 for the Democrats and the high votes obtained by Roosevelt, Tobin and Walsh in the recent past tended surely to offset the pull that men like Saltonstall and Lodge had with independents and some of the ethnics. The only doubt enters when one notes that the Democratic "lows" at the time were below similar figures for the Republicans (the former could score only 667,000 in the Senate election while the lowest statewide Republican figure— for treasurer—was 805,000), but this could be due to the greater discipline of the Republican Party and also the enormous popularity of Saltonstall on the other side. The number of registered voters in 1944 was 2,296,000, suggesting that a rough balance at this time was to be found by splitting this vote into three equal parts, Democrat, Republican and Independent (if Mullins' figure of 1,500,000 "committed" voters is close to correct). A few years later, the "undesignated" voters at registration time numbered as many as 50 percent, but this would include many voters leaning to one or the other of the parties even if they preferred not to be registered as party supporters.[62]

Party allegiance continued to be a notional concept in Massachusetts for many years after the period under discussion. The

above-mentioned newspaper reporter was still pointing out the
significance of the independent vote in 1954:

> It has been asserted that Massachusetts is the third most
> independent state in the Union in the matter of voting the
> split ticket. Only Ohio and Colorado exceed us in that re-
> spect. We have a large element that votes for the man not for
> the party.[63]

It is this latter tendency that encourages caution over fixing too
early a date for the final transformation of the state into one than
can be firmly labelled "Democratic." Huthmacher, in his otherwise outstanding survey of the 1919-1933 period, states that those
years "witnessed a striking transformation in the political status of
Massachusetts, from a rock-bound Republican stronghold to a
"Democratic state."[64] Despite the erosion of the Republican position after the highly significant election of 1928, to describe Massachusetts as a "Democratic state" by the mid-1930s, or even by
the mid-1940s, is more than a little tendentious.

From 1930 to 1944, in eight biennial elections, with six constitutional offices at stake each time, the Democratic "score" is twenty-
two to the Republicans' twenty-six. If the three major offices alone
are taken, the figures are ten and fourteen respectively. Apart
from 1931-37, the Republicans retained one of the two U.S. Senate
seats in this period, while they kept their majority in the U.S.
House and their majorities in the Great and General Court. Only
the vote for the Democratic presidential candidates from 1928
through 1948 shows a uniform Democratic bias and this is no
more a decisive indicator than is the vote for Eisenhower in 1952
and 1956 indicative of a reverse swing. There was a dichotomy
in these years, one that David, Moos and Goldman noted in
1952 when introducing the state into their study of presidential
nominating politics. Acknowledging the pull of the Roosevelt
and Truman candidacies, they noted that nevertheless "the
Republican Party has continued to hold great strength in state
and local elections."[65] This is a fairer assessment than that
of Huthmacher quoted above and it is pure hindsight to be
more sweeping than this about Democratic success in the '30s
and '40s.

If the decisive watershed in Massachusetts electoral politics
did not come in the 1930s, when did it come? That it is now a

"Democratic" state few would deny, which suggests that the post-World War II period was the crucial one. The fifteen or so years following the end of this war marked the final phase of the "transformation," and the changing electoral patterns of three years are probably the most critical ones for an understanding of the emergence of Massachusetts as a great bastion of the Democratic Party.

Chapter Four
The Politics of Change

If the most profound of the political changes in twentieth-century
Massachusetts did occur in the years after World War II, what
were the reasons at the root of them? It must be emphasized that
they are of a piece with earlier economic and social change in the
state. But that they are real is indicated by the voting figures in
the two decades or so following 1945. Austin Ranney placed Massachusetts in his list of "two-party states" when drawing up an
"Index of Competitiveness" a few years ago and, since the Republican Party is still a force to be considered within certain districts
and also in the elections to constitutional office, this was a reasonable comment.[1] Ranney tends to relegate voting patterns for presidential and congressional elections in terms of the individual
state to a secondary position in favor of elections for purely state
office, whereas one would prefer to go along with V.O. Key's assessment that "the states do not operate independently of these
broad national sweeps" and emphasize that there there is some
link between the two areas.[2]

Sectionalism, as Key also surmised, has tended to decline so
that, within broad limits, the ebb and flow of national politics
is more clearly reflected at local level than it was once; however, there are those who see the rise of new sectional patterns
which seem to reverse former ones.[3] If this is so, and some special
pleading may be involved here, Massachusetts could find herself
one of the factions of a minority party coalition instead of, as it
has been over the past two generations, moving itself from membership of the majority party coalition of the post-Civil War years
to the new one of the mid-twentieth century (i.e. Republican to
Democrat).

The indications of political change could be cited as five in
number: the presidential vote, the vote for congressmen, that
for senior constitutional office, separately for junior constitutional office and for the Great and General Court. The vote for
U. S. senator is highly personalized and more useful in individual
elections than in determining trends. Of these, the presidential

vote had hardened towards the Democrats at a time when it was beginning to weaken nationally and was to suffer a temporary erosion only at the hands of Dwight Eisenhower.

However, the state's delegation to the U.S. House had never presented a Democratic majority (though in 1934 the split had been 8-7 only in the Republicans' favor) and was not to produce such a balance until the 1958 election; there are questions of personal loyalty here which make rapid changes less likely. The senior constitutional offices (governor, lieutenant governor and attorney general) were consistently in dispute between the two parties, the first and last of these being the two most coveted posts in state government—the governorship for obvious reasons, the attorney general's office because of its key position in the legal structure of the state, giving its holder the opportunity to establish an independent power base. The junior constitutional offices —secretary of state, treasurer and auditor—are "less visible" and, except for treasurer before 1964, they are susceptible to "long runs."[4] It is often argued that they should be appointive, not elective, offices. No Republican has occupied any of them since 1948. The legislative balance was in favor of the Republicans in the Great and General Court even at the height of the "New Deal."

After World War II, the legislature gradually slid into Democratic control, a trend stemmed briefly in the early '50s but complete since the 1954 election for the House and the 1958 election for the State Senate. Thus, the legislative majorities in the General Court and the congressional delegation are as near secure for the Democrat as anything can be in elective politics, while only the senior constitutional offices offer real opportunities for Republicans to make policy at state level. Political change of this nature demands an explanation, but we can do no more than suggest probable causes. As we shall see in the next chapter, the relative isolation of the constitutional offices from the overall trend may be linked to the performance of some Democratic office holders, but this and the overall trend only makes sense when seen against certain background factors in post-war Massachusetts.

In a state such as this, much of the political pressure for change or any dynamic action comes from the weight brought by groups in the community, whether "reference" in character or more akin to "pressure" or "interest" groups. One is reminded of Dahl's definition of the "normal" American political process, while remem-

bering that much of the peripheral political activity of the last
few years prevents its acceptance as readily as we did once, Dahl
suggested that this process was:

> . . . *one in which there is a high probability that an active and
> legitimate group in the population can make itself heard effec-
> tively at some crucial stage in the process of decision.*[5]

Many groups make themselves heard in Massachusetts and the
party system itself depends on the reference groups that one has
referred to many times, particularly when one considers how many
voters regard voting for someone of their ethnic group as a satisfying outlet. Yet the contrasting pattern of group activity, that
based on the narrower "interest," especially economic interest, is
also important if, in this context, it is probably subservient to the
biting effect of racial origin which is such a feature of Massachusetts politics.

The cleavages that exist in the body politic are well illustrated
by the group pressures of an economic and sectarian variety in
the post-war history of the state. Edgar Litt has illustrated the
conflicting forces at work during the period 1940-1963 in making
key decisions in policy areas.[6] Economics dominates the majority
of the interest groups that he lists, running from the AFL-CIO as
the main representative of organized labor to the chambers of
commerce, taxpayers' associations and small retail associations.
Sectarian groups are active in more limited fields usually, such
as the birth control legislation debates that have occured from
time to time.

Lockard suggests that the two-party nature of Massachusetts
legislative politics allows interest groups less leverage than in the
"one-party states" in northern New England.[7] Despite the changing balance in Massachusetts politics in particular, and in New
England politics in general, since the 1950s (when Lockard's
book was written), there is little doubt that interest groups retained about as much influence in the 1960s as in previous decades,
no more and no less. Latham and Goodwin, writing at about the
same time, found that the "lobbies" spending the most money
in the late 1950s were those connected with insurance, banking
and real estate, with other commercial and industrial interests
also well represented among the top spenders.[8]

The exact effect of interest groups on a great deal of the legislation that comes before the Great and General Court is not es-

pecially easy to assess. When a "big" issue comes up, one can see the ranging of groups on either side, and the occasional public hearing that airs legislation of overriding public interest is the one occasion for a completely clear picture of the arguments that interest groups hold about policy making at state level to be presented. At other times groups do tend to make their position clear on pending legislation to anyone who may be interested enough to inquire.

Simple lists of those for and against pending legislation are usually contained in newspaper reports and can virtually be predicted if one knows the implications of the issue before the legislature or other branch of state government empowered to make decisions. In April 1966, for example, the General Court was considering a bill which was to require disclosure of the finance charges on installment sales in terms of simple annual interest and in cash payable. This was a "liberal" measure, one which, it was argued, would prevent simple citizens from being "conned" by door-to-door salesmen in particular.

In this context, one would expect commercial and industrial concerns to oppose the bill on the "caveat emptor" principle, and they did. The Boston Retail Trade Board felt that the scheme was unworkable, while the American Textbook Publishers' Institute fought a proposed cooling-off period by which the victims of door-to-door salesmen would have a brief period to cancel the contract. On the other hand, the bill's backers among organized groups included the Massachusetts Federation of Womens' Clubs, the Massachusetts Consumers' Council and the AFL-CIO, i.e. organized labor and the representation of housewives and others who expected some protection (perhaps from their own weaknesses) in the terms of the bill.[9]

In cases such as this, the groups expect to find a certain amount of support within one party or the other the (AFL-CIO can always expect many Democratic legislators to be friendly to them) and decisions to enact legislation of this type will depend on the relatively less committed legislators who will vote according to their consciences, the pressures of their colleagues and assessment of the probable reaction of their constituents to the issue. On occasions, of course, pressure groups decide not to oppose legislation which may seem to be against their special interests on the grounds that its passage is inevitable or that long-run considerations would not balance against short-terms gains in

killing a bill. At about the same time that the case just cited
was before the General Court, the Legislative Committee on Labor and Industries reported favorably a bill to raise the state's
minimum wage, a move one would expect to be treated with dis-
may by industry and commerce. Yet both the Associated Industries of Massachusetts and the Greater Boston Chamber of
Commerce, through their spokesmen, declined to oppose the bill
because it stayed "within the bounds of similar legislation on
the federal level," i.e. it could have been much worse.[10] Public
pressure of the type just described is, if anything, encouraging
to those who support a "pluralist" interpretation of the American political system.

There are less pleasant aspects of interest group activity in
a state such as Massachusetts. Is everyone represented by such
a group and how many people are left to suffer the fate of a buf-
fer, squeezed between interests that are not theirs? How much
unpublicized influence on legislative and executive government
exists in the shape of the pressures of lobbyists on individual
legislators? As Latham and Goodwin pointed out, it is not so
much a question of "gross and indictable corruption" but of the
"invisible government" which may not even be representative
because of the tendency for "the few to lead the many," i.e.
legislators are persuaded that large numbers of votes (or small
numbers of influential voters) back a certain position.[11] Any frequent visitor to the galleries of the state's Senate and House of
Representatives will soon get used to the occasional tense little
man at the time of a crucial vote, sitting to one side and ticking
off the names on a list, showing who is voting for and against
the motion. There are still suggestions too of free hotel accom-
modation available for upstate legislators, the bill being footed
by one of the more prosperous interest groups. To introduce a
fresh metaphor, there is always the fear that the part of the activities of interest groups that one sees without difficulty may be
the tip of an iceberg and one would like to know what exists be-
neath the surface of the water.

The crux of this is that there is a potential for activity by interest groups in the state that is not conducive to good government. That it does not seem to provide a great deal of concern
among those who are trying to improve governmental standards
may be due to two reasons. One is that the very real problems of
corruption in politics that have been uncovered, from time to

time, especially in the early 1960s, have involved individual and isolated firms rather than interest groups as such. Secondly, as noted earlier, political parties still offer a degree of competition and, to use the now well-known categories of Gabriel Almond, the functions of the articulation of interests on the one hand and their aggregation on the other are fairly well separated in Massachusetts with the Democrats and Republican parties influenced by, and receptive to, the views of sets of interest groups but neither dominated by them nor likely to abdicate the right to look at these opinions critically.[12] This tendency is reinforced by the very wide range of interest groups that exist in the state, making it more likely that what is sometimes termed "countervailing power" will appear from a group when another has taken up a position on an issue. This is dissimilar to some other New England states in recent decades when, as Lockard notes about one of them:

> *In few American states are the reins of government more openly or completely in the hands of a few leaders of economic interest groups than in Maine.*[13]

The economic changes that have taken place in Massachusetts over the last few decades have tended to produce a changing variety of interest groups, not only because of the decline of those based on older industries and the emergence of many newer ones stemming from the industries that have recently taken root, but also because the expansion of an educated and articulate middle class in such an economically sophisticated state has produced a number of "cause" groups, some working for example for the general improvement of state government.

The inter-war economic decline stemming from the decay of a conventional industrial base was checked to some degree by the war, which produced a demand for the sort of goods that Massachusetts could produce and, by 1944, a fair comment by one magazine was that "its goods and plants produce everything from the $60 million aircraft carrier 'Lexington' to G.I. shoelaces."[14] Almost as soon as the war was over, the New England economy slipped back again because it was essentially "oriented to nineteenth century conditions."[15] Some movement of industry within the region helped certain of the New England states; the footwear industry declined in Massachusetts whereas it expanded in Maine and New Hampshire where wage rates were lower.[16]

The textile industry experienced a great deal of migration out of the region altogether, mainly towards the South, where lower wage rates, less militant unionism and financial incentives for the establishment of new factories made up a combination difficult to resist. The wage differential between Charlotte, North Carolina, and the major New England textile centers in 1950, for example, was as much as thirteen cents an hour.[17] Worcester County, the Plymouth area and the Merrimack valley experienced a considerable number of liquidations in the 1950s. The Northeast Committee of the National Planning Association summed it up in 1954:

> *If the management of a textile mill determines to close or re-locate, it tends to let its plant and equipment run down. Some day when the industry is caught in a slump, the mill closes its door permanently. A new mill may be built, but it is built in another region. Many of the mill's workers may be left stranded.*[18]

Personal tragedy, as suggested in that last sentence, is inescapable at a time of economic depression, but there was another side to the state's post-war economy. As employment in the "non-durable goods" industries dropped (44,000 from 1947 to 1953 for example), the "durable goods" industries were expanding (by 85,000 jobs) in the same period.[19] Electrical products, plastics, and optical instruments were among the growth areas of this period starting around 1950 and both the textile towns and the Greater Boston area (especially symbolized by the industrial complexes on the Route 128 ring road that almost encircles Greater Boston) benefitted. On this occasion, Massachusetts benefitted from the wage differential for it was competing with the very high wage area of the Middle Atlantic states, such as New York and New Jersey.[20]

There may still be dangers in the technological makeup of the state, especially since the invasion of the new technologies based on research and development owes some of its expansion to the provision of defense equipment for the United States government—almost ten percent of the personal income in the state came from the defense industry by the early 1960's.[21] The sign of a general cutback in defense spending from the late 1960s onwards has seemed to suggest a need for a substitute for this sort of demand on the state's economic capacity. If, however, the state's economy can make any adjustment necessary to allow for this, the future balance of the economy should be healthier than that in the recent past.

One of the most significant effects of economic change on any society is that it brings about consequent change in the roles of the actors and Massachusetts is a good example of this. In the gradual expansion of the labor force in the period 1950-1960, there was a drop of 48,000 in those occupied in "manufacturing" (virtually all in non-durables) while the category known as "professional, technical and kindred workers" expanded by no less than 70,000.

By 1960, the managerial and professional classes stood at twenty percent total occupied persons in the state, a rise of two percent over 1950.[22] It is especially the "professional" segment of the white-collar classes that is expanding and one recalls Robert Lane's description of occupations that "facilitate political expression." He contends that one can denote them as follows:

(i)   *intellectual or social skills helpful in political understanding and expression.*

(ii) *patterns of social interaction with like-minded others or with politically minded others.*

(iii) *higher than average stakes in government policy.*

(iv) *occupational roles congenial to "civic-mindedness," "ward heeling," "agitation" or some other socially recognized types of political behavior.*[23]

Lane suggests that a technological society encourages an expanding middle class which is more active politically. It must be admitted that research into the degree of political participation exercised by an expanding middle class has achieved somewhat conflicting results, but in a society changing in the way that Massachusetts has, with the professional classes enjoying the brunt of the expansion, one would tend to agree with the 1950 diagnosis of Woodward and Roper, who produced an index of political activity which placed those of better education and higher income (including the college educated, executives and professional peoples) at the top and their opposites at the bottom; the sub-groups here included laboring people, those with grade school education only, Negroes and housewives.[24] The trend in the state is for the "top groups" in this ranking to increase absolutely and proportionally; even the absolute value given to the lower-ranking groups may have shifted, for certain housewives, for example—mainly from high-income groups, it must be admitted—are intensely active politically through groups like the League of Women Voters.

C. Wright Mills suggested that " . . . on the political market-place of American society, the new middle-classes are up for sale."[25] This does not ring true in the context that he was using. Anthony Downs equates low income with the tendency to abstain from voting because of the greater difficulties that those on low incomes have in achieving the level of information necessary to make a decision and because the act of voting hurts them more in terms of relative cost.[26] This may be too mechanistic a view, but most evidence suggests that, in Western societies, it is more difficult to get high turnout in working-class than in middle-class districts. Participation, and intense identification with issues, are more middle-class than working-class traits.[27]

The suburbs of Boston provide the clearest illustration of the presence and power of this burgeoning professional middle class which now plays such an important part in the political life of the state. Writing of one of these—Newton, with a "white collar" element that amounted to 65.8% of the population—Edgar Litt isolated the politically active element as follows:

The politists are liberally educated, tolerant, supporters of the intellectual community and positively engaged in their professional work. Their political style values participation, conflict and social rewards.[28]

This particular suburb is of special interest when one looks at the politically active element in terms of its political allegiance. It was once regarded as being solidly Republican and the figures in Table Nine indicate how true this was in the late 1940s and early 1950s. These were the years when that favorite cliché of post-war political speculation held sway, i.e. that movement to the suburbs tended to make Republicans of Democrats.[29]

More acute observers saw that the reality was otherwise, that early migrants to the suburbs were more likely to be middle-class Republicans than Democrats and that as the number of Democrats in the suburbs grew, it became less of a problem to assert Democratic allegiance if it had been held as a central city dweller.[30] It seems likely that the post-war decade or so was one of mainly Republican movement; the upwardly mobiles moving from city to suburb and rural Republicans moving into the city to take their place.[31]

In Newton, it seems that the number of registered Democrat voters rose considerably though perhaps less dramatically than Table Nine suggests because, in the early period, many Democrats may have been reluctant to register as such because of social pressures in a predominantly Republican community. Democratic activists in Newton estimated (in conversation with the writer) that the increase was from about 3,000 in the early 1950s to near 16,000 in 1964.[32] The rank and file included many French, Irish and Italian voters, while the leadership was mainly Yankee, Jewish and Irish. By the mid-1960s, however, the "independents" in Newton were the key group since they were larger in number than the voters registered for the two main parties.

That there is something in the idea of a new "suburban" ethos seems to be borne out by research done in the early 1960s on three communities in the Greater Boston area, one of which is relatively near the core city and two that are of the type of residential suburb that we have been describing above. Malden, the old Democratic stronghold of the three with a near traditional pattern of Democratic Party structure, appears to have had at that time typical leadership of a highly personalized type where personal betterment came from taking on roles which helped in the election of Democratic candidates and in generally furthering the cause of the party. In the suburbs, Lexington and Concord, politics was less of a vocation, more of a part-time and public-spirited activity, oriented to the state rather than the local organization but ready to oppose even convention choices of candidates if they appeared to be weak on the issues that the activists felt to be important. Admittedly, there is an added factor in that in Lexington and Concord the Democrats are in a minority, unlike Malden, but this is difficult to see as the main cause of this difference of outlook.[33] The middle-class suburbanite, the "wave of the future" as it were, does not divorce politics from everyday life and rarely considers that one either must spend virtually all or none of one's time at it. He rarely wishes to become a professional politician but is prepared to spend a limited amount of time in issue-centered political activity that will not benefit him individually but rather the community at large.

The reactions of this type of political individual must be considered against the climate of political ethics that has been a feature of the state in the twentieth century. The term "corruption" has tended to be almost synonymous with professional politics at certain times when a wave of disclosures about political corruption has taken place. It must be admitted of course that one cannot see a low standard of ethics in political life, when it exists, standing in isolation from society as a whole. The Massachusetts Crime Commission, reporting in 1965, put this into context with the following statement:

The Commission recognizes that, fundamentally, the values and attitudes of the general public will determine the quality of government, but we do not subscribe fully to the common assertion that people get the kind of government they deserve. We believe that the citizens of Massachusetts deserve, badly need and can get a far better government than they have had recently.[34]

The first sentence of this statement is unexceptionable; the second may be open to some argument, though probably not much. Corruption in the political system must echo some low ethical standards elsewhere in the social system. The bribing of public officials by private citizens suggests private as well as public enterprise corruption. A telling paragraph in the above-mentioned report sums up the position of businessmen who were engaged in corrupt transactions to reap political favors or to cut corners on the procedures by which their businesses were regulated in the public interest:

The heads of such corporations who know about the corrupt methods used are as corrupt as those who obtain results from them by such methods . . . insulation from moral responsibility is cloaked in such clichés as "being realistic" and "meeting competition." It constitutes a specious failure to oppose corruption."[35]

Is it then a paradox to suggest that the "suburban ethos" is a force conducive to "good government" when business and industry, run often by the suburban managerial set, is occasionally subject to corrupt methods itself? To moderate this paradox, one can argue that the sheer size of the industrial-commercial networks, compared to the political, ensures that corrupt practice of the more blatant kinds may be more diffused in the non-political systems. It is probable that corruption that involves the relationship between the two areas is concentrated in those undertakings that expect returns from political decision-making of an immediate and direct order, for example the contracting industry where some, though of course not all, firms have profited unfairly or unethically from public works contracts, i.e. the building of high-ways and the like. Although private enterprise in the United States demands of the suburban executive a fierce identification with and loyalty to his firm and its interests over those of its compet-itors, this is usually kept within general ethical bounds and does not preclude his being a good citizen in the sense we have tried to describe.

If the industrial and commercial interests are not the villains of the corruption scenario, then who are the villains—the politi-cians? This latter group will argue that the corrupt politician, like the corrupt businessman, is a comparatively rare specimen, especially when the temptations of office and the pressures on the politician are taken into account. Chief among the pressures is the need to acquire money to pay for the vast expenses of American electoral battles. The increasing use of television in particular has added considerably to the cost of campaigning over the post-World War II years and total costs for a single campaign from the pre-convention period through the primary and biennial elections are now at a peak that most politicians will deplore in private if not in public. A one-time political aide in the state alleged in an interview that "the biggest source of corruption in political life is the amount of money it takes to get elected." Few politicians believe that it is possible to cut down these amounts for, as a member of the legislature put it, "Americans are advertising-conscious and expect campaigns to be well-publicized."

The size of these sums can be gauged from some actual figures. In 1958 the Republican and Democratic candidates for governor spent $502,278 between them, but by 1964 the gubernatorial cam-paign cost the considerable sum of $2,438,996.[36] Even much lower down on the ballot, where constituencies are smaller, the sums are not inconsiderable for a politician with meagre resources or an aspiring politician with none! In 1964-65, members of the General Court claimed that a campaign for the House could cost the individual anywhere between $2,000 and $12,000 and for the Senate $15,000—$30,000 with some senatorial elections costing a contender as much as $40,000. No doubt inflation has affected prices in this region as elsewhere in the last five or six years. It must be difficult to run for governor these days without a sum in the region of a million dollars at one's disposal. But not many individuals have this sort of money readily available, nor do the lesser men for minor offices have the ready money in most cases. It must often be solicited from friends or "fat cats" who are prepared to stake them for one reason or another. Out of the forty state senators, for example, it was estimated that in the mid-'60s there were perhaps five who could finance their own campaigns out of personal wealth. The percentage in the House was not likely to be greater.

The 1965 Crime Commission referred to "the thin line that separates bribes from campaign contributions."[37] Most legislators feel that they are lucky if they can gather their war chest from a large number of small contributors for this tends to cut down the dependence on a few individuals who can call for later favors in return for the gifts. Money from contractors is suspect to those politicians who like to keep themselves aloof from possible "strings." The financing of American political campaigning is a major problem that is perpetually worried over but rarely tackled directly. The failure of a recent Congressional attempt to tap taxation revenue for campaign funds illustrates this point admirably. The only short-term hope for most individual politicians is to encourage the spread of giving to the "politician of your choice" and an expansion of the view that this is an investment in good government rather than a payment for future concessions of a personal nature.

Whatever the pressures on politicians may be, it is difficult to create a frame of reference which excuses the worst of the scandals that made the newspaper headlines in the early 1960s but which extended over much of the '50s and the beginning of the '60s, at least. Scandals, for example, like the Worcester case, in which a firm of building engineers, headed by Harvard-educated Thomas Worcester, provided $275,000 in bribes for state officials in order to net contracts to design or build highways and other projects for the state. This 1960 case seemed to show that Worcester was a relative dupe and that others involved were the real villains; the presiding judge claimed that Worcester had identified:

former members of the state legislature, a former candidate for the Republican nomination for governor, and a present member of Congress as recipients of what may, with some euphemism, be called the Worcester Bounty.[38]

Involved in this and later scandals was the chairman of the

Massachusetts Turnpike Authority, William C. Callahan, described by Anthony Lewis of the *New York Times* in 1961 as "regarded by some as the most powerful force in Massachusetts government" and a few years later (prior to his death in 1964), by the Crime Commission as "a czar accountable to no one."[39] Lawmakers were put on the authority payroll and insurance commissions were funneled into the pockets of members of the legislature to ensure the passage of legislation favorable to the Authority's road-building program.

The Worcester case does not stand alone, nor is the Turnpike Authority the only public agency to be affected by the lax moral climate that infected the public service. When the Boston Common Garage was planned and the Massachusetts Parking Authority was entrusted with its construction, the Authority's head, George L. Brady, appears to have determined on a share of the ten million dollars allocated to the project and $800,000 was illegally secured by Brady and his accomplices, three of whom were eventually jailed though Brady himself eluded capture.[40] By the mid-'60s, it must have seemed that Governor Foster Furcolo's anguished complaint that peculation by officials was "an occupational hazard of modern government" was something of an understatement.[41] The Department of Public Works was an especial target of the "muckraking" that went on in the early '60s, while exposures of graft inside the Metropolitan District Commission of Greater Boston resulted in a number of convictions of MDC officials and at least one state representative.[42]

Apart from the institutional problems referred to above, there is a cultural context in Massachusetts which makes corruption thrive in a way that might be more difficult elsewhere. Elliot Richardson's 1961 comment following his description of some of the scandals ran:

> *The most striking feature of the Massachusetts political scene, as I view it, is the subordination of programs and principles to personal relationships.*[43]

This could appear like the supercilious complaint of a Yankee politician in a political system where he seems increasingly isolated, but it is gainsaid by Richardson's follow-up, which suggests that the isolation of ethnic community from ethnic community stemmed originally from the Yankee attitudes towards the Irish and Italian *arrivistes* of the later nineteenth century. In fact even today, Massachusetts, despite its high standard of living and its firm technological base, retains some of the attributes of a "developing country" in that loyalties are not to the political system as a whole but to the ethnic group, to the "tribe" rather than the community at large. Writing about corruption in developing countries, Wraith and Simpkins see one of the "cures for corruption" as:

> *The passage of time, during which, given steady economic progress, loyalties will gradually move from family, clan and tribe to nation-state.*[44]

Other forms of cure include education ("which will enable people to understand what politics are about, instead of regarding them as a tribal or partisan form of excitement"—a phrase which seems an excellent description of the outward show of much of Massachusetts politics!), evolution of public opinion, strengthening of the middle class, growth of a professional class, etc.—almost all reflective of the general argument that we have been trying to develop. Increasing "mobilization" of the polity as a whole towards the community rather than the private good over an area of human endeavor is the obvious solution, as is the cliché that this is bound to take time. Many observers see it coming and share the view that what is often crudely termed "embourgeoisement" will play its part:

> *Massachusetts is changing. It is witnessing the rise of a discriminating suburban population which has disavowed the politics of private gain and will tend in future to elect to major office those men who reflect high standards of public service.*[45]

This is a bald and rather optimistic statement, but despite cross-currents like the seeming hatred of the suburban ethos by many of the young, hopefully it has the seed of the future in it. There are signs of an improved political climate in the state. The middle and professional classes, too narrowly based and divided in the past from the rest of society by ethnic, economic and social barriers, are now more widely based in their ethnic and economic antecedents and are able and willing enough to ensure that the state does have the standard of government that any state deserves.

Some of this feeling is reflected in an increase in the volume of activity by the highly specialized type of pressure group that is mainly concerned with the improvement of the standards

of government within the boundaries of the state. Two of the
most active reform groups of recent years are the League of
Women Voters of Massachusetts and the Council for Constitutional Reform in Massachusetts. The former is one of, if not
the largest "league" in the United States and brings together
about 12,000 women (almost all middle-class whites) in an
extensive civic action program of which government reform
is probably the largest overall commitment at any one time.
In V. O. Key's words, the fifty-year-old League "has a long
record of lobbying in support of governmental measures or-
dinarily in the general interest."[46] It has been in the vanguard
of attempts to strip state government of archaic structures
like the Governor's Council and to make the Great and General
Court (in its view) more efficient by cutting the size of the
House of Representatives. Its most successful year was probably
1964 when two measures that it supported were on the ballot,
one restricting the powers of the Governor's Council and the
other extending the terms of all six constitutional officers
from two to four years. Both became effective as a result of a
favorable vote in the referendum. The success with the four-
year term was especially notable in view of the fact that eight
years previously, when the four-year term was turned down
by the General Court in joint convention, most people with knowledge of the legislature's and the people's attitude felt that the
task was hopeless. The League's enquiries reaped replies like
"It is a lost cause—the General Court refuses to break with
tradition and neither party really wants this reform."[47] The
climate of opinion following the disclosures discussed above
must have assisted in the 1964 result, for the majority (58.3%
of the total vote, 75.5% of the "yes-no" vote) was a clear one.

The Council for Constitutional Reform was active for a relatively brief period. It claimed to be nonpartisan and did have
support from both main parties (e.g. Herter and Furcolo among
ex-governors) but was weighted towards the Republicans, probably because of the sensitivity towards the corruption issue
among the Democrats as the majority party in the legislature.
The Council's program was by now the familiar one of strengthening the executive branch, abolition of the Governor's Council,
cutting the size of the legislature and extending the privilege
of "home rule" to cities and towns subject to legislative veto
over their powers to control their own destinies. Reform move-

ments generally, perhaps rightly, are less suspicious of strong executive power or local democracy than they are of the log-rolling in the General Court, where the temptations alluded to earlier can so easily undermine the attempts to further the general good of the people of Massachusetts.

Other reform organizations have tried to work through one or the other of the main parties. The Americans for Democratic Action (A.D.A.) grew out of the Independent Voters of Massachusetts. Though its prime orientation was towards liberal candidates in both parties, its basic orientation was towards the Democrats and, in particular, behind platform planks that promised reform of a constitutional nature. "COD"—its original full title of Commonwealth Organization of Democrats was taken away by a Democratic state committee chairman with a court order—was another middle-class organization, this time working inside the Democratic Party for the support of "liberals" and in specific opposition to old style leaders like the late John Thompson and Frankie Kelly. It dissolved itself in 1964 after a four-year run in the hope that Edward Kennedy and the then state committee chairman, Gerard Doherty, were about to reform the party organization in COD's own image, a belief far from fully realized.

The Republican Party in the state has appeared to be less polarized in its attitude towards reform than the Democrats, probably because it has tended to be in a minority position since the mid-'50s. It cannot be due to the relative purity of the party, for Republicans as well as Democrats have been exposed by the investigations of the 1960s. One contributing feature may have been the ideological split that existed for several years during the height of the public interest in the corruption issue, a split that was national in origin yet which percolated down to local level. It was, of course, best represented by the circumstances surrounding the presidential election of 1964. A group like the Ripon Society, originating from Harvard and MIT Republicans, tended to take a national rather than a state view of politics. One ostensible reform group, the Jefferson Lincoln Union, based in Essex County, seemed to stand on the far right of the Republican Party. It combined a basically "national" issue, opposition to world Communism, with support for fiscal responsibility and included a blanket attack on Democrats, old style and new!

By the later 1960s, reform was rather like apple pie and one could not hope to be against it and expect a statewide level of support. In the Democratic primary of 1966, for example, the three Italo-American but otherwise quite diverse candidates for the attorney general nomination, Frank Bellotti, Foster Furcolo and Robert De Giacomo all plumped for this issue and it was reported that "all three say the time has come for drastic reforms in controlling campaign contributions and expenditures."[48] The interests of voters and politicians in this particular issue had converged in that, as we observed earlier, the parties and the candidates found it difficult to raise the amount needed for mass media advertising while the public now recognized that expensive campaigns laid politicans open to near bribery as a source for meeting their bills. There was an attempt at a voluntary moratorium in 1966 when Democratic leaders put forward a plan to limit expenditure in the election period but, despite support from Governor John Volpe, the state chairman of the Republican Party refused to cooperate on the grounds that only legislation would effectively limit campaign spending, and then only legislation with strict sanctions for infringement.[49] Six years later, in the 1972 legislative session, a new law, paralleling a federal law of the same year, placed a ceiling on campaign spending but it remains to be seen how effective its implementation will be.

Far-reaching reforms in the shape of legislative action may well have to wait for the gradual evolution of the Great and General Court, where, on the whole, younger members seem more sympathetic than the older ones. The legislature, usually regarded by reformers outside it as the greatest roadblock to improving the quality of state government, now contains a number of younger members who, despite the constraints of party discipline, tend to be more "public-regarding" than legislators of the recent past. Democrats like Beryl Cohen and Michael Dukakis, Republicans like John Quinlan and Martin Linsky are a few of the names that spring to mind for the period under discussion (Cohen and Dukakis are now both out of office).

One specific "reform" candidate was Independent Chandler Stevens, who served two terms in the House, elected in 1964, re-elected in 1966, and defeated in 1968 when he ran for the U.S. House, once again as an Independent. He stood for the Thirty-fifth Middlesex District in 1964 after working for the Council for Constitutional Reform in Massachusetts and realizing that, as he put it, "the one hold-out was the legislature" as far as reform

was concerned. [50] His argument was that the policies he favored
were based on the theory that the economic battles had largely
been won and that social issues (civil rights, education, mental
health, etc.) were now the important ones but they should be
accompanied by measures of political reform. He attacked the
rigid social and economic structures of the past and sponsored
legislation to abolish the Governor's Council, set up an ombuds-
man's office, revise the structure of county government and give
the cities and towns more "home rule," but few of these became
law. Well-educated candidates of Stevens' background (he was
educated in three different disciplines—engineering, mathematics
and economics) both reflect the economic development of Massachusetts and provide able men to operate its government.

Of course, it would be foolish to suggest that the increasing influence of the enlarged middle class is likely to be an unmixed
blessing in the future political life of the state. It is likely to produce its own problems and some of these have already been hinted
at by some writers:

> *Since duty tends to be little more than a middle-class version of
> noblesse oblige, it is not nobility status which obligates but
> bourgeois status. Political volunteerism derives from citizen
> duty, and malrepresentation of social groups in legislatures is
> one consequence."* [51]

As yet, these problems are not especially marked in a governmental process where the pressures until recently have tended to be
from groups other than this "new class" we have been describing.
In the short run, one envisages this group providing more than
its share of "reformers" and, in a state where social class as such
is becoming less noticeable as a divisive agent, the dangers of
"malrepresentation" in favor of an established middle class seem
less obvious than they were when a small bourgeoisie dominated
a largely working-class polity.

At the present time the "reformers," recognizing that many of
the problems lie in the machinery of government itself, are
emphasizing reform in this area and are also encouraging the
recruitment of—as they see it—a higher standard of legislator
and administrator in state government. Although there have
been a few—perhaps more than a few—relative villains un-
masked, or suspected in recent years, it should be emphasized
that the overall standard is not a low one, certainly no lower than

in the state at large. In fact, many of the supposed old-style politicians have tried to be effective decision-makers within the system as they found it. The truth is that the demands on the state political system have diversified as the need to provide for no more than a basic regulation of social and economic life has given way to a demand for government to intervene in the wholesale protection and improvement of life-styles. The technologically mature society is incredibly complex and calls for more subtle and sophisticated responses from its political leaders than was the case in the past. It is this agonizing realization that had overshadowed the pattern of politics in Massachusetts in the postwar era.

Chapter Five
The Post-War Watershed

If one were to choose a period of ten or fifteen years when the political complexion of Massachusetts changed from basically Republican to basically Democratic it would undoubtedly be following World War II, the fifteen years between the end of the war and the time when a Massachusetts man once again won election to the U.S. presidency. It was a time when state politics seemed comparatively trivial compared to the events in the world at large which dominated the news, since the country was now the leading Western power. Against the backdrop of cold war abroad, with occasional "hot" war as in Korea, McCarthyism at home represented the heights of disillusionment with the "peace." Under Eisenhower, confidence slowly recovered but fell off again near the end of his two terms, especially when the Russians made their first technological advances into space. Much of this international involvement reacted on state and local politics, adding another dimension to the usual range of "bread and butter" issues that had dominated the inter-war period. The Democratic "coalition" seemed badly bruised in the country as a whole by the 1950s, but by and large Roosevelt's handiwork survived the immediate post-war strains and, once the war hero Eisenhower was no longer available and "Communism, corruption and Korea" became a decaying slogan, it reasserted itself by 1960.

Ignoring for the moment the external or "extra-societal" influences on the state's politcal system, one can divide the major problems into two areas: (1) the peculiar ones faced by the state and the region as described in the last chapter, and (2) those that were the stuff of politics in the other forty-seven, later forty-nine, states, such as education, transport facilities and the welfare program. These major "demands," in Eastonian terminology, must be seen against the backdrop of the political culture of the state, its high degree of ethnic consciousness, the urbanized (and suburbanized) character of most of it, the tensions between metropolitan Boston and the rest. More than in earlier periods, the "state," in the philosophical and constitutional meaning of the

term, came to be looked to as a provider of services which had
once been the prerogative of private enterprise, services like transport of the mass transit variety and post-public school education.
As we saw earlier, money is crucial to the election of office-
holders. It is also the stuff of politics in that it redistributes the
utility factor in the social system and provides services that
the individual, however wealthy, could not do.

Massachusetts has been termed a "high tax state" and tends
to be in the top half-dozen or so of all American states in this
respect.[1] It depended on a flat rate income tax for a large part
of state revenue until the eventual adoption of a sales tax after
the election of 1966 (Table Ten indicates the sources of revenue
and the per capita expenditure in 1960). Much of the income
tax revenue in the post-war period was returned to towns and
cities to meet local expenditures, for their own range of taxes
is small, the property tax and motor vehicle excise (especially
the former) comprising their chief sources on income. The state
does have a miscellaneous set of minor taxes, those on cigar-
ettes, alcoholic beverages and motor fuel, but has for a long
time coveted the sales tax as an additional source of revenue. Until 1966, this was a recurring theme for political debate and the
stuff of many an electoral dispute. As early as 1933, Governor Ely
had indicated that a general sales tax or a higher state income tax
was needed to allow the state to aid the localities and relieve their
high dependence on property taxes.

Nowhere in the state was the out cry against the property tax as
shrill as in Boston itself. A comparison made in the 1950s between
Boston and twenty other large American cities put the Bay State
city at the head of the table of equalized property tax rates.[2] This
is a fact well known to Bostonians if newspaper comment is any
guide, but it is a little misleading since most American cities
levy supplementary taxes that Boston is not allowed to use because of the reluctance of the General Court to extend the city's
taxing powers. When these other taxes are taken into consider-
ation, Boston does not appear to stand out as much from the mass
of urban America:

> *When the* total *tax burden of Boston is compared to the* total
> *tax burden of other cities, Boston is by no means as badly off as
> it appears when only property tax rates are compared.* [3]

Even if this is true, it is difficult to erode the belief among Bos-

tonians that they live in the most highly taxed city in the country
or at least one of the two or three most highly taxed. Pressures to
spread taxation, particularly by means of the general sales tax,
have been evident in both major parties. Within the Democratic
Party though, where Bostonian dislike of the property tax could
be expected to surface, it was offset by the belief that the sales
tax was essentially regressive and that relief from property taxes
should be met by a higher rate of income tax.

The thesis that no one votes for a tax, only for increased services, seems illustrated by the tax history of post-war Massachusetts and even by looking back to the pre-war experience. When
Governor Volpe's aides were producing a "kit" to help his supporters in the sales tax battle of 1965-66, they were able to quote
from the 1937-38 Special Commission on Taxation and Public
Expenditure which asserted that:

> For almost a decade, we have drifted from year to year, looking
> mainly for an improvement, pursuing fiscal mirages and devising
> stop-gaps of questionable merit. To continue that way is unsafe
> from a financial point of view and a reflection upon our compe-
> tence to govern ourselves. We cannot postpone the adoption of a
> sound policy for the relief of the tax burden on real estate.[4]

This was equally as apt for the '60s as for the '30s and indeed for
much of the time in between. Tax reform in urban society is never
easy and the problems in Massachusetts have been especially
acute. Fiscal crises seemed to be impending from time to time in
the fifteen post-war years but were averted either by wartime
expansion of the economy or, at one period, by instituting a withholding system that virtually brought in two years' income taxes
in one, a device that cannot be repeated.

The "rising expectations" of the post-war generation were
hampered by the difficulty of funding the new programs generally
desired. Despite this factor, it was found possible to undertake
a considerable road program, for example, including the magnet-
for-industry Route 128 which looped around Boston on three
sides and the Massachusetts Turnpike, even with the latter's
aura of corruption. From the late '50s, concern about the state's
place in the provision of college education grew, though the
realization of some of these programs belong more to the '60s
than the '50s.

It might be argued that pressure for a widening participation

for the state in satisfying the basic demands of the individual instead of leaving them to market forces was bound to benefit the
Democratic Party which, during the twentieth century, has come
to be regarded as the "spending" party of the two that dominate
American politics. Although this is likely to be a contributory
factor, it is unlikely to provide a simple one-to-one relationship
as far as Massachusetts is concerned. Republican governors in
the whole post-war period—men like Herter and Volpe—have
not been adverse to providing programs if they can be funded
without excessive borrowing. The shift in the state's political
allegiance is in fact a more than complex mix of changes in the
state and nation: decline in relative size and assurance of the Yankee population, coming-of-age of the ethnic minorities, a shift
in the national balance inside the parties so that, for example, the
Republican Party has gradually become less the party of a north-
eastern establishment and more a party of the spread-out West
and the border-state status aspirants. This is a regional phenomenon and even Republican strategists who foresee the possibility
of a new majority coalition in favor of their party have virtually
written off the whole Northeast, once a bastion of Republican
power. Kevin Phillips admits that:

> *From the peak years of the New Deal, the power of the North-*
> *east has been declining as the influence of the South has been*
> *rising . . . The Republican Party is no longer the party of the*
> *Northeast.*[5]

Although it is a regional phenomenon to a great degree, it is
equally true that different states within the region have drifted
towards the Democrats at a differing rate and that, for example,
northern New England is less—far less—committed to the drift
than is southern New England. Vermont and New Hampshire
went for Nixon in 1968 and Maine might have done so if Muskie
had not been the Democrats' vice-presidential candidate. In
Massachusetts, the transition has been a jerky, labored and
sometimes uncertain one, and the behavior of individual politicians and the emergence of specific issues have thrown up cross-
patterns, as has the influence of a national figure such as Eisenhower.

The only clear way to underline the changes is once again to
look at the period 1945-1960 in chronological terms. Inevitably
this means examining the administrations of the five governors

—Tobin, Bradford, Dever, Herter and Furcolo—whose terms of office spanned these years even though the division into Republican governor and Democrat governor is itself not as significant a guide to political trends as might be thought. Governors do tend to focus attention on themselves even if their real power is limited. Their power is executive and therefore dramatic; the public can in turn focus on the pronounced intentions of one man far more easily than the more diffused, often contradictory statements of the legislative leaders and their followers. The reality of power may be that it is divided and separated at the state level as it is at the federal, and legislative leaders are fond of reminding one that "the governor proposes, the legislature disposes."

But a governor will leave his stamp on two, four or six years of office clearer than any legislative leader can. This is particularly true in Massachusetts where, since the lieutenant governor does not preside over the Senate, there are two presiding officers (the President of the State Senate and the Speaker of the House of Representatives), without mention of majority and minority leaders etc., to divide the legislative leadership. Governors rarely meet with acquiescence from the legislature for their programs and when major problems arise, such as the patent need for raising extra revenue, the General Court itself will be the seedbed of alternative solutions that conflict with those put forward by the Governor. This built-in tension is a vital fact of American political life, as students of the relationship between president and Congress know only too well. It is to American politics what competition is to the private enterprise system of economic distribution. Without entering into philosophical debate about American institutional practice, it is obvious that the nature of the separation of powers makes what is often termed sustained power, i.e. the pressing of a definite program into law, extremely difficult. The governor who sees a high percentage of his program on to the statute book is usually proud of this fact and generally uses it to fuel a reelection campaign.

To return to the elections and administrations of the 1940s, one needs to look at Massachusetts at the time when the Second World War was ending. Maurice Tobin had been in office less than a year and the initial fear was an economic one, the governor having foreseen this to some extent in his inaugural address of the preceding January:

The concept that mass unemployment will follow this war, we must reject. We also reject a philosophy that government should control and permanently regiment the economy and direct the daily lives of our citizens. [6]

Curiously, one symbol of the public concern with the problems of economic adjustment and, in particular, a feeling by its citizens that Boston was down-at-heel and depressed as a city, despite wartime prosperity, was the emergence of James Michael Curley for his fourth and final victory for the mayoralty in November 1945. Studies of this election suggest that Curley's reputation as a man who could get things done helped him in 1945; his support came from low income groups and the ethnics, as one would expect, rather than from those with high incomes or the Yankee and assimilated immigrant voters. Surprisingly though, support came from younger voters rather than older ones; Curley's appeal was that of a man who could get things done through personal dynamism.[7] Despite the impending trial in the Engineers' Group case which was to lead to Curley's conviction and a term at the Federal Penitentiary in Danbury, Connecticut, Curley succeeded in netting 45.7 percent of the vote in a six-sided contest, no mean feat and an indication that the Boston voter, at least, hoped for dramatic answers to the problems of eastern Massachusetts.

Curley was a disappointment to Bostonians in the late 1940s, which was why this was his last term as mayor. His former pupil, Maurice Tobin, impressed himself little more than Curley on the electorate. His defeat in 1946 was probably as much due to his political style as to anything else. Although his personal manner was smoother than that of Curley, he had progressed little from the Curley era in other ways. When John Gunther interviewed him for his book on the United States he felt the Tobin entourage was a recollection of things past:

Instantly I remembered days when I was a cub reporter in Chicago twenty years before. This was politics. These were politicians.[8]

Brokerage politics was the basis of the style and the spoils system, curbed to some extent under Salstonstall, reappeared in blatant fashion. State employees in career grades who had supported Tobin in 1944 found that they were discriminated against in favor of political appointees.[9] This was paradoxical to some extent in that Tobin was proud of one of his main legislative attainments, the

passing of the Fair Employment Practices Act which outlawed
discrimination on the grounds of sex, race and religion for all
state employees (but not, it will be noted, on grounds of political
loyalty!).[10]

Signs of Tobin's potential weakness came in the primary election
when his little-known opponent, Francis D. Harrigan, secured a
quarter of the statewide and over a third of the Boston vote.
Although this was noted as a sign that Tobin should "mend his
fences," attention was for once centered more upon the primary
for lieutenant governor where Paul Dever beat an opponent,
Mayor Roger Putnam of Springfield, who, like Dever, had once
opposed Saltonstall for the governorship. Putnam had been
endorsed by John McCormack, then majority leader of the U.S.
House of Representatives, and was a strong candidate. Dever, who
had stood up better to Saltonstall than had Putnam, reaffirmed
his superior appeal to Putnam on this occasion.

The newspapers suggested that the campaign was being fought
in a low key and that the "man in the street refused to become
excited over the political situation."[11] Tobin tried to heal the
ten-year-old feud with Curley, but the declaration made by the
two men was certainly lukewarm on Curley's part and his supporters in Boston are reputed to have defected in considerable
numbers to Bradford on election day. Saltonstall linked Tobin to
the Democratic administration in Washington, a useful device in
a year when it was on the defensive nationally.[12] Since Tobin
could not rely on the Boston Irish as a bloc, he appealed to other
ethnics such as the always tenuous, but theoretically large, Can-
adian-American vote, as one advertisement in the *Boston Herald*
made clear:

> *Canadian American Voters re-elect Governor Maurice J. Tobin.*
> *As Mayor of Boston and Governor of the state, he has always*
> *shown us co-operation and understanding. Like most of us, he*
> *comes of humble, hard-working stock and he knows our*
> *problems.*[13]

The mid-term Republican sweep of 1946 regained the Congress
for them for the first time since 1932 as well as a bare majority of
state governorships. Their successes were reflected in Massachusetts and the *Boston Herald* headline, "Republicans Sweep State,
Nation" was an expected reaction to the GOP successes.[14]
Tobin and David Walsh both went down in defeat. Walsh lost

even Boston to Lodge, a clear indication that the aging senator
was regarded as no longer fit for service when compared with a
younger opponent with an efficient organization and a good war
record. Tobin's loss was not as great, but even he lost seven of
the city's twenty-two wards including the one in which he lived
(Ward Nineteen, Jamaica Plain-Roslindale). In general, Tobin's
worst losses were in the eastern counties of the state where he had
made some impression in 1944 (see Table Eleven). Tobin suffered
from the general reaction to Democratic executive control but
also from a divided party in which a number of the leading figures
were opposed to him. His administration had not been of a high
enough quality for independents to be attracted to supporting
him. It had been a highly "political" administration in the narrowest sense of the term with over-use of patronage and poor
appointments to public office two of the reasons for the 150,000
deficit instead of 150,000 majority that Tobin received in 1944.

The gubernatorial victor was Robert Bradford, the Republican
lieutenant governor during Tobin's term of office. As district
attorney of Middlesex County he had made for himself a reputation that led to comparisons with New York's Dewey and,
although his political touch was not always very sure, his integrity and quiet manner seem to have long outlived his brief
term as governor. Like many of his predecessors, he had never
served in the General Court, an experience that is generally regarded as being invaluable to a prospective chief executive.
Service as lieutenant governor is no substitute in Massachusetts,
since unlike most states of the Union, the Massachusetts lieutenant
governor does not preside over the State Senate. Hence Bradford's
two years as Tobin's lieutenant governor had been of only limited
value as political experience. As in Washington, executive-legis-
lative relationships in a state capital are more often strained than
amicable even when governor and legislative majorities are of the
same party.

In Bradford's case, the clash came inevitably over the taxation
issue. He proposed a two percent sales tax designed to relieve
the property tax burden by subsidies that would at least hold the
rate and provide some aid to education in the localities.[15] It
suffered the fate of all other sales tax measures proposed up to
1965. He did achieve some successes, such as in the degree of independence he allowed to state agencies, including the Public
Health Department, enabling some relief of political pressure

on day-to-day administration. Other measures helped the Boston metropolitan area, such as the establishment of the Metropolitan Transit Authority as recommended by the Coolidge Commission, chaired by the then Senator Arthur Coolidge who had now become Bradford's lieutenant governor.

The MTA provided a major issue for the election of 1948. A report published just before the election showed that the deficit for the first nine months of 1948 was almost twice as much as for the first nine months of 1947. There were rumors that a fifty percent fare rise was on the way to offset this deficit, the basic ten percent fare in the inner city, for example, going up to fifteen cents. The Democrats pushed this home by advertising that "Your Only Chance to Fight the 15¢. MTA Fare is by Electing Dever Your Governor, " while in a late October radio broadcast, Paul Dever claimed that tokens for the higher fares were already being tested for use in the rapid transit cars.[16] Since this was a time of fairly rapid inflation, threats of higher prices in the public sector and suggestions that Bradford supported a two percent sales tax were reasonably effective campaign material.[17]

Divisions in the Democratic Party nationally were reflected to some degree at state level. The "Dixiecrat" revolt, in the person of Strom Thurmond, had virtually no effect in Massachusetts, for Thurmond was not on the ballot—but Henry Wallace was and his Progressive Party challenge, breaking away sections of the liberal wing of the party, was looked upon as a possible threat. In the Tenth District, where the formidable Christian Herter was the incumbent congressman, a "Progressive (Wallace) Democrat" was his only challenger but Herter won by more than two to one. Wallace did manage to attract 8,000 people to his rally in Boston Gardens in September, but the main bulk of the Democratic cadres stayed with the Truman ticket even though the hoped-for nomination of John McCormack as vice-presidential candidate did not take place at the Philadelphia Convention in July.[18]

This air of uncertainty stemming from Truman's seemingly weak position in his bid for reelection in 1948 appeared to induce a defeatist air in the state Democratic Party. They should have taken heart from the higher turnout for the Democratic primary (320,039) than for the Republican (271,209) in September 1948. This was especially true since the gubernatorial contests in both parties, always one of the main centers of interest, should have attracted a higher Republican than Democratic vote. Bradford

faced a fairly strong challenge from Senator Edward M. Rowe
of Cambridge who described the Governor's administration to
date as being one of "broken promises and extravagance."[19]
Paul Dever would have contested Maurice Tobin for the Democratic nomination and this would have been a close fight, but
Tobin was appointed Secretary for Labor by the President only
a few weeks before the primary, too late for his name to be taken
off the ballot though he tried to offset this ostensibly by asking
his supporters not to give him a "complimentary vote." In fact,
21.1 percent of the vote did go to Tobin but Dever's 69.3 percent was clear enough to save him great embarrassment. Bradford,
facing a real opponent, did well with 77.6 percent as against 16.1
for Rowe.[20]

In general, and as usual, the Democratic primaries provided
the most excitement with shades of the "name's the same" game.
Frankie Kelly won the Democratic nomination for attorney
general despite confusion caused by the appearance of a John
Kelly on the ballot. A West End politician and one-time aide to
Martin Lomasney, John I. Fitzgerald, won a five-cornered fight
for the senatorial nomination with 24.9 percent of the total vote
though John F. Fitzgerald was convinced that he was trading on
the name of "Honey Fitz."[21]

The final stages of the election were fought warily on "bread-and-
butter" issues like the MTA fare and the need, on the other hand,
for expenditure on services such as an improved highway system.
Local polls, showing Bradford ahead, were as inaccurate as the
national ones that showed Dewey in the lead over Truman at a
late stage.[22] Thus the result of the election, which returned
Truman to the White House and also swept in the entire Democratic slate for the six Massachusetts constitutional offices, was
an almost complete surprise to the state Democratic Party. At the
same time, the state House of Representatives went Democratic
by a majority of four and both parties secured twenty seats in the
Senate. The cumulative effect of all this is to mark 1948 as a
watershed in the electoral history of Massachusetts. Short-term
and long-term trends came together, suggesting 1948, despite
subsequent ebb and flow, as the most "critical" election in the
creation of a firm Democratic majority in the state. What 1928 had
started, 1948 consolidated. In Boston, for example, the Republican enclave shrunk to Ward Five only (Back Bay-Beacon Hill);
even the West Roxbury-Roslindale Ward Twenty "went Demo-

cratic for the first time in a presidential year."[23] Massachusetts
had been an uncertain devotee of the "New Deal" in many respects,
but the ethnic and religious makeup of the state ensured that,
once the Democratic coalition began to assume a majority position in the state, it would be more durable than in many other
states.

The Democratic victory in 1948 was given point by the appearance of several vital referenda "questions" on the ballot. Referenda
have been a feature of Massachusetts elections ever since the
"progressives" at the 1917 Constitutional Convention succeeded in
making them part of the system and are based on initiative petitions or laws referred to the people by the General Court. One that
must be singled out from the nine on the 1948 ballot was a virtual
repeat of a 1942 question aimed at the repeal of Massachusetts'
notorious birth-control law which prevented doctors from dis-
seminating birth control information to their patients. It was
even more decisively defeated in 1948 than in 1942 and it may well
have encouraged the Catholic vote, heavily Democratic at this
time, to turn out to defeat the amendment and incidentally vote for
the Democratic candidates. Table Twelve shows the relationship
between the vote on the amendment, the two-party vote for the
senatorial and gubernatorial elections and the percentage of Catholics in the population, all county by county. The similarity between the Catholic and Democratic "votes" are noticeable, with
exceptions, and the tie-in between the gubernatorial vote and opposition to the amendment is even stronger, suggesting that the
one benefitted from the other as far as the Democrats were concerned.[24]

As well as the "birth-control amendment," there were three
referenda aimed at restricting the privilege and rights of organized labor. All were heavily defeated. These three "questions"
were tied to the Republican Party and, in particular, to Attorney-
General Barnes, noted as a supporter of the Taft-Hartley Act and
the regulation of union activities. Although the turnout in 1948 was
not especially high for a presidential election year (1944—87.5%;
1946—73.7%; 1948—87.1%; 1950—78.7%; 1952—90.9%;), it could
be argued that high turnouts are likely to produce more working-
class Democrats and that they were likely to have their allegiance sharpened by the birth-control and labor referenda. Rossiter's
description of the Democratic party as "urban, working-class, new
stock, union orientated" fits the Massachusetts party at this time.[25]

The character of the 1948 election pointed up these denotations and encouraged the faithful to exert themselves for the sake of the party.

1948 (or more strictly speaking, January 1949) instituted a run of four-year governorships which lasted until the election of 1960. Paul Dever, Christian Herter and Foster Furcolo were very different types and in fact represent what can be considered the three major ethnic strains in modern Massachusetts politics, Irish, Yankee and Italian (although Furcolo is half-Irish). The first two are considered in retrospect to have had some qualified success in office; Furcolo is less highly regarded, not because he lacked ability but because the governor's chair was not the appropriate political niche for him. Each faced the problems we have discussed earlier and each was forced back on solutions which often blurred the supposed party-oriented difference between the Republican and the two Democrats.

Dever's inauguration ended the political career of Robert Bradford, evidently because his political acumen was not the equal of his administrative ability. Robert Wood described him as a "bright young man who lost ground."[26] Dever was quite different, an acute party leader described by Shannon as "a professional politician, known and trusted by other professionals" and a man who possessed "a quick, shrewd, sceptical mind."[27] Politicians in the 1960s still considered him to have been "progressive" in ideology, able as an administrator and of course every inch the politician, an all-around governor of his period who had progressed beyond the private-regarding attitudes of pre-war Democratic politicians. Nonetheless, he still found the roles of broker and pragmatic political leader difficult to reconcile. Early in his first term, the unfulfilled expectations of spoils-seekers were, in an exaggerated fashion, said to be costing him "1,000 votes a month" and his former campaign manager, Senate Floor Leader John E. Powers, was trying to deal with two hundred job-seekers a day. The tradition dies hard in Massachusetts.[28]

Interviewing leading politicians (past and present) and political journalists in 1965, I tried to find out why it took twenty years for the "Democratic hegemony to seep down" as one of them put it, i.e. from the constitutional offices to the General Court and beyond. It must be made plain that sudden change in the composition of a legislature is comparatively rare, even when all the seats are up for reelection every other year. Legislators tend to establish close ties with their districts and can often ride out short-term trends against their party; this is especially true in state legislatures (as compared with Congress) where the "coattails" effect of presidential elections is less evident. In Massachusetts, the Republicans had two added advantages, good organization and monetary resources (being the "middle-class" party of the two). A third often adduced, but one that needs to be probed more deeply, is the power of the majority party in the legislature to control the boundaries of the House and Senate districts. "Gerrymandering" is a term that originated in Massachusetts and has had some reflection in the twentieth as well as the nineteenth century, for boundary lines often helped Republican incumbents to keep their seats. However, its effect is limited. Latham and Goodwin point out that the 72nd Amendment to the State Constitution lays down firm rules for the drawing of districts but this does not mean that some adroit manipulation is not possible.[29]

Before the Supreme Court decisions, starting with *Baker* v. *Carr* in 1962, there was some imbalance and gerrymandering in districting in Massachusetts and it generally favored the majority party of the day as far as the General Court was concerned. In the late '40s, there were examples of urban areas being split up and added to contiguous suburban ones, a device which could help to dilute the Democratic vote. Twelfth and Thirteenth Bristol, for example, took precincts from Fall River and married them to Westport and Somerset respectively and made two Republican-tending districts out of an area which, apportioned differently, would have provided one Democratic representative at least. In 1948, the swing was enough to topple both of these Republican districts.

One of the reasons for the 1948 swing may well have been the influence of returning veterans after World War II. Ex-Speaker John Thompson, now deceased, told the writer in an interview that he and others of his generation wanted to take an active part in a governing process that had helped to send him and his contemporaries off to war. This may have been a rationalization of other motives, but the veterans were certainly a new wave. Nineteen forty-eight saw the emergence of names that were to be active participants in the top reaches of the state's politics in the '50s and '60s: men like Thompson, Maurice Donahue and Joseph Ward among the Democrats, and Sidney Curtis, later House minority leader, among the Republicans. The Democratic Party, using a "fighting fund" controlled by, among others, Representative T. P. "Tip" O'Neill, but owing much of its origin to the belief of Congressman John McCormack that the House could be won for the Democrats, concentrated on marginal seats, almost forty in all, and the candidates for these (mostly youngish men and including many veterans) were victorious in most cases.[30]

This election, a crucial one in the state's history, produced the possibilty of a consistent Democratic program from the Governor and the Democratically controlled House (the Senate was divided 20-20), but the lack of real ability in his fellow constitutional officers hindered Dever and inter–and intra–party bickering in the General Court made policy-making difficult, although measures like Dever's transportation legislation were pushed through by the younger elements in the legislature.[31] The Republican Party, in defeat, tended to splinter as the Democrats had often done; personal factions appeared backing Saltonstall, Lodge and others.[32] Neither party was happy about imposing tax increases to pay for new services, but Dever eventually reconciled himself to the fact that borrowing on a large scale was necessary if new schemes were to be floated. In 1949, a bond issue provided a hundred million dollars for a new road program. [33] This inevitably encumbered future generations with interest repayment and eventually capital redemption (capital repayments were often deferred for a considerable number of years). There seemed no alternative to this unless and until the general public could be persuaded to support new methods of taxation (like the sales tax) or big increases in existing tax rates.

Despite these fiscal problems, 1950 was not an especially critical year for the Democrats, now seemingly on the ascendancy in the state. However, there were external forces that were to have effects on their climb up from the underdog position. The Korean War broke out in 1950 and, at the same time, Joseph McCarthy was claiming attention in the months following his notorious speech at Wheeling, West Virginia, in February of that year. The high proportion of Catholics in Massachusetts tended to encourage the anti-Communist outbursts that broke out in the state as elsewhere in the Union. This surge of feeling was in an early phase in 1950 but was to be critical in the election of 1952.

What made the Democrats relatively safe in 1950 was the continuing disarray of the Republican Party in which conflicting views were apparent, some wishing to retain old practices like

the "escalator" system in the person of Arthur Coolidge, Bradford's lieutenant governor, defeated with his chief in 1948 but
now an active candidate for the gubernatorial nomination. Bradford himself pressed Coolidge's claim:

> *The Republican Party is crying out for responsible leadership*
> *. . . What the present situation calls for is the wise head, the*
> *background and character of Arthur Coolidge.*[34]

The counter view was that "new faces" were needed, but the result was a divisive Republican gubernatorial primary in which
Coolidge was pitted against five opponents, including a brigadier,
an admiral, a judge and former Attorney General Clarence Barnes.
Coolidge won but on a minority vote, about a third of the total
cast. It was this election that Duane Lockard examined when
considering whether the so-called "friends and neighbors" pattern was relevant to Massachusetts voting, and he concluded that
it had little effect on the result.[35] Lockard took the county as
his unit as a test of whether a candidate would gain the support
of his own area, but county voting is not of great use with the
"friends and neighbors" type of analysis because counties are
relatively large and often not especially "local" in character. The
pattern does work for the immediate locality, i.e. the town or
city, rather than the county, and Table Thirteen illustrates the
phenomenon (an obvious one) for this particular election.

The ticket produced for the Republican Party was an all-
Yankee one, although strong contenders for the attorney general
and treasurer nominations were George Fingold and Roy Papalia whose Jewish and Italian backgrounds respectively would
have given some diversity to the ticket. One of the unsuccessful
candidates for the lieutenant governor nomination was Robert
Welch, a Belmont candy manufacturer, later to win political
notoriety as founder of the John Birch Society, but an active
Republican at this time.

The Democratic primary was much quieter on this occasion
than the Republican and Dever had no opponent at all but did
suffer the slight indignity of over one-third of the Democratic
primary voters "blanking" him on their ballots. The general
election however, was another victory for the Democrats, since
the Republicans' only real success was their recovery of overall
control of the Senate. The Democrats retained all six constitutional offices and both the House and the Governor's Council

remained under their control. Dever led Coolidge by a quarter of a million votes and the whole election was a mirror image of the past—an efficient Democratic organization had trounced a poorly organized and under-financed Republican one. The Democratic slate was not a strong one but, in comparison, the Republican one was pathetic and, for example, made no concession to the multinational heritage of the state's voters.

Democratic joy at the plateau they had reached in 1948 and 1950 was short-lived; 1952 is a year which exemplifies the effect that external forces—national and international—can have on a state election but, at the same time, it shows that such influence need not be, and rarely is, decisive. The combination of Dwight Eisenhower and the legacy of twenty years of White House domination by one party made the desire for change almost overwhelming, particularly when taken alongside the hysterical overtones of the Korean War and the use made by Joseph McCarthy of the public fears over the possibility of Communist activity inside the United States.

The influence of McCarthy in the Bay State was almost inevitable given the affinity that the large Irish-American population had for one of its own who echoed their fears, even if he was a Republican. They were encouraged in this by the new proprietor of the one newspaper that the Democrats had been able to rely on in the past, the *Boston Post*. John Fox, who had purchased the *Post*, tried to enliven its rather dull image but also used it to further his views and especially his support of McCarthy. Fox's constant emphasis on the McCarthy "crusade" made him an equivocal supporter of the Massachusetts Democrats and only a late and personal appeal by Dever brought a reluctant endorsement from the *Post* for the Democratic ticket. [36]

Dever had other problems. His programs in the areas of road building, workmen's compensation and mental health had been ambitious ones. The depressed state of Massachusetts industry at the turn of the '40s and '50s helped to encourage a free-spending administration, though the economy seemed over the worst by 1952. Public interest in Dever's programs seemed at a relatively low ebb by 1952, perhaps because of the preoccupation with affairs of state in Washington and overseas. Dever's own image suffered a blow when his great opportunity to be the keynote speaker at the Democratic Convention in July 1952 was missed by his losing his voice and by the (literally) sweaty appear-

ance he presented on the television screen (he was a big man and
the television lights were an obvious trial to him).[37] The Democrats (and Republicans) in the General Court supported a move
to give generous pension rights to state employees, including
themselves, and this so-called "pensions grab", which had to be
curtailed by Dever after public protest, seemed to weigh against
Dever because he had not opposed the original bill.[38] In the
Democratic primary, Dever was "cut", falling behind his junior
constitutional officers in the vote given him in a largely uncon-
tested election.[39]

Republican recovery contrasted with this. Christian Herter had
been persuaded to leave his relatively safe Congressional district
to run against Dever. Republican organization, under Daniel
Tyler who had taken over from Mason Sears as Chairman in 1950,
was improved greatly in the two years up to the 1952 election
and an army of "doorbell ringers" had been recruited by Tyler,
one-time "Chief of Military Staff" to Governor Saltonstall.[40]
Tyler caught the new mood of the party, trying to broaden its
appeal by appointing four "ethnic" deputy chairmen, John Volpe
(Italian), James Gaffney (Irish), Robert Beaudreau (French) and
Edwin Olander (Swedish).

In order to underline the hoped-for recovery and, in particular,
to produce a "balanced" ticket to appeal to all ethnic groups, the
Republican leadership wished to bring together leading Republicans in the state in something resembling a convention. The party
convention has had a checkered history in Massachusetts and,
prior to the 1950s, the pre-primary convention existed for only
two elections in the 1930s. A 1932 law allowed the conventions of
1934 and 1936 to take place and the result was a "balance" in
both party slates that had barely existed before. When the
pre-primary convention law was repealed in 1937, the reason
given was "vote-buying," but it is also said that the convention
opened up the factional fighting (often of the physical variety)
that was so prevalent in the Democratic Party at that time (and
most of the time since).

Republicans, being more addicted to "party responsibility"
theories than the Democrats and remembering the need to get
away from Anglo-Saxon slates of the 1950 variety, were anxious
to reintroduce the convention. This was eventually passed into
law in 1953 and the convention has been a major political
event in election years since.[41] Adoption by the convention is no

guarantee of getting on the ballot as party nominee, especially in the Democratic Party, but any candidate who can sweep convention and primary against real opposition is likely to be a reasonably strong contender in November, although this is always contingent on the strength, or lack of it, of the opposite party candidates.

Since in 1952 a "convention" was not legal, the Republicans gathered together in an "Assembly" at Worcester. The so-called "Miracle of Worcester" was a superbly balanced ticket which included in the six constitutional offices and one U.S. senatorial nomination, three Yankees (Lodge, Herter, Whittier) even though one (Whittier) was "swamp" and another (Herter) was part-German; two Jews (George Fingold and David Mintz); one Irishwoman (Mrs. Beatrice Mullaney) and one Italian (Roy Papalia). The ticket held together through the primaries and Herter, Whittier and Fingold took the top three constitutional offices from the Democrats in November 1952.

Herter's victory was by a hairsbreadth (14,000 votes in nearly 2.5 million) compared to his running mate. Sumner Whittier, whose good record on Beacon Hill helped him to a six-figure majority. Dever was said to have lost the election in the industrial centers, especially Lawrence, New Bedford, Fall River and Pittsfield.[42] A public opinion survey carried out in Pittsfield showed that "desire for a change" was a paramount attitude and this appears to have spilled over from the national to local level, rather than vice versa. Eisenhower's "coattails" obviously were an important feature in the Republican alternatives that were open to the voter. That eleven incumbent Congressmen were returned in the state, that the Democrats retained their majority in the delegation, and that John Kennedy wrested the Senate seat from Lodge, suggest that 1952 was a marginal rather than a profound shift at state level.

The presidential election which brought Eisenhower to the White House had reached down into the two state party organizations to show some division on the choice of respective candidates. In the Republican Party, Senator Robert Taft was supported especially by the influential *New Bedford Standard-Times* whose editor, Basil Brewer, became the Ohio Senator's campaign manager in the state. In the presidential preference primary, Eisenhower carried the state two to one and Senator Lodge, as the head of the national "Eisenhower for President"

committee, spent perhaps too much time for his own electoral
good health in running the Eisenhower campaign nationally.[43]
The Massachusetts delegates to the national convention, in addition to being heavily pro-Eisenhower, were noticeable for their
considerable ethnic mix, another radical departure in Republican
tactics.[44] The Democratic delegation to their national convention was more firmly under Dever's control and, when he eventually declared for Stevenson, the majority (twenty-five out of
thirty-six) followed his lead.[45]

Eisenhower's victory is usually ascribed to a great deal of ticket-splitting among Democratic and independent voters all over
the USA and this is broadly true.[46] However it takes two to make
an election and it is undoubtedly true that Adlai Stevenson was
not a strong Democratic candidate in Massachusetts, especially
amongst the Boston Irish (the Stevenson percentage of the
Boston vote was 59.5% as compared with Truman's 71.5% in
1948).[47] Both the issues—the Irish dislike of anyone who could
remotely be termed "soft on Communism"—and the personality
contrast between the two candidates helped to trim the Democratic presidential vote.[48] Dislike of Stevenson's divorce and
intellectual complexity was less marked upstate if the Pittsfield
Survey figures are any guide.[49] The Massachusetts Irish found
in Eisenhower an eminently respectable family man—a "father
figure" in fact—and their whole ethos found him more acceptable than the somewhat alien Stevenson.

Nineteen fifty-two, then, was a limited comeback for the
Republicans but not a pivotal year except that it was the last
time that the Republicans gained a reasonable spread of electoral
successes. It was the last time that they secured a majority in
both houses of the General Court (Senate 25-15, House 124-116).
Most political observers now felt that the state was essentially
Democratic, with a tendency toward split-ticket voting of the
type that produced the 1952 result.[50]

Christian Herter, like Dever before him and Furcolo afterwards, had little difficulty in securing two terms in office. His
election and reelection were in line with the gubernatorial election
tradition in the state, that of "voting the man" rather than the
party as far as this highly exposed office was concerned. Although
of the opposition party, he was not unlike Dever in some ways,
both being able politicians who could persuade the public that
they were addressing themselves to the problems of the day. Her-

ter had been both a Congressman and state legislator (he was Speaker of the House before entering Congress), and concentrated during his time as governor on administrative reorganization, such as the creating of new state agencies, rather than on dramatic programs as a Democratic governor might have.

A rematch with Dever seemed quite likely for 1954, but the Democratic ex-governor chose not to run and the decision came before the pre-primary convention in the first instance, Herter having signed the Republican-controlled General Court's pre-primary law in 1953 (a previous bill had been vetoed by Dever in 1951).[51] The convention endorsement was given to the minority leader in the House of Representatives, Robert F. Murphy, preferred over "Sonny" McDonough, the only remaining Democrat in the Governor's Council, and State Auditor Buckley. Although it has been claimed that Dever supported Murphy, if at all it was a covert support and the vote ran to five ballots before the final decision was made. [52] Murphy had to face the perennial Frankie Kelly in the primary but brushed this challenge aside with 62.7 percent of the total primary vote of over four hundred thousand, Kelly receiving little more than a quarter of the vote (the remainder—10.8%—were blanked). [53]

Murphy, although honest and hard-working, was something of a lackluster candidate and, although his support stemmed from his image of sincerity as against the cruder styles of men like Kelly and McDonough, little attempt was made to capitalize on this as an asset, except in a mild "Mr. Integrity" publicity campaign. Murphy's campaign though was poorly financed and lacking in professional skills because his immediate lieutenants were afraid of the "contamination" that the "pols" were likely to bring to this attempt at running a campaign divorced from the usual Democrat ground rules.[54] The rest of the Democratic ticket for the constitutional offices was Irish and unexceptional. This was the first year that "name's the same" John Francis Kennedy of Canton made a successful bid in both primary and general elections, a bid made easier by the fluid situation after Foster Furcolo had held the post prior to contesting the Senate seat of Leverett Saltonstall in 1954. Even Furcolo, nominally the "Italian" candidate, was half-Irish!

Unlike the Democrats, the Republicans, now guided by state Chairman Elmer Nelson, managed to include a degree of diversity once more in their ticket. Herter, Saltonstall and Whittier

were the Yankees at the head of the ticket and the nomination for
treasurer went to a real "blue-blood", Augustus Gardner Means,
against Nelson's advice, for the latter had hoped the Republican
Convention would choose Senate President Richard Furbush, a
self-made man who had risen from factory bench to the vice-
presidency of a manufacturing company. The three "ethnic"
representatives were Michael J. McCarthy (secretary), Willaim
P. Constantino (auditor) and George Fingold (incumbent attorney general), covering Irish, Italian and Jewish aspirations
respectively. There was even a degree of geographical spread not
possessed by the Democratic ticket, heavily centered once
more on Boston. [55]

A post-election comment was that the Democrats had fielded
a "second team" for the election.[56] Since the party, though retaining the three junior constitutional offices, again lost the
senior ones and failed to oust Saltonstall, this seems a fair comment. Once again, though, it was not a rout for the Democrats.
Apart from the junior constitutional offices, the Democrats won a
Congressional seat and regained control of the lower house of the
General Court. It was the Eighth Congressional District that
switched its allegiance. At this time, the Eighth District stretched
from Somerville to North Reading, a residential and agricultural
district sixteen miles from Boston. A shift of about five percent
of the vote between 1952 and 1954 ousted the Republican in-
cumbent Angier L. Goodwin, and let in Democrat Torbert H.
MacDonald. When one notes how relatively slim the incumbent
Leverett Saltonstall's majority was in the contest for the Senate
seat, the Democratic share of the 1954 victories seems a good one.
Furcolo ran well in most parts of the state, especially as compared to Murphy's gubernatorial vote as the figures in Table
Fifteen show (one can ignore the statistically insignificant Dukes
County). As one would expect, Furcolo did especially well where
there were high concentrations of Italian voters (e.g. East Boston,
North and West End of Boston), but not as well as Murphy
where the Irish vote was concentrated (e.g. South Boston).

Herter's aim as governor, according to his own publicity, was
twofold:

> . . . to improve the quality of the service given by the state to
> its citizens and to increase the opportunities for gainful em-
> ployment by reversing a dangerous trend of industry away
> from the state.[57]

That the second of these two desires was accomplished to some extent was fortuitous and not due to specific action on the part of the governor. As we mentioned earlier, Herter's emphasis was on the bureaucratic structure of state government. He established a clearer career structure for state employees, for example, enabling those with ability to rise to positions of responsibility on merit alone.[58] Programs, though perhaps not as forceful as Dever's, were put in hand, such as a start made on low-rent housing for the elderly with an initial state guarantee of five million dollars that rose to something like 140 million by the mid-1960s. There was no determined onslaught on the fiscal problems of the state. Herter was prepared to sign a sales tax bill if passed, but he did not campaign for one. Because of the shortfall in revenue, demands like those arising from pressure on higher educational institutions were put off and it was the subsequent administration that had to deal with them.

In February 1956 Herter stated that he was not a candidate for reelection.[59] Although recent history suggested that it had lost its charm, the party tried to revert to the "escalator" system by nominating Sumner Whittier, the lieutenant governor, to fill Herter's position and he pledged that he would stand on the record of the retiring governor.[60] Another "balanced" ticket was produced by the Worcester convention of July 1956 and it held through to the general election. The Democrats, encumbered by a pre-primary convention that they had not sought, attempted but failed to agree on a pledge to which all candidates would adhere and which would bind them to accept the convention choice and not make a primary challenge.

Foster Furcolo prevailed over "Sonny" McDonough in the gubernatorial nomination contest by a good majority (806-524), but the many hard fights for nomination right down the ticket led to an acrimonious atmosphere and it was said that they "left a legacy of profound antagonism."[61] Robert Murphy defeated four candidates for the nomination for lieutenant governor. John Francis Kennedy, trying to secure renomination for the treasurer's post from the Convention, cut a pathetic figure when he lost to Clement Riley by 36 votes to 980.[62] Kennedy, however, vindicated himself in the primary by taking 35 percent of the vote against runner-up Riley's 23.9 percent in a five-man contest. Edward McCormack, nephew of John McCormack, also defeated Convention choice Joseph Ward for the attorney

general nomination. [63] The convention choice was an upstate
man (from Fitchburg), a "popular and articulate Democrat in
the House."[64] The Boston-bred McCormack, with the city
casting more than a quarter of the primary vote, had a considerable advantage over Ward because of this and consolidated it by
running an efficient organization which "covered the state like a
court plaster, missing not a single voting precinct."[65]

Furcolo came out of the primary with enhanced prestige,
winning convincingly over his only opponent, Thomas H. Buckley of Abington. Not only upstate in the Connecticut Valley did
he do this, but also in Boston where he came close to a 3-1 lead
over Buckley. Furcolo, of course, was the one amongst the
"Springfield veterans" who had gone straight to the U.S. Congress
and might have remained happily in the House (where he was
respected as a man of potential) if Dever (in order to appeal to
the Italian vote) had not persuaded him to take the appointment
to the vacant post of treasurer in 1952. Having narrowly failed to
unseat Saltonstall in 1954, he was now hoping to become governor, a post which (as it turned out) he was less suited to than the
legislative area that he started in and to which he almost returned
in 1954.

Had the Republican recovery in Massachusetts been at all deep-
rooted, 1956 would have been a good year for the party. With
Eisenhower running for reelection, the presidential coattails
were as wide as they had ever been for them in recent times and
the international atmosphere of the fall of 1956, with events in
Hungary and the Middle East taking up much of the newspaper
headlines, should have benefitted the party of the incumbent
president. Eisenhower appealed to what Fuchs has termed "Irish
Anglophobia" in his treatment of the British at the time of the
Anglo-French Suez adventure and opinion poll findings in Pittsfield give some indication that, in that part of the state, well
removed from "Irish" Boston, Eisenhower was preferred to
Stevenson as a man who would keep the country out of war.[66] In
fact Stevenson's statewide vote slumped from 45.6% in 1952 to 40.5%
in 1956. In Boston, the respective figures were 59.7% and 53.7%.[67]
The circumstances behind the Suez confrontation did alienate
some of the "Jewish" vote from Eisenhower though. One substantial
township, the so-called "gilded ghetto" of Brookline, a good indication of the (relatively small) Jewish vote in Massachusetts, gave
Stevenson a vote of 45.6% as against 40% in 1952 (and 43.8% in 1948

for Truman).[68] Eisenhower's 19% lead over Stevenson in the state as a whole was the most dramatic victory for any Republican presidential candidate in Massachusetts in the last generation.

Once they had voted in Eisenhower at the top of the ballot, Massachusetts voters "split their tickets" more than ever before.[69] George Fingold, a popular and respected attorney general, was the only survivor on the Republican ticket and, with a higher turnout than in 1954, his majority was cut from fifty-seven thousand to thirty-nine thousand. McCormack, relatively untried in state politics, almost managed the hundred thousand majority in Boston that is the tradition for a winning Democratic candidate (actually 96,000 in this case) but fared badly elsewhere and the declining importance of the Boston vote relative to the state as a whole was reflected in his defeat. It was now evident that Republicans would have to nominate exceptional candidates, or the Democrats men of poor vote-getting abilities, to be sure of Republican victory in the constitutional offices.

This was especially illustrated in Furcolo's victory over Whittier, for the former was the ethnic candidate to end all ethnic candidates (half-Italian, half-Irish) while he presented a program that had wide appeal, including as it did promises to adapt the state's tax structure to contemporary needs, to spend more on services like health and education and to attract revenue to the state by developing it as a "vacation-land".[70] Once elected, Furcolo would face problems, especially financial ones that would make his administration a contentious one because of his attempts to cope with them.[71]

The low point in Furcolo's career came many years later, well after he had left office, when he was tried but acquitted on the charge of arranging a bribe for members of the 1960 Executive Council when the name of Anthony di Natale was before the Council for confirmation as Commissioner of Public Works. Four members of that Council were eventually found guilty and imprisoned on bribery charges. The general impression given by much of the press in the 1960s is that the late 1950s was the highest point of corruption in Massachusetts executive and legislative politics.[72] In retrospect, it seems wrong to make Furcolo the scapegoat for this period although he does appear to have been lazy and casual in his oversight of the administration responsible to him and distinctly unwise in some of his appointments (though not all, for several of those working with him were able and reputable). He did provide a program, however, for the "needs" of the state, aided by such "eggheads," as they were termed at the time, as Kermit Morrissey, Martin Lichtermann, John Mallan and "Chick" Mahoney. He was an "ideas" man essentially, not an administrator, which is perhaps why he allowed other aides to raise campaign finances by methods that should have been checked and controlled. His one claim to literary fame, the novel "Let George Do It," published in 1957, a satire on ethnic politics with two main protagonists, honest Peter Martin and cynical George Clancy, suggests that he found it difficult to reconcile the two sides of his character in one political animal.[73]

Furcolo was certainly determined that his "audit on state needs" would benefit education above all else. A special commission, fortified with the information that Massachusetts then stood last in the league table for per capita support to higher educational establishments, pressed for greater overall spending in salaries, loan schemes and scholarships, but especially for a network of regional community colleges to provide a relatively inexpensive "junior college" level of high education.[74] The finance for these schemes was to be found from a "limited" sales tax (i.e. one exempting certain necessities). It would also relieve the pressure on the property taxes in the towns and cities.[75] His own party was cool toward it, as were the A.D.A. and A.F. of L., while newspapers and the Republican establishment in the state at large were for it.[76] Paradoxically, at the end of the long drawn-out fight, it was the Republicans in the House (plus some Democrats) who defeated the sales tax bill despite Republican pressures from outside the House. They had, it seems, "a desire to administer a defeat to a Democratic governor."[77] The financial crisis, in fact, did not materialize, but only because the G.N.P. was rising rapidly and because a windfall was also secured by the institution of a "withholding" system of tax collection at this time.

His failure to prevail in the sales tax dispute might have harmed Furcolo in his 1958 bid for reelection if his formidable rival, George Fingold, had not been removed from the scene by a cruel stroke of fate. Fingold, attorney general since 1952, the first Jewish candidate to reach high office in the state, was respected as a crusader "against crime, graft and Communism."[78] On August 31st, he lay dead after his second heart attack that summer and the Republican Party, having been united behind

Fingold as their gubernatorial candidate, had to find another candidate quickly. The party executive managed to push Charles Gibbons, one-time House Speaker, through the primary although the dead Fingold still received 23,000 votes out of the 267,000 cast.[79]

It was a quiet year in the Democratic primary, the most noteworthy contest being the stiff fight that Edward McCormack had to put up for the attorney general nomination. After winning handsomely in the Convention against Joseph Ward and the Yankee Endicott Peabody (McCormack, 651; Ward, 262; Peabody, 131), the primary was relatively close with Peabody making a good showing with 39.6% of the total vote as against McCormack's 47.6%. McCormack even found that the Bostonians were not wildly enthusiastic about him.[80]

If there was any glamor in the 1958 elections in Massachusetts, it was to be found in the senatorial contest in which John Fitzgerald Kennedy was trying to amass a record majority with the 1960 presidential nomination foremost in his mind. The results do provide something of another milestone in the political evolution of the state since, for the first time, not only were all the constitutional offices and the senatorial seat at stake won by the Democrats, but they achieved a clear majority in both houses of the Great and General Court. The Senate, which had never been lost in modern times by the Republicans (and only been split 20-20 with the Democrats once), produced its first Democratic majority with two seats in the Boston area, two in Essex County, and one in the Berkshire district changing hands (in Middlesex County, there was a double switch, the Fifth District being lost by the Democrats as they won the Seventh).[81]

One of the results of such a victory would be that the Democrats in future would control the drawing of boundaries in the legislative districts:

A Democratic redrawing of the boundaries of the legislative districts should assure the party of legislative control for years to come. The disproportionate balance of power which the towns of [sic] held over the cities may be expected to be eliminated.[82]

We noted above that some limited gerrymandering has been the perquisite of the majority party in the legislature, and some of the changes introduced by Democratic re-districting after 1958 seem to have benefitted the majority party. The senatorial district known as First Hampden, for example, was Republican up to 1956, partially at least because the Democratic-leaning wards of Springfield were diluted by the neighboring town of Longmeadow which was Republican despite the fact that it was Foster Furcolo's home town. By 1960, the district contained the Democratic town of Ludlow instead of Longmeadow and had a Democratic majority in that year of about fifteen thousand.[83]

A Democratic governor and a Democratic legislature might be expected to work hand in hand to effect at least some of the proposals that the governor had been propagating over the previous two years. A certain amount of Furcolo's legislation did get through, but his relations with the Democratic legislators were far from good and the general tenor over the years 1959 and 1960 was one of "bickering and backbiting" as the press termed it, as the 1960 election loomed near.[84] Certainly the persistent attempts to push through the sales tax soured relations between Furcolo and the Democrats in the General Court. In January 1960 he was still trying to persuade the legislature that his three percent limited sales tax would provide property tax and income tax relief, but the support was minimal.[85] Criticism in the state as a whole generally circled around Furcolo's appointments which were felt to be motivated more by patronage considerations than by ability. A Republican victory in a special election for a State Senate seat in the New Bedford area in the fall of 1959 was put down to the unpopularity of the Furcolo administration with the voters. The Republican victor, Howard Young, used the once familiar Republican slogan of "Had Enough?" and suggested that his rival was another Furcolo "helper."[86]

The last years of the 1950s, then, were perhaps disappointing to any Democrat who was expecting great things from a combination of the executive and legislative branches both under the party's direction. This short term failure to grasp the opportunity that electoral victory had brought the Democrats cannot hide the fact that, by 1959, the party had reached the other side of the watershed and was in a position to dominate both elective branches of state government if it used the minimum of discretion about choice of candidates and in meeting its internal dissensions. The electoral shift did not signify any great ideological movement in the state. Lockard's descriptions of the Massachusetts Democrats as embodying "liberalism in moderation" and the state's Republicans as representing "conservatism in moderation" are apt. [87] From an ideological standpoint, the differences between Saltonstall and Herter on the one hand and Dever and Furcolo on the other were slight and their respective party allegiance is more explicable in terms of ethnicity and economic background than in any difference of fundamental approach to state government. One of the first backers of Furcolo's sales tax proposals was Herter! Ethnicity and the social groups represented by the two parties remain a decisive factor differentiating the two parties and there is certainly no consensus in the legislature or in executive politics.[88]

Before making some assessment of the state of Massachusetts politics in the 1960s in an attempt to see what the Democrats made of their inheritance we should briefly look at what has become very much the "first family" of Massachusetts politics and the relationship that its members have developed with the political system of the state.

Chapter Six
The Kennedys and Massachusetts

For the politically active members of the Kennedy family, Massachusetts was less a home state than a launching pad to national prominence. This is not entirely unusual with political figures who consider that their destiny is to lead the nation, but it inevitably creates tensions because it can never be admitted in public for fear that the political base, vital to the politician, may be eroded. Added in this case is the dislike that the Kennedy brothers, especially the late President, have had for both the tawdry patterns of Democratic politicking and for the "dull" minutiae of state politics. It was John Kennedy who made this remark to Arthur Schlesinger one day when both were in the vicinity of the State House:

I hate to think of myself up in that corner office deciding on sewer contracts.[1]

None of the three Kennedy brothers, active though they were in state politics in Massachusetts and New York, has ever had to concern himself with the petty details of budgeting and program building that a governor must master, although as U.S. senators they have all had to pay attention to the broad economic and political needs of their states. Robert Kennedy's brief electoral career, cut short by the second of the tragic assassinations that have helped decimate the current generation of Kennedys, impinged little on Massachusetts, but the dead President and the state's present senior Senator have between them wielded a considerable influence over two decades of the state's political development, due to their prestige, position and the political values that they came to represent.

The Kennedy brothers started their political careers with two immense advantages. One they held in common with a number of fellow Irish-Americans in Massachusetts and that was a political heritage handed down from their paternal and maternal grandfathers, John J. Fitzgerald and Patrick J. Kennedy. Both "Honey Fitz" and Pat Kennedy had been "politicos" of the traditional Irish-American type, essentially limited in their political and social attainments in comparison with their grandsons.[2] The second part of the Kennedy heritage, and one that was a little more unusual, was the wealth amassed by the successful economic adventures of Joseph P. Kennedy in the following generation. As John Kennedy recognized when he visited Ireland a few months before his death, the emigration of his great-grandfather to the United States led to opportunities not available in Ireland. Referring to his great-grandfather he said at the time:

If he hadn't left, I would be working at the Albatross Company across the road.[3]

Whatever truth there is in that remark, the combination of political and economic heritage meant that political contacts could be combined with the availability of large capital sums to fight elections. This in its turn meant that the Kennedys were respected as politicians, not only for their evident ability and appeal to ethnic voters, as well as to some Anglo-Saxons, but also because, in that classic comment of the cynical voter, "at least they are too rich to steal."

Since class division and poverty kept the Boston Irish-American of several generations back in a subservient position, it was a shrewd move on the part of the young Joseph Kennedy to use his early financial success in Boston to take the family out to a wider world, a move which took them eventually to the Court of St. James's following his support of Franklin Roosevelt and his involvement in the "New Deal." As the children of the Ambassador to Great Britain at a critical time in the diplomatic history of the Atlantic powers, the younger Kennedys were drawn into a milieu which contrasted vividly with the circumscribed political world of their grandfathers. The Ambassador's second son, feeling that Boston politics was "pretty small potatoes in the winter of 1938-39",[4] spent the summer of 1939 touring the troubled mainland of Europe and reporting back to his father whatever he could glean of conditions and public opinion there. This outward-looking characteristic was shown in John Kennedy's use of much of his observation of English and European politics in the months prior to the outbreak of the War in 1939 in writing his bachelor's thesis at Harvard, later published as *Why England Slept*. It was the resulting amalgam of these cosmopolitan influences that probably prompted Paul Dever to describe John Ken-

nedy as "the first Irish Brahmin," although this may well have
been a description that made the late President wince![5]

There is little point in speculating whether John Kennedy
would have entered political life if his elder brother had survived
the war, though it seems likely that, just as John became the political pacemaker for his two younger brothers, Joseph Kennedy,
Jr., would have done the same for John and Robert Kennedy
at least. Joe Kennedy, Jr., was the only Kennedy son to be em-
broiled in active politics prior to Pearl Harbor, for he was active
in support of Jim Farley's presidential aspirations in 1940, possibly as a reaction to his father's disappointment at the Roosevelt
third term bid, one which cut off any hopes of Joe Kennedy, Sr.,
becoming the first Catholic president![6] By the end of the war,
with the eldest son killed in action and the father's political career
at an end, the way was clear for John Kennedy to enter political
life as a war hero of the Pacific and with a Congressional seat—
the Eleventh District of Massachusetts—vacated by James Michael Curley after his recovery of the Boston mayoralty in November 1945.

Given the importance of local ties in Congressional elections,
it was evident that opponents in the decisive Democratic primary
in 1946 would use the epithet of "carpetbagger" to try to keep
John Kennedy out of the Eleventh District seat.[7] In fact, John
Kennedy had political contacts through his still-active grandfather John F. Fitzgerald and through associates of his father like
Francis X. Morrisey and a Kennedy cousin, Joseph L. Kane.[8]
The family money was used fairly discreetly, though inevitably
allegations were made during the primary campaign that the
election was being "bought." The family helpers were certainly
believed to be responsible for the introduction of a candidate
named Joseph Russo to cut the vote of an existing candidate with
the same name.[9]

The original Joe Russo, a member of the Boston City Council,
was one of the main rivals in the election. John Cotter, Curley's
Congressional secretary and Michael J. Neville, a former mayor
of Cambridge, also commanded considerable support—Cotter
in Charlestown and Neville, as one would expect, in Cambridge.
Kennedy's support was evenly based though and, as one newspaper reporter pointed out, he could win overall "even if he fin-
ished second in every section".[10]

Neville did push Kennedy into second place in Cambridge as

it happened, but was no match for Kennedy elsewhere. Cotter was the runner-up in Boston, while in Somerville Neville and WAC major Catherine Falvey split most of the non-Kennedy vote (see Table Seventeen). The runaway victory in a complex election with ten candidates was a good beginning for Kennedy, though he recognized that, in addition to his name, the identification of the veteran vote with his fine war record was a considerable factor and that as far as experience was concerned:

> . . . *people voted for me because of the things I might do, rather than for anything I have done.* [11]

Needless to say, the Republican challenge in November of 1946 was negligible in this case and John Kennedy's share of the two-party vote was 72.7 percent.

The Kennedy "personal organization" grew from the small beginnings of this campaign, and the old-time professionals who were in evidence in 1946 slipped more and more into the background as time wore on though they never entirely disappeared as long as John Kennedy needed his Massachusetts base. The outward appearance of the Kennedy "style" was to be in direct antithesis to the "derby hat and cigar" era of Democratic Party politics, even though many of the roots of Kennedy-type political organization do go back a long way. [12] Organization independent of the state party and even intense use of family and friends were not new in Massachusetts, nor indeed in the politics of many other states. What was new was the pragmatic combination of the old and new, wealth, personality, organization, an impression of integrity and ability, welded into an amalgam which possessed great elective potential. Yet even in all of this, some very human hangovers from the past, like the feud with Foster Furcolo, creep in from time to time.

Much of the political potential in John Kennedy may seem to have developed slowly in his six years in the U.S. House of Representatives. Few of those who knew him while he served these three terms will give him high marks for doing more than the bare minimum to keep his constituents happy. Like one of his political models, the nineteenth-century English Premier Lord Melbourne, his interest in being a minor unit in the legislative politics of the day was slim. [13] Leaders like Sam Rayburn and John McCormack were said to despair of him because of his erratic attendence at crucial votes in the House.

Even if his rating with the Democratic leadership in Washington was not high, electoral fences were kept in good repair in Massachusetts. The organization dedicated to furthering his political career was extended beyond the Congressional district by recruiting local Democratic activists or potential activists without known affiliation to any other personal organization, and relying on these "secretaries" to develop an organization faithful to Kennedy first and the party afterwards. Much new blood was brought into political activism in this way, the "secretaries" being in the main, professional or business men and women, inevitably college-educated and what one well-known academic has described to the writer as "a cut above normal".

The Kennedy hold on the Eleventh District was a firm one and, in 1948, no contenders appeared in either the primary or general elections. In 1950 a quintet of aspiring Congressmen challenged him in the primary. Out of the five (Bevilacqua, Diehl, DiSessa, Martelucci, and Zona), four were Italo-Americans and therefore would tend to split the Italian vote.[14] In fact, Kennedy took 67.3 percent of the total primary vote and went on to win 75.1 percent of the total vote in November, when his opponents were Republican Vincent Celeste and a Prohibition Party candidate. The primary support rivalled Paul Dever's vote in the Eleventh District even though Dever had no opponent in the primary.[15]

Three terms in the House and John Kennedy was in a position to fulfill the family expectation that he would run for, and win, a seat in the U.S. Senate. His 1952 opponent was Henry Cabot Lodge, Jr., whose grandfather had defeated "Honey Fitz" in 1916 and it became a point of honor that the rematch would go to the Kennedys. Paul Dever had decided not to run against Lodge. If he had done so, only the gubernatorial election would have been a possibility for John Kennedy and this was a far less attractive prospect. The alternative would have been to wait for 1954 and to compete against Saltonstall, but it may be that Kennedy's later respect for Saltonstall had already taken root and it would have been a less pleasant duty to defeat the latter rather than Lodge.[16] Not that Lodge did not look a strong candidate; he was Eisenhower's national campaign manager and stood to gain reflected glory from this position.

The Kennedy organization, however, was ready for the election, as Lodge's biographer notes bitterly:

He [Kennedy] *had a network of 286 "secretaries", many of whom were independents or even registered Republicans. To give them a workout, since he was unopposed in the primary, the Kennedy clan decided to have his people collect a record number of signatures for his nominating petitions. He only needed 2,500, and he wound up with 267,324.*[17]

The Kennedy strategy was to downgrade Lodge's performance as a senator, suggesting that Kennedy would do better. Lodge's counter to this was to attack Kennedy's voting record in the House and to attach himself firmly to Eisenhower. Unfortunately for Lodge, his presence on the ticket was resented by a body of pro-Taft Republicans in the state because of his support for Eisenhower's nomination instead of the Senator from Ohio. Prominent among these men was newspaper owner Basil Brewer, whose *New Bedford Standard-Times* bolted the party on the Kennedy-Lodge issue, supporting the Democrat instead of the Republican. Southeastern Massachusetts is a particularly volatile area politically and in the 1952 election there is a wide discrepancy between the support for gubernatorial candidate Paul Dever and senatorial candidate John Kennedy in Bristol County (and especially in New Bedford itself), as well as in Barnstable County where Brewer also had newspaper interests. It would be stretching the power of the press to suggest that the Brewer papers were the sole cause of Kennedy's good showing in southeastern Massachusetts, but they must have contributed to his relatively high vote for a Democrat in that area.

The part played by another newspaper in the 1952 campaign, the *Boston Post,* has been referred to before and it may be conjectured by some that the elder Kennedy's aid to Fox in the shape of a substantial loan helped to persuade the newspaper proprietor's switch to Kennedy and the Democratic ticket at a late stage of the campaign.[18] Fox claimed in 1958 that the *Post* support of Kennedy turned the scales against Lodge and that it was largely because of the Brewer use of Tydings Committee testimony that Fox had been persuaded to switch to Kennedy after being equivocal about the campaign.[19] This committee (a special sub-committee of the Senate Foreign Relations Committee) had criticized Senator Joseph McCarthy for his allegations about Communism in the United States, but Lodge as a member of the committee had dissented from the majority report and his dissent had been supported by the Republican Policy Committee chaired by Brew-

er's hero, Senator Robert Taft![20] Brewer's own contention was
that his arguments with Fox had been based on Lodge's lack of
firm conviction on general policy matters but, whatever the reason, Kennedy seems to have benefitted from the quasi-alliance
of these two newspaper owners.[21]

Since the ideological differences between Lodge and Kennedy
were slight, it seems likely that Kennedy won in 1952 because he
had taken the type of organization that Lodge had developed
and improved on it to such an extent—with devices like the
relatively apolitical secretaries—that he beat Lodge at his own
game. The November margin of seventy thousand votes was not
overwhelming though good enough at the time of the Eisenhower
presidential sweep and the failure of Dever to retain his position
as governor. Some indication of the problems that Kennedy
had to overcome to oust the incumbent senator can be seen by
comparing the August 1952 Pittsfield survey with the follow-up in
October of the same year. In the August sample, only 35 percent
could identify John F. Kennedy, while 68 percent could identify
Lodge (and 97 percent Eisenhower). By October, the Kennedy
figure had risen to 52 percent and Lodge had in fact dropped a
little (but not significantly) to 65 percent.[22]

It has been suggested to the writer by an active Republican
official of the period that the Kennedy campaign secured for
him many first-time voters in 1952 who might otherwise have
voted a straight Republican ticket. Apart from Suffolk County,
Kennedy's uniform lead over the Democratic gubernatorial candidate (see Table Eighteen) suggests that his relative aloofness
and independence from the state Democratic organization paid
excellent dividends. In fact, it is from 1952 that one can date the
emergence of a new "Kennedy coalition" in Massachusetts, rival-
ling, say, the Walsh one of earlier decades. While retaining the
bulk of the "ethnic" vote that traditionally supported the Democrats, it added support from young, professional people from a
variety of ethnic backgrounds who might easily have been seduced into regular Republicanism.

The six-year term from the 1952 election was the only full term
that John Kennedy was to serve in the U.S. Senate. It might be
said to be the time when he reached political maturity. The bouts
of ill-health that he suffered, one of which was near-fatal, seemed
to temper his character and eradicate the physical immaturity
that had made him appear as a "boy Congressman." One occa-

sion, the severe sickness that kept him away from the McCarthy censure vote in 1954, may have been a blessing in disguise for, although there is evidence to suggest that he would have pursued the line that he found so admirable in his book *Profiles in Courage* and voted for censure, it was a line that would not have endeared him to many of his pro-McCarthy constituents.[23]

Unlike some of those newly elected to Congress in the 1960s, freshmen senators in the 1950s were still expected to defer to their seniors in senatorial experience. Apart from attending to the special interests on his constituents, Kennedy seemed almost too pleased to ignore the dull legislative grind. One of his closest English friends, Lord Harlech, recognized that his gifts were not attuned to the legislative process:

> *He became increasingly serious about his political career after he became a Senator, although perhaps detailed legislation was not the thing that chiefly interested him. He was very interested in international affairs, and made some very notable contributions on foreign affairs topics; and I think that this has led to the suggestion that he wasn't as keen on attending Senate in order to push through legislation. I think this is possibly true.* [24]

His interest in foreign policy was recognized when he (and not Kefauver who was his senior in Senate experience) secured a vacant place on the Senate Foreign Relations Committee. During his time in the Senate though, he remained a comparative "maverick," preferring to build a political reputation that owed little to the party hierarchy in this august body.

The creation of this reputation was a necessity if the upward swing towards the great prize of the presidency was to be maintained.[25] The struggle for the vice-presidential nomination in 1956 may have been a strategic error, for a place on the defeated Stevenson ticket could have been a blow to the Kennedy mystique of success (although Edmund Muskie in 1968 saw his political career enhanced by taking second place to the defeated Hubert Humphrey). As it was, the publicity accorded by the strong challenge that Kennedy provided for Kefauver in the Democratic Convention made his a name that would be regarded as "presidential timber" in the late 1950s.

This intrusion into the highest ranks of electoral politics was,

in a minor way, a challenge to Kennedy's ability to dominate
Democratic Party politics in his own state. As the 1956 Convention approached, it seemed desirable to ensure that the state
committee was at least sympathetic to the Kennedy aspirations
for a place on the Stevenson ticket and that a slate of convention
delegates was produced which would be acceptable to the Senator. This was unlikely unless the incumbent state committee
chairman, William "Onions" Burke, a protege of John McCormack, was removed. Burke wanted to see McCormack as the
delegation's "favorite son" at the Chicago Convention, while
Kennedy was reluctant to see this happen. He favored a commitment to Stevenson, thus opening up his chance for the vice-presidential nomination. There was no option but for Kennedy to go
down into the muddy arena of the state's factional politics, to
pressure the state committee into electing a pro-Kennedy chairman, Pat Lynch, thus producing a more favorable atmosphere
towards the Kennedy strategy for the Convention. Lynch received
a majority, replacing Burke as state chairman, but the state committee split into two factions, one sympathetic to McCormack
and the larger one supporting Kennedy. Policy decisions could
only be taken after lengthy debate with roll-call voting. Lynch's
position was virtually nominal because of the division, but at
least Kennedy had stripped Burke of his power.[26]

The "Onions" Burke incident was one of the few occasions
when the Kennedy organization showed that it could take on the
old-style political machinery and beat it at its own game. It indicates in fact that there were carry-overs from the earlier style
of Massachusetts politics in the Kennedy approach. This was
seen even more clearly in the circumstances of the two major
feuds that the Kennedys carried on, one with the McCormack
family (illustrated by the Burke affair) and the other with Foster
Furcolo. The former was the more gentlemanly of the two feuds
and might have been buried completely if the Massachusetts
senatorial primary of 1962, with two of the younger members of
the family contending for the seat, had not revived it. Earlier
in 1962, John McCormack called it a "feud that never was" and
insisted that he had been a reluctant ally of Burke in 1956. He
cited the many occasions on which he had helped John Kennedy,
seconding the vice-presidential nomination in 1956 and earlier,
in 1952, taking responsibility at a crucial moment of the senatorial
campaign of that year for what seemed to some an anti-Israeli

amendment to a House foreign aid bill, an amendment which would have hurt Kennedy with the small but useful Jewish vote in Massachusetts.

The Kennedy-McCormack feud was played down by both sides because of the harm it might do to those from either side who served conspicuously in Washington where this style of in-fighting might not be appreciated. With Foster Furcolo, a man with less of a national reputation than John McCormack, the necessity for disguise was less and the feud could easily be contained within the Massachusetts political system. Paradoxically though, the feud had dated from the time that both John Kennedy and Furcolo were young Congressmen in Washington and Furcolo had "passed the buck" to an unprepared Kennedy on an occasion when the Massachusetts delegation had an "audience" with President Truman. Certainly the rivalry was well developed by 1954 when Kennedy refused to endorse Furcolo for senator after a quarrel in a television studio prior to a telecast in support of the Democratic ticket. There was some attempt to make it up in 1956 when Kennedy endorsed Furcolo's gubernatorial attempt, but the feud lingered until 1960 when Kennedy opposed Furcolo's attempt to take over the Senate seat vacant as a result of the presidential election.

The basis of the division between the two men was partly personal, partly ethnic, partly factional. Burns suggests that:

Many in Massachusetts considered the rivalry in part a sign of the mutual suspicion between the Irish and the Italians.[28]

Whatever Furcolo's parentage (remembering that he is half-Irish), it is likely that, as a potential alternative center of power in the state Democratic Party, he would have clashed with Kennedy, just as the Kennedy-McCormack coolness stems from the same power rivalry. The Kennedys, despite the disdain that they have felt for the creaking, factional apparatus that comprises the party machine, have ensured since the early '50s that no star would rise as high as theirs in the Massachusetts Democratic heaven.

The 1958 senatorial election proved to be the last occasion, except for the 1960 presidential election, that the Massachusetts electorate would express its support for John F. Kennedy. Nineteen fifty-eight was a landslide for Kennedy and created a record for the size of the vote given to any statewide candidate in Massa-

chusetts up to that time.[29] While holding fast to the traditional
Democratic support, Kennedy could reach out and attract groups
normally tending Republican. Republican newspapers such as
the *Boston Herald* and Brewer's *New Bedford Standard Times*
joined with liberal groups such as the Americans for Democratic
Action in his support and he successfully appealed to a wider
ideological gamut than virtually any other candidate in recent
Massachusetts electoral history. The *Boston Globe* summed it up
as follows:

> *It seemed that perhaps the biggest ingredient was Kennedy's
> ability to present the public image of being both a safe middle-
> of-the-roader standing high above party (not unlike the early
> Eisenhower image) and of being a red-hot liberal. Even before
> returns came in, there was interesting proof of Kennedy being
> able to sell himself as a Democrat in a button-down collar
> shirt for whom a Republican could vote without permanently
> tainting himself and also hold the city Democrats and the Cam-
> bridge liberals.* [30]

Although, right to the end, there was a solid hard core, of Yankees especially, who would not be won over to the Kennedy image, the consensus reached by Kennedy with the state's voters
by 1958 gave him the "inclusive" image that would stand him in
good stead in 1960.

One factor that presaged a similar national trend in 1960 was
the appeal of an attractive Catholic candidate to some at least of
the non-Catholic voters. In Massachusetts, an Irish Catholic has
an obvious advantage but the existence of a "Catholic bloc" could
have encouraged non-Catholics into united opposition. (Certainly
something of this sort seems to have happened in 1960 in some
parts of the United States.)[31] Table Nineteen though, based on
figures for the "Catholic vote" that are not 100 percent reliable,
suggests that in 1958 especially, many non-Catholics voted for
Kennedy. In 1960, even the "favorite son" image could not entirely eradicate the attraction of the Nixon/Lodge ticket for Yankee Republicans. Kennedy showed in 1958 that religious and ethnic lines could be blurred by a candidate who looked and talked
like a Brahmin even if he was not one by heredity.

With his victory in the presidential election of 1960, John Kennedy's preoccupations were almost totally divorced from the specific political problems of Massachusetts. His farewell speech

to the Great and General Court, with its reference to the "city upon a hill," was regarded as a parting indictment of the quality of Massachusetts government (which he had done little to improve) and, fending off Furcolo, he ensured that his senatorial seat was to be kept warm for the next two years by an old college friend, Benjamin Smith II. The horror of November 22nd, 1963, meant that he would never emulate another Massachusetts man who became president, John Quincy Adams, and return to Congress after his time in the White House. With Robert Kennedy's eventual decision to pack his carpet bag and make his political base elsewhere in the few short years before his equally tragic assassination, the role of the Kennedy family in the state soon came to be associated with the activities of the youngest of the Kennedy brothers, Edward.

In retrospect, it may appear to have been a foregone conclusion that the Kennedy role in Massachusetts politics would be carried on by another of the brothers, but it would be an error to believe that it was devoutly desired in all corners of the Democratic Party in the state. There were some in the party who were jealous of the special position that the Kennedys had carved for themselves in a relatively short time, some who believed that the Kennedy influence on the party organization was a mixed blessing, to say the least, and a few with personal reasons for disliking the family, such as those who had been taken up and later dropped as part of the personal organization that John Kennedy had created. Some Democratic Party activists of the period claimed that the Kennedy influence in the 1950s had been "divisive" and that the then senator had done nothing for the party as a political instrument. [32] A less firmly committed political commentator was even more biting: in his view, the Kennedys had used Massachusetts as a vassal state—"Call it home but never come."[33] The reply to this by those closer to Kennedy usually runs along the lines found in the Schlesinger biography, i.e. that John Kennedy "found . . . a collection of rival tongs" and "beat the pols on their own ground and in their own language."[34] Other political figures in the state often pay a more generous tribute to the example that Kennedy set for those beginning to take an interest in politics in the 1950s.

The Kennedy brothers epitomize the Weberian concept of "charismatic authority," long since popularized by the columnists. John Kennedy's electoral successes, in his two senatorial campaigns especially, helped to provide what is occasionally described as the "third wave" of the Democratic rising tide in the state (1928, 1948, 1958). It is possible that the Kennedy "gift of grace" could have been used to put the Democratic Party organization in Massachusetts on a more efficient and responsible tack, but this might have been an act of virtual self-effacement in that the Senator's own drive to the presidency would inevitably have been slowed down in the process. Therefore, even if it seems a desirable role in retrospect for John Kennedy to have played, it is inconceivable that, in the circumstances of the time, he would have adopted it. Neither is it at all certain that he would have been successful, for the divisions in the Massachusetts Democracy might have been harder to heal than the reconciliation he tried between contestants at national and international level! If the job was to be done, it was now left to Edward Kennedy to carry it through.

By the latter part of 1961, it was assumed that the new Kennedy candidature would be announced in the New Year. Referring to the 1962 senatorial elections, John Fenton wrote in The New York Times:

> It is considered a foregone conclusion that one of the Democratic candidates will be Edward M. Kennedy, the President's younger brother. But his announcement is expected to be held in abeyance until Feb. 22 when he will reach the statutory age of 30 required of Senators.[35]

The biographer of Joseph Kennedy paints the old man as saying (though, he confesses, apocryphally) "I spent a lot of money for that Senate seat. It belongs to the family."[36] There is little evidence that President Kennedy saw it that way but he must at least have acquiesced to the candidature. During this time, Edward Kennedy was appointed as an (unpaid) assistant district attorney for Suffolk County and, when he became an official candidate, attempts were made to create a record of "community service" for him, one that could have been rivalled by hundreds of young professional men in the state.[37] It was evident though that the name was to be the focus around which the campaign was to revolve.

By a strange quirk of fate, the 1962 senatorial election was to be fought by no less than four candidates who were related to famous political personalities. Edward Kennedy's primary opponent was Edward McCormack, nephew of the Speaker of the U.S. House, while the general election opponents were to be Republican George Cabot Lodge, son of Henry Cabot Lodge, Jr., and Independent Stuart Hughes of Harvard University, grandson of one-time Chief Justice and presidential candidate Charles Evans Hughes. It is little wonder that murmurs were heard about the contest being between several dynasties, and the *New York Times* suggested that the entrance qualification seemed to be an entry in the American equivalent of "Burke's Peerage," adding:

Accomplishments usually impress the voter more than heredity. This does not justify discriminating against the relatives of prominent officials, but it does mean that they must present some solid evidence of talent before they make the sacrifice of starting at the top.[38]

It was the primary election that was Edward Kennedy's main battle, for his rival was more than a vehicle for nepotism. Edward McCormack had a following in the party based on his family connections and on the record that he had built up as a reasonably liberal attorney general. It was probably this latter factor that gave him a broad-based support from the "intelligentsia of the Democratic Party," twenty or more leading academics from the Harvard, Brandeis and Boston College faculties. Edward Kennedy countered this with a letter of support organized by two of the best-known liberal academics in the Democratic Party, Samuel Beer of Harvard and Robert C. Wood, then of MIT.[39] The letter, signed by a group which included Professor James Burns and a number of lay members of the COD organization, implied that Kennedy was going to identify himself with party reform, and it stung McCormack to reply to the effect that it was "an obvious shift by the Kennedy forces to get away from his lack of experience, lack of a record and lack of qualifications."[40]

This fight between what some called "the best of the old (McCormack) versus the worst of the new (Kennedy)" persisted through the convention and primary stages of the summer of 1962. McCormack, perhaps because of the family implications (his uncle was unlikely to welcome too bitter a public war between the two families), failed to exploit one of his main advantages, the rumor that the White House was interfering in the contest.[41]

Certainly, the Convention gave McCormack little ground for hope, for only in Berkshire County (where the influential *Berkshire Eagle* had backed him) did he have a delegate lead over Kennedy and that only by four votes, 31-27. Elsewhere, Kennedy's lead was decisive, rising in Middlesex County, for example, to 266-89.[42] The smooth working of the Kennedy organization, so reminiscent of that which had given the elder brother victory in Los Angeles in 1960, was noted by the press. Almost every delegate had been worked on by the Kennedy team, and the candidate himself had "rocked on front porches" all over the state.[43]

Murray Levin has suggested that the primary campaign was a "pseudo-event," and, in particular, scorned the television confrontation between the two men.[44] To those who supported each side, however, it seemed to be more than that. Kennedy supporters, intellectuals and middle-of-the-road Democratic leaders alike, saw the young candidate as a means of strengthening the party organization and image within the state, while they feared that McCormack would concentrate on a Washington-oriented career, virtually ignoring the needs of that party and state. McCormack supporters, on the other hand, and as we have suggested they included more intellectuals than the Kennedy team, disliked the "dynastic" issue and preferred an experienced candidate instead. It is noticeable that, of the few towns that McCormack won in the primary, two were the college towns of Williamstown and Amherst.

None of the towns supporting McCormack in the primary was of great importance—one (Hawley in Franklin County) produced only three voters (two for McCormack and one for Kennedy), while among the largest were Weston in Middlesex County and Longmeadow (Foster Furcolo's home town) in Hampden County. Kennedy captured all the counties and all the major towns and cities: his total vote was 66.7% of those cast.[45] The turnout was almost double that of the Republican primary (853,339 compared to 458,425) in which George Lodge defeated Laurence Curtis. The triumphal march was concluded by Kennedy's decisive win over Lodge in the general election, which compared well with his brother's win over Lodge senior in 1952 (see Table Twenty). The Kennedy candidature in 1962 was of course a much more powerful one than that of 1952 and the comparison between father and son on the Republican side was hardly to the latter's favor.

For the greater part of 1963, the three Kennedy brothers made political history in the mere combination of three of the predominant political offices of the United States — president, attorney general and a United States senator — in the same generation of one family.[46] This "Kennedy era" seemed to come to an end on November 22, 1963, when John Kennedy was assassinated in Dallas, Texas. In Massachusetts, once some of the shock had worn off, conjecture turned on the effects that the assassination would have on Edward Kennedy's future and that of the Democratic Party in the state. More specifically, the fact that the youngest Kennedy brother would have to run for a full six-year term in 1964 revived interest in the relationship between senator and party. At the time of his election, he had evidently agreed that the party organization needed strengthening by specific measures including, for example, an increase in the number of professional staff and a stricter control by the committee over fund-raising formerly dominated by the Jefferson-Jackson Dinner Committee rather than by the state central committee. His 1962 academic support had provided the backbone of a "Research and Development Committee" which looked at the organization in detail and submitted a report late in September 1963, specifying those areas where specific proposals might produce, in the report's title, "More Democrats for Massachusetts." It is worth reproducing the final lines of the report, "a thumbnail summons for an immediate action program":

To Local Committees:
Recruit more members, stressing Associate Members. Give members status on the Committee, a sense of belonging—and work to do. Appoint action Committee Chairman—for registration, education and liason with Boston, etc. Broaden local Party finances through membership subscriptions, party dues, social functions and the like. Modernize by-laws and Democratic procedures.

To The State Committee:
Appoint and direct regional Field Representatives who will inspire and work closely with Democratic leaders and Committees. Establish a centralized registration program that will make 1964, and all the election years thereafter, banner years in the extent of voting in Massachusetts.[47]

Although this was a high-powered committee which had put a great deal of work into the report, it received little publicity and few of the recommendations appear to have been acted upon. On the wider question of the direction of the state party, although his ties are closer than were those of his eldest brother, there has been little sign that Edward Kennedy is trying to take effective command to provide a controlling force within the organization. It is debatable, in fact, whether he could have done so, however much he wished to. As a senator, less direct influence could be wielded in the form of patronage than was held by the governor (and a Democratic governor, who did work closely with the Senator, served for only two of the first eight years of the Senator's term). The hard fought primary and convention system meant that chosen candidates needed backing against rivals and that, if the Senator's man lost, his prestige would suffer. Therefore, endorsements have been relatively rare, although when made the Kennedy machine worked with full vigor. An example was the 1964 special election to the State Senate when Democrat Beryl Cohen, a former Kennedy coordinator faced Republican Freyda Koplow in the Norfolk and Suffolk district. Cohen won narrowly and the Kennedy pull, especially in the Brighton (Boston) part of the district, was perhaps decisive in this victory.[48]

Whether Edward Kennedy could have prevented the faction fighting at the 1964 Democratic Convention at West Springfield is conjecture, but in any case another Kennedy catastrophe intervened. He was severely injured in a plane crash while en route to the Convention (two of the passengers were killed) and this "cast a pall over what was to be a pretty gay convention."[49] The result was that Kennedy lay on his back at the New England Baptist Hospital during the 1964 campaign and made only one videotaped TV speech. His own victory was virtually a foregone conclusion, even if he could not discipline Democratic contenders for other offices. His Republican opponent in November 1964 was Howard Whitmore, a sacrificial lamb who had to be content with only 25.5 percent of the two-party vote and lost every county in the state.

After his recovery and return to the Senate in 1965, Edward Kennedy soon began to establish a reputation for political ability, unusual in a senator with his youth and relative lack of experience. His handling of the administration's immigration bill was commended for example. The only blunder of the period seemed to be his attempt to secure a federal judgeship for Frank Morrissey, a family crony, and it met with so much opposition in the Senate that Morrissey's name was eventually withdrawn. [49] In Massachusetts, there were suggestions that Kennedy was still reluctant to endanger his reputation by a wholehearted involvement in the issues that racked party and state. Press comment occasionally highlighted this:

> *Until now, Kennedy has steered clear of political involvement in any of the major issues facing the state this year. . . . There are those who have felt that he could take strong public positions on issues such as the sales tax, the Willis Report and the Crime Commission's status to promote Democratic Party philosophy.*[50]

In an interview in December 1965, he refused to support "any candidate for governor prior to the convention or during the convention."[51] It was only during the late stages of the 1966 campaign that the Senator worked actively for the Democratic ticket, emphasizing the party unity theme, but it did not save the top of the ticket for constitutional office from going down to defeat.

Since 1966, personal misfortune has continued to attract itself to Senator Edward Kennedy. His brother Robert's death by the hands of another assassin in June 1968 led to his virtual withdrawal from the 1968 presidential campaign at a time when it was evident that he would have been heavily involved in the support of his brother. He controlled the state committee and, in the person of Lester Hyman, had a state chairman who appeared to be his man even more than Gerard Doherty had been. However, the degree of confusion after the assassination is perhaps shown by the substitution of Hyman by House Speaker Robert Quinn as vice-chairman of the Democratic delegation to the Chicago Convention.[52]

In the following year came the Chappaquiddick incident and the long pall that it cast over Edward Kennedy's political future. By this time he was Majority Whip in the U.S. Senate and it was taken as a foregone conclusion in the first part of 1969 that he would be the Democratic presidential candidate in either 1972 or 1976. He repudiated the idea of contending for the presidency in 1972 after Chappaquiddick and many felt that he would not make a showing in his 1970 reelection bid for the Senate that would compare in any way with his 1964 vote. In fact, given all the circumstances, he did reasonably well in November 1970[53] and by the end of the next year, 1971, much lost ground had been made up.

It was still not possible, if it had ever been, to "control" the Massachusetts Democratic Party an any meaningful way. Although yet another Kennedy appointee, David E. Harrison of Gloucester, took over the Chairmanship of the state committee in December 1968, the 1970 primary and pre-primary convention was the usual "scramble" in the words of one newspaper and Kennedy obviously felt unable to imprint his personality on the campaign for constitutional office and to transform the warring factions into anything approaching a team.[54] "Transference" of the Kennedy magic or "charisma" to the party as a whole now seems impossible. Perhaps a chance has been missed but it is more likely that the process of transference is no more a valid object in Massachusetts today than it has been in the past.

Many of the Democratic activists with whom one talked in the mid-'60s had felt that some reform of the party organization been effected by the Senator and his aides, but few were clear about the extent to which this could be followed through in the future. There is little doubt though that Edward Kennedy is closer to the party organization than his brother was and that he is committed to working through it. John Kennedy never seems to have felt that the Massachusetts Democratic Party could be saved or was worth saving, and his personal feuds hindered rather than helped the emergence of the party as a responsible organization with a high degree of unity.

The youngest brother has avoided many of the errors of the late President in his dealing with the state party: perhaps his sudden appearance at the top of the organization with the family prestige acquired in the ten years prior to 1962 had something to do with this. If he had not been concentrating on his own re-election in 1970, which had been transformed from a victory march to a testing time, it is just possible that he would have taken charge of picking the ticket.

If he can do this in 1974, then he will show a reincarnated Kennedy image that can only do him, and the Democratic Party, a great deal of good and perhaps lead to a presidential bid in 1976. If the Kennedy "legend" is now so impaired that the presidency is out of reach (and the failure to retain the position of Senate Majority Whip in January 1971 might indicate this), the local base will still retain its importance, and it is possible that more attention will be paid to creating a more responsible Democratic Party organization in the state. It seems unlikely that the Kennedy influence in Massachusetts will wane or die in the foreseeable future and it may yet regain its former degree of dominance within the state and even the nation.

Chapter Seven
The Latest Phase

It is never easy to place events that are near-contemporary into perspective and it may be a few years before the many strands of Massachusetts politics in the 1960s can be seen in their proper place. Already though, one can make some assessment of the major events that took place within this political system during the first half of the decade, stretching this to take in the 1966 election. For the first time, there was to be a four-year gap in the choosing of constitutional officers and this provided more of a breathing space in the intensity of political action than has usually been the case in modern times. As a further rough generalization, the late '60s were not as turbulent as the early years of the decade when issues like the sales tax and the backlash of the corruption probes gave an intense edge to the polity as a whole. All of this justifies a close examination of the electoral politics of the state up to 1966, with only a sketch of what has happened since then.

During the early '60s there was an air of crisis hanging over the state and its politics. It was the time, for example, when it became fashionable to refer to the citizens of the state as "alienated voters," a term which has gained currency far outside Massachusetts but which was largely based on research into the Boston mayoral election of 1959 and the state gubernatorial election of 1960.[1] As so often happens, the Boston mayoralty election in 1959 became infused with personal rivalries inside the Democratic Party, with State Senate President John Powers being opposed by a former state senator and city council member, John Collins, who had a modest record at that time in state and city government. Powers was one of the most influential members of the party and commanded support from many men of great political status in this nonpartisan election, including both U.S. senators, Kennedy and Saltonstall. Despite this, and a convincing win in the preliminary election when he led the field with 34 percent of the votes as compared to Collins' 22 percent, he lost eventually to Collins by 24,000 votes in a total poll of over 200,000 and, although he remained President of the Senate until 1964, his career never fully recovered from this defeat.

Powers has since claimed that a combination of the mayoralty and the Senate presidency in his hands for even a brief period might have allowed him to break the vicious spiral of rising property taxes by the device of raising the state income tax (rather than promoting a sales tax) and using the revenue to help Boston and other cities, an ambitious and frankly unlikely aspiration. Collins used the symbol of Powers' name — "power politics," for example — and stressed his own underdog candidacy with, for him, a final windfall in the raid on a bookie joint just prior to the election; the place was owned by a man well known to Powers and the press story included photographs of the two men fraternizing in public.[2] It is doubtful whether this event did turn the tide. More than likely, the Powers image seemed dated in 1959, closer to the politics of revenge than of reconciliation, and a relatively fresh face was more attractive.

The result of this election and the victory of Volpe over Ward in 1960 was said to be the result of "alienation"—"political powerlessness, meaningless, estrangement from political activity, and normlessness."[3] The alienated voter does not weigh both sides and vote for whomever he thinks is the "best" candidate as the classical democratic model would suggest, nor would he vote for a man out of habit or traditional party allegiance:

> *If he votes at all, it is because in his judgement one candidate is less crooked than the other . . . The alienated voter is therefore likely to depend upon intuitive feelings or gut reactions.* [4]

The phrase "alienated voter" continues to be brandished on occasion. In the mayoral election in Boston in 1967, newsmen commented, for example, that "Boston voters are alienated," and Mrs. Louise Day Hicks, who eventually lost to Kevin White, suggested that:

> *The greatest issue of all is that we feel alienated. No one in City Hall listens to us.*[5]

The phrase has thus passed from academic currency to a more general one though this does not necessarily make it any the more acceptable if one believes it to be, at the least, overdrawn as a picture of the Massachusetts voter.

Some critiques of "alienation" see it as little more than the "conventional expressions of discontent" which "appear to be indigenous to the style of politics in America." [6] Although it is presented to us as a new interpretation of voting attitudes, much of the character of the alienated voter seems close to more traditional apathy which, as Lipset and Key have long since pointed out, tends to be common among "socially and economically disadvantaged groups," and examples of these are especially to be found in big cities and urbanized locations generally. [7] One of Powers' research staff has suggested that the sampling in the Boston mayoralty study was faulty because it ignored those (few) wards in which Powers led Collins and therefore exaggergerated the trend to "alienation" or anti-Powers feeling. [8]

"Alienation" is a package with little in it that is new. Voting "against" a candidate rather than "for" one is a common enough phenomenon and indicates a degree of interest in the political process insofar as an outcome of a particular election is willed by the voter. There is little that is "anomic" (in the sense that this is used by Merton, Lane and others) in the concept of alienation; voters are not withdrawing from the political process but are reacting to it. [9] In fact, the Massachusetts voter is relatively sophisticated when compared to those in many would-be democratic situations in other parts of the world. He has learned to evaluate the "man" as well as the party and to punish those who, rightly or wrongly, he feels to be unsuited for office as well as to reward those whom he prefers to see installed in positions of power. In short, the concept of "alienation," fashionable when applied to Massachusetts politics in the 1960s, must be used with care, to say the least. [10]

The 1960 election, one of those used to support the "alienation" thesis, was certainly a year when Democratic voters defected from several of the main standard-bearers of their party. This was not true of course for the presidential election where John Kennedy secured 60.3 percent of the two-party vote in contrast with his wafer-thin majority in the country as a whole. At state level, there was some reaction to the whiffs of corruption that were strengthening and centering on the conduct of the Democrats rather than Republicans. During the course of the election itself, Democrats played into the hands of their opponents by such actions as that of the Democratic Convention gubernatorial nominee, Secretary of State Joseph Ward, who allowed the primary ballot to be printed in such a form that it appeared to favor his own chances by its very layout.[11]

During the conventions, some concessions were made by both parties to the pressures to diversify the "ticket"; no longer could parties ride to success on simple emotional appeal to single ethnic blocs. The Republicans produced a ticket headed by the Italo-American John Volpe who was preferred to three rivals, all Yankees. Volpe's climb from apprentice plasterer to head of a construction company and then experience in the appointive positions of State Commissioner of Public Works and Federal Highway Commissioner made him what one account terms:

> . . . *the embodiment of the Horatio Alger hero, the poor little immigrant boy (almost) who rose to riches.*[12]

He had no connection with the temporarily discredited General Court. He was both a successful business man and a proved administrator, which combined with his Italo-American ancestry to make him highly attractive to the Republican Covention at Worcester even though his opponents and their supporters smarted under the defeat. As well as the selection of Negro Edward Brooke for endorsement by the primary as Secretary of State nominee, a Pole and a Jew appeared among the members of the ticket recommended by the Convention to registered Republicans.

The Democrats' only concession was still the person of Foster Furcolo, put forward by John Powers at the party convention despite the latter's former opposition to Furcolo's sales tax, now shelved. Furcolo was unsuccessfully opposed for the senatorial nomination by the Mayor of Springfield, Thomas J. O'Connor, who claimed that the Powers-Furcolo rapprochement was "a shot gun wedding, involving a combination of desperate, grasping men."[13] Apart from Furcolo and Ward, who came from upstate, the ticket was composed of (five) Boston Irishmen which meant that the non-Irish representation was still slim.

Although leaders like Dever and Powers had come to realize in the 1950s that a narrow ethnic and geographic basis for the ticket was no longer a viable electoral gambit, this belief took a considerable time to percolate down to the rank and file if indeed it had by the end of the '60s. The Democratic primary in September 1960 reflected the fierce degree of intra-party competition with no less than seven candidates competing for the gu-

bernatorial nomination—Ward, Robert Murphy, John Francis
Kennedy, Frankie Kelly, Endicott Peabody and two Italo-
Americans, Gabriel F. Piemonte and Alfred Magaletta. Peabody,
the one Yankee on the ballot, turned out to be the chief threat to
Ward. Peabody was to be one of the key figures in Massachusetts Democratic politics in the 1960s (and the party's only
successful gubernatorial nominee at this time). As the son of an
Episcopalian clergyman and grandson of the founder of Groton
school as well as the bearer (in Christian name and surname) of
two of the most famous of Yankee names, he could hardly be
more removed from the world of "The Last Hurrah." Yet he ran
Ward a close second in the primary with 25.5 percent of the vote
to Ward's 30.2 percent.

Peabody's good showing in the primary was an indication of
two factors. One was the disquiet felt with the "old guard" but it
also indicates the diversity of the party by this time, a true coalition of ethnic, religious and economic types, Peabody carving
out support presumably from those Yankees, intellectuals, middle-class and other minority groups that distrusted the existing
leadership who were still reluctant to move far from the "all-
green" ticket. This is not to say that Ward was entirely rooted in
the past though his range of attitudes on public affairs, bitterly
anti-Communist like so many fellow-Catholics, yet liberal on
"bread and butter issues," was not dissimilar to the majority of
his party contemporaries while the press emphasis on his being a
"seasoned scrapper" and having "seven lovely daughters" has a
familiar ring about it.[14] Yet he seemed to believe quite genuinely
that his twenty-three point program with its emphasis on educational improvement and other forward-looking provisions could
be implemented and would bring inevitable change to the state.
He is another example of the way in which the old and the new
often coexist in politician and party in Massachusetts.

At least Ward won his primary election, but Furcolo lost to
O'Connor (O'Connor 43.3%, Furcolo 35%, Edmund C. Buckley
of Cambridge 11.3%, the rest mostly blanks). It was generally
assumed that Furcolo had "coasted" in the primary, conserving
his energies for the general election campaign against Republican
incumbent Leverett Saltonstall. The postmortem in the press
suggested that the growing publicity about irregularities uncovered in the MDC and DPW as well as the poor campaign, the
sales tax fiasco and his strained relations with the legislature all

hurt Furcolo.[15] Yet it should be noted that his opponent was an articulate Irish-American who was helped by the heavy Irish coloring of the primary vote as well as by a hard-hitting campaign well financed from sources that could only be guessed at (there were rumors of Saltonstall and even Kennedy money being involved). Yet the defeat of Furcolo could do little but rekindle the suspicions of Italo-Americans towards the Irish Democrats and siphon their support away from the top of the Democratic ticket in November.

Certainly, Volpe's win over Ward in the general election was aided by defections from Italo-Americans who usually voted the Democratic ticket.[16] It would seem that the impression of a Ward-Powers-Furcolo clique at the Convention had also led to deviance on the part of many voters who could usually be relied upon: "split ticket" voting was a marked feature of the election. Ignoring the presidential vote, the difference between the total vote for Democratic nominees for the Governor's Council (1,314,853) on the one hand and for the two Democratic nominees for senator and governor (O'Connor and Ward) on the other is quite striking (1,050,725 and 1,130,810 respectively). Lower on the ticket, the "normal vote" for the Democrats reasserted itself. Edward Brooke did not, in 1960, show much sign of his later ability to win the independent vote, since he lost to Kevin White for the Secretary of State position by over 100,000 votes. Edward McCormack's lead over Republican George Michaels in the attorney general contest was well over 400,000.[17]

In the Great and General Court, the Democratic majorities moved from 146-94 and 24-16 to 156-84 and 26-14 respectively.[18] It was therefore the gubernatorial and senatorial votes that were the exception. Volpe's victory we have explained and Saltonstall, being what the press termed "a sort of Bay State institution," was obviously more attractive to independents than the less well-known O'Connor.[19] Massachusetts may have been a "Democratic state" by 1960, but the voters still expected candidates of stature and proven ability at the top of the Democratic ticket.

With the extent of the Democratic victory over the rest of the spectrum, John Volpe's position as the Republican survivor was not entirely to be envied. His experience as primarily an administrator rather than a politician was itself a mixed blessing, for it took most of his first term for him to acquire the political expertise required and by this time he needed a renewal of his mandate from the electorate. With a Democratic legislature, although it was under some popular pressure to be positive rather than present a negative opposition to Volpe, he would need to dramatize issues to secure cooperation and he lacked this flair at first. Neither were his relations with the Republican Party organization entirely happy for he put little patronage through its hands and retained his own political and electoral organization, by now a common phenomenon, yet he expected the state committee under its new chairman, Philip Allen, to help in wiping out the debt left by his campaign.

Familiar problems faced Volpe during this term of office, especially those concerned with the Boston metropolitan area. Some reorganization of the much-criticized agencies was initiated and some vital transportation legislation did get through. There was a degree of legislative opposition to other measures, including some transportation bills, led by the late John Thompson, then Speaker of the House.[20] At the same time, publicity about the moral standards of the state's public life continued to grow. On television, the DPW was attacked in a program entitled "The Great Highway Robbery," while another telecast, "Biography of a Bookie Joint," with its disclosures of police protection of an illegal bookmaking establishment, resulted in the forced resignation of the Boston Police Commissioner.[21] Volpe persuaded the legislature to agree to the formation of a "Massachusetts Commission on Crime and Public Morality" composed of citizens of known integrity, which was to be invited to take a detached and apolitical view of the moral crisis in state government in Massachusetts and to report on possible remedies to raise standards.[22]

It was at this time (1961) that the *Atlantic Monthly* and *New York Times* articles on political corruption in Massachusetts appeared and that cases such as *United States* v. *Thomas Worcester* began to reach the courts. In 1962, a poll of Massachusetts voters showed that taxes and corruption were the two most important problems to the people of Massachusetts.[23] Democrats and Republicans in office reacted to the public concern by admitting that some housecleaning was necessary although exactly what was needed was an issue that did not meet with general agreement. Among the constitutional officers, Attorney General Edward McCormack opposed the Crime Commission because it would lead "to trial by hearsay, by rumor, by innuendo and denies the accused even the basic right of confrontation."[24] At the same time, McCormack was building a liberal record in office, setting up a Civil Rights Division and taking a positive stand in initiating "legal and legislative action to confine the rights of citizens."[25] The General Court, especially sensitive because of a widespread suspicion that several legislators were involved in the scandals and conscious of the unfavorable publicity that the Charles Iannello case aroused,[26] was becoming more susceptible to limited change encouraged by the few younger, more articulate and issue conscious members already elected to its ranks.

By the 1962 election, discussion of the extent to which corruption had become entrenched in the political life of the state was a major feature of political campaigning. Republican Edward Brooke, aiming for the attorney general's chair to be vacated by Edward McCormack, insisted that the state was "literally plagued with crime, graft and corruption" and put forward the view that the state's chief law officer should bring forward legislative recommendations that would "close up loopholes and build safeguards."[27] When John Volpe formally announced his intention to seek reelection in May 1962, he seized on the curbing of corruption as his main theme and claimed that the failure to reorganize the DPW was solely the fault of the Democratic majority among the legislators.[28]

At the Republican Convention in June of that year, serious contests arose for the lieutenant governor and attorney general nominations. Francis Perry won in the former contest and Edward Brooke in the latter. The Brooke victory was another of the symbolic events that occur from time to time. Brooke's choice of the Republican Party may seem unusual although his rise may well have been more difficult if he had tried to challenge the ethnic stranglehold held by the Democratic Irish leaders. His rival Elliot Richardson's experience encompassed service with Felix Frankfurter, Leverett Saltonstall and the U.S. Department of Health, Education and Welfare (he was also U.S. attorney for Massachusetts at the time of the Goldfine and Worcester cases). Brooke had achieved some prominence as a Chairman of the Boston Finance Commission which had cracked down on unethical conduct by city officials. Brooke's victory seemed to have been due to the better discipline of his supporters at the Convention, for Richardson was almost victorious on the

first ballot but was defeated on the second one. The old-stock
Yankee would have probably been a clear winner a generation
earlier but now Brooke was launched on a meteoric rise (and, to be
fair, Richardson was only held back temporarily.)[29]

The Democratic Convention was dominated by the Kennedy-
McCormack duel and all else paled by comparison. Yet the endorsement of Endicott Peabody for the gubernatorial nomination (defeating incumbent Lieutenant Governor Edward Mc-
Laughlin) is as symbolic in its way as the Brooke victory, for
Peabody was a progressive Yankee Democrat and was to become the first governor in this category since Ely thirty years
before. Like Ely, he had good friends among the leading Irish
Democrats of the day (i.e., for Walsh, read the Kennedys). The
Springfield Convention has been epitomized as a carryover of
the derby-hat era but this is an exaggeration of the truth.[30] The
party platform, in particular, was more specific than usual, advocating reform of state agencies, a strict code of ethics for public employees, constitutional reform and increased fiscal support of educational institutions and locally-run welfare services.[31]

The only surprise that came out of the primaries was the defeat of Democratic Convention endorsee James Lawton by
Frankie Kelly for the nomination for attorney general. In the
five-man contest, Kelly's Boston support was the crucial factor
and he also led in a number of other industrial centers such as
Worcester, Fitchburg and Lynn. Kelly was the epitome of the
old-style candidate; newspaperman Cornelius Dalton wrote of
him:

> *A specialist in crowd appeal, he had come a long way in three
> decades. In the 1930s, he was promising the people free elec-
> tric light bulbs. Now, with his sweepstakes plan, he is promising
> them lower taxes and the chance to become a millionaire.*[32]

Kelly was a contrast to the head of the ticket. Peabody had worked
for Governor Bradford in the 1946 election but quickly found
the Democratic Party (nationally) closer to his own liberal views.
His blue-blood Yankee background, "All-American" football
record at Harvard, and prowess as a gunnery officer in the Pacific in World War II made him good material for the campaign
biographers.[33] In 1962, he was a useful example of the party's
good faith in purging corruption where it could be found. As
what was described as "an intelligent supporter of COD," his lib-

eral credentials were close to impeccable.[34] Since Volpe seemed
to be near impregnable, some Democrats may have conjectured
that Peabody was little more than a stalking-horse until they
could field a more orthodox candidate.

Republican discipline held up as usual in the primaries and the
Brooke nomination survived with a clear majority over Richardson of forty-two thousand. Presumably because of the interest
in the senatorial nomination, the total vote in the primaries rose
by 200,000 as compared with 1960. Since 1962 was an "off-year"
election, the general election vote was down and the percentage
of primary vote compared with general election was 65.0 percent in 1962 compared with 35.1 percent in 1960. There is some
significance in this in that it may well have altered basic party loyalties and cut the "independent" vote. Certainly, what the press
termed "the blizzard of ballots" for Ted Kennedy and Chub Peabody in the Democratic primary" should have dimmed the confidence that John Volpe seemed to be exuding up to that time.[35]
Even the reformers in the Democratic Party were happy with
the ticket, with the exception of Kelly who was excluded from
the endorsement given by COD to the ticket and condemned for
his "demagogic campaign" by the reform organization's board.[36]
Yet Volpe, while he recognized that the rest of the Republican
ticket was vulnerable, felt that he was not. Opinion polls that he
commissioned showed him ahead of Peabody and only reinforced his view. Remarks in his speeches like, "Massachusetts
doesn't need a debater, Massachusetts needs an efficient manager," were intended to indicate his lack of respect for the challenge mounted by the Democratic nominee.[37]

The win that Volpe expected turned out to be a defeat, a narrow one, but a defeat nevertheless, and it upset the expectation
that an efficient governor has generally had for reelection in the
last twenty years. Peabody's victory was a little unusual for a
Democrat (though it carries echoes, oddly enough, of Tobin in
the 1940s). He led Volpe by only 52,000 in Boston, whereas the
standing "rule" has been that a Democrat needed a 100,000 vote
lead in Boston to offset upstate Republican votes. On the other
hand, once out of the city, Peabody made gains in places usually
Republican or marginally Democratic.[38] Peabody's Episcopalian background may well have helped him in the areas with
a normally high Republican vote although he also did well in
communities with large Italian minorities, perhaps because the

Democratic candidate for lieutenant governor was Francis X.
Bellotti who, in fact, ran ahead of Peabody in places like Revere,
Everett and Lawrence. Further down the ticket, Kevin White,
John Driscoll and Thomas J. Buckley also ran ahead of Peabody,
though this was only to be expected.

The one Democratic failure was Kelly, who succumbed to
Edward Brooke by 239,000 votes and the reports emphasized
that:

> *Brooke carried such Democratic cities as Waltham, Everett,*
> *Pittsfield and lost Springfield by only 1,300 votes. Kelly's*
> *strength was centered in such Democratic cities as Lawrence,*
> *Lowell, Lynn, New Bedford and Fall River.*[39]

Some years later, the received view on this election was that
Brooke "defeated a Democratic machine candidate, who was
picked for the race only because the incumbent, Edward Mc-
Cormack, was locked in a senatorial primary fight with Teddy
Kennedy."[40] In fact, Kelly was "picked" as a minority candidate
in the primary against the wishes of the Democratic leadership
(if this is what is meant by "machine" in this context) and failed
partially at least because the party was not behind him.

Looking at 1962 in retrospect, it appears to be the finest electoral success enjoyed by the Democrats in recent years. Although
it was a time when the party was suffering from a spattering of
mud from the first phases of the "corruption" issue, its well-bal-
anced ticket, relative unity of purpose, coherent platform plus the
Kennedy personalities both near and far, gave it a clear mandate
at the constitutional office level as well as in the General Court.
In the years following 1962, jealousy and rivalry within the
leadership plus a certain lack of purpose threw away the natural
advantages that the party enjoyed. The administration headed
by Peabody, which took office in January 1963, was soon riven by
feuds and ambition. The governor clashed with his fellow Democrats over his tactics and his general lack of political acumen. The
natural suspicion of the still predominantly Irish-American Democratic hierarchy for a Yankee was compounded by the Governor's unfortunate sense of timing, as for example when he was
publicly advocating the abolition of capital punishment at a time
when three policemen had just been killed in the course of duty.
The all-American football player was ridiculed with comments
that he had played "too much football without a helmet."

Endicott Peabody was a controversial governor but not an incompetent one. His program was ambitious and liberal but "got over" to the reform groups that had been pressing for changes in state government and improved education and welfare programs. It did not "get over" to the general public, in part because insufficient trouble was taken with press relations and in part because Peabody projected so poorly as a public figure. Though a man of intelligence and sincerity, he had no feel for the mass media, suffered from "mike fright" and was stiff and awkward when using the electronic media, now an essential part part of any statewide political impact. Since his power base was a limited one, he was open to attack from associates who appeared to believe that his reelection was impossible and jockeyed for position according to their personal ambition. After a cool start when, for example, he backed an attempt to remove John Thompson from the position of Speaker of the House at the beginning of 1963, Peabody, oddly enough, received support for his legislative program from both Thompson and John Powers in the Senate. This was probably the basic reason for his high "score" of 85 percent of his legislative program becoming law, a figure he claimed to be "the highest record of legislative success of any Governor in modern times."[41]

Among Peabody's greatest achievements in office was the successful reorganization of several of the state agencies which had been criticized for several years. The DPW had been described as "a cesspool of political pestilence" by a Congressional investigation reporting in 1963.[42] Although opposed by the DPW Commissioner, Jack Ricciardi, Peabody worked hard for the passage of the bill and it passed the General Court late in the year. Ricciardi resigned immediately afterwards.

The Department of Commerce was also reorganized as the Department of Commerce and Development with the Commissioner serving at the pleasure of the governor. Another major scheme was the transformation of the Boston transport network, now renamed the Massachusetts Bay Transportation Authority (MBTA), into a larger organization including seventy-eight cities and towns in eastern Massachusetts. The Peabody bill allowed for a two hundred million dollar bond issue and improvements to the services, including subsidies for some lines, with day-to-day management vested in a general manager and a six-man Board of Directors ultimately responsible to an advisory board representative of the towns and cities. Some opposition in the House came from upstate legislators, but the final vote for the bill was a clear majority (132-80) even if not as overwhelming as that of the Senate (21-6).[43]

Other measures of note included ensuring a substantial financial appropriation for the work of the Crime Commission, some expansion of state aid to higher education and the reference of measures of constitutional reform to the voters for a decision, including the recommendation to curtail the powers of the Governor's Council and to lengthen the terms of office of the six-man executive branch to four years. Peabody's efforts to fulfill what he considered was his mandate from the people led to criticism from those who felt that he lowered the dignity of his office by personally intervening in many cases to persuade legislators to support his program. On the other hand, many citizens' groups, such as the League of Women Voters and the Junior Chambers of Commerce, found government more responsive to change than at any previous time due to sympathy from the executive branch and thus were highly appreciative of Peabody's work.

Pressure groups and reform-minded politicians alike found that the public climate by this time was in favor of a limited program of house-cleaning in state government. In addition to Peabody, Attorney General Edward Brooke used the public concern to good effect in pursuing a campaign against those public officials and their associates who had been involved in the corrupt practices of the immediate past.[44] John Kennedy is reported to have described Brooke's 1962 victory over Kelly as "the biggest news in the country" in terms of that year's elections,[45] and the black law officer inevitably attracted considerable publicity both inside the state and in the nation at large.

The state, despite its historic connections with the abolitionist movement, is not markedly more liberal on race issues than others in the Northeast and, in its urban "ghettoes" like Boston's Roxbury, it has problems of integration, educational, economic and social that are only modified by the relatively small size of the Negro minority compared with some other urbanized states. Brooke did not have a particularly large ethnic support, both because of this factor and because he insisted that "I am not a civil rights leader, and I don't profess to be."[46] Even Peabody had some group affinity with liberal Protestant Democrats of which there are a number among the intellectual middle class, but the number of those who could directly identify with Brooke (middle-class, well-educated black people) was obviously relatively small in the mid-1960s. Yet his career has been as successful and has moved upwards as Peabody's has declined from relative success to relative obscurity.

The truth is that both had ability but that Brooke was articulate and projected well while Peabody had, as we noted earlier, a poor public personality. There was a unique quality about Brooke—a black politician trusted by the white community and a man who allowed that community to exercise a certain "token" liberalism—while Peabody lacked any such feature except insofar as he was from a social and ethnic group once closely identified with Republicanism (but Brooke was equally paradoxical as a black Republican).

By 1964, the "Goldwater" year for the Republicans, the party in Massachusetts could produce a strong team of candidates for the top three offices. Brooke resisted the temptation to try for the gubernatorial nomination (ostensibly because of his obligation to pursue the indictments for corruption still pending[47]) and Volpe persuaded the state Republican Convention to allow him to attempt a comeback by assuming the party's gubernatorial nomination. After an unchallenged primary, Volpe, Brooke and Elliot Richardson (nominated for lieutenant governor) presented a "top of the ticket" varied in ethnic line (Italian, Negro, Yankee) and credible as office-holders.

Inside the Democratic Party, the reaction against Peabody could be seen as the Irish-Yankee dispute breaking out afresh although the participants claimed otherwise. One claimed that Peabody was a "total disaster" who over-reacted to issues but, whatever the reason, a rival soon appeared in the shape of Lieutenant Governor Francis Bellotti. Bellotti, although Italian-American, is said to have felt himself "sociologically and culturally more Irish than Italian" because he was brought up in an Irish section of Boston.[48] Bellotti failed to oust Peabody from the nomination at the Democratic Convention, probably due to the support given to Peabody by Edward Kennedy's organization (it will be remembered that this was the Convention that was overshadowed by the Senator's near-fatal air crash). Bellotti claimed that the failure of the Convention to support his plea for a secret ballot showed that the Convention was "rigged" or at least "controlled" by Peabody.[49] As an incumbent with a reasonably good record and a man who was accepted by the nominal leader of the party, it was perhaps as natural for Peabody to receive support from the Convention as it was for Bellotti to seize on this excuse to take the decision "to the people."[50]

Bellotti's reversal of the Convention decision in the primary rests on a number of factors. His organization seems to have been more successful at making an impact than was Peabody's, which was once again hampered by the problem of "projecting" the governor.[51] Bellotti used a clever commercial based on favorable comments made by Edward Kennedy about him some time earlier while Kennedy's hospitalization prevented his making an outright endorsement for Peabody until just before the primary.[52] Whatever Bellotti's upbringing may have done for him, he certainly received considerable Italo-American backing in the primary, especially in areas such as the North End and East Boston which backed him 3 to 1 against Peabody. The latter may not have been helped by John Power's eve-of-poll suggestion that Bellotti was trying to create an "Italian" party to support him.[53]

Peabody did well only in those areas that were mainly Republican in tendency. These are usually areas with Democratic Party organization based on the Yankee middle class, and it seems obvious that the centers of traditional Democratic blue-collar support felt more at home with Bellotti than with the more "aristocratic" Peabody. On a county basis, Peabody did best in Berkshire and Barnstable (see Table Twenty One), a reflection of the point just made and also possibly a preference for a man less redolent of the politics of urban Boston than Bellotti seemed to be (though both candidates lived on the fringe of Boston, Peabody in Cambridge, Bellotti in Quincy). Some may argue that Peabody's weak position with the hard core of Democratic voters shows that he would have lost against Volpe by a greater margin than Bellotti, but this ignores the importance of the "independent" vote which might have preferred him to the more traditional Bellotti when November came.

On the face of it, Bellotti did appear to be in an advantageous position for the general election in November. There was no incumbent to beat, Bellotti having already defeated him, and his opponent had been defeated two years previously. Moreover, there was always the possibility of hanging on to the "coattails" of Lyndon Johnson who seemed likely—unless opinion polls failed to show the "backlash"—to sweep the state and nation. Republicans were cool in the main to their presidential candidate. When Goldwater spoke at a rally in the Boston arena, Volpe attended (reluctantly, it was reported), but Brooke did not, and the latter stated quite flatly about Goldwater that "his statements are incompatible with my principles."[54] The Republicans' main hope for the top of the ticket was that the divisive primary and the known penchant of Massachusetts voters for "ticket-splitting" would let Volpe in and see that Brooke was reelected.

It was estimated soon after the 1964 election that Bellotti had amassed about one million dollars in campaign funds. Yet in the post-primary stage of the campaign, this command of resources appeared to benefit him less than in the earlier stage. He was evidently unwilling to delegate decisions to his assistants and his campaign lost its incision, probably because it lacked a defined point of view apart from his nebulous slogan, "Don't go back, go Bellotti." Volpe was more specific in his campaigning, tending to pose issues such as the fiscal problem of the towns and cities, which he intended to help with the sales tax. Some of the press reports suggested, for example, that the tax was "an albatross around Volpe's neck."[55] His election and the fact that the 1966 referendum supported its introduction suggests that this was a misinterpretation. He also emphasized his part in "creating" the Crime Commission and his support of the referendum question which would limit the powers of the Governor's Council. A little maliciously, Volpe queried whether Bellotti supported the retention of the Council's powers "because its members helped him in his conspiracy against Governor Peabody."[56]

The slim size of Volpe's majority (23,000 in a ballot of nearly 2.4 million) stresses the importance in the defeat of Bellotti of the support he lost as the challenger of an established incumbent. Many of Peabody's erstwhile supporters seem to have "sat on their hands." Even Mayor Collins, who apparently had been a Bellotti supporter, seemed to cool, perhaps over the sales tax issue or perhaps because the mayor wished to run for the Senate eventually and preferred to do without a Democratic governor who might control a future convention. Bellotti did especially badly in the Boston area. In the city itself and in many suburban areas, he ran well behind Lyndon Johnson and Edward Kennedy. Even in his own home town of Quincy, he could only manage a majority of 3,299 against Volpe, whereas the Johnson and Kennedy majorities were in excess of 20,000. Further out, in towns where the State Committee's registration drives had been effective, results were better for Bellotti, though not dramatically so.[57]

Bellotti blamed the "difficult primary" for his general election defeat and seemed surprised at his poor showing in "the peripheral Route 128 area."[58] Yet it was this area that contained elements of the Peabody organization. Virtually all of the Collins organization was in Boston itself and it was noted that "the defection from Bellotti was mainly concentrated in the upper wards of the city where the mayor has most influence."[59] The ethnic advantage, useful in the primary, disappeared in the general election where the opponent was a self-made Italian with whom even many Democrat Italo-Americans might like to identify. A survey of Springfield carried out immediately after the election produced a finding that voters felt that (unfair as it may have been) "Volpe was known and thought to be honest, Bellotti was unknown and possibly corrupt." The post-primary erosion in Springfield was shown by the figures indicating that only 52 percent of those who voted for Peabody and 66 percent of those who voted for Bellotti in September voted for the latter in November.[60]

The contrast between the vote for the Democratic gubernatorial candidate and that for the party's presidential and senatorial candidates was especially marked in 1964 because of the popularity of the Johnson-Humphrey ticket (or the dislike of Goldwater) and the large sympathy vote given to Edward Kennedy, hospitalized as a result of his airplane crash, although he would obviously have received a handsome majority under whatever circumstances the election had been held.[61] Any reasonable assessment made just before the election would have assumed that the Democrats would succeed in these two sections of the ballot and they did not offset the loss of the three senior constitutional offices. In fact, Elliott Richardson in second place on the Republican ticket did better than Volpe (though not as well as Brooke who produced a mirror image of the Johnson vote).[62] Richardson aides claimed that this was due to their study of the 1960 vote, noting those places where Saltonstall ran well ahead of the Nixon vote, and concentrating attention on them in terms of appearances by Richardson, distribution of literature, etc. This may have helped but a look at the results shows that Richardson did especially well in Yankee towns like those on the Essex coastline. All three men—Volpe, Brooke and Richardson—had their careers significantly advanced by this election and by the end of the '60s were in Washington in elective or appointive office. Brooke especially was singled out by the press as "the GOP's No. 1 vote-getter," "a qualified, honest, ambitious candidate who is Negro; rather than a Negro candidate who is qualified, honest and ambitious."[63]

The three junior constitutional offices remained tightly in control of the Democrats even though a last-minute replacement for Thomas J. Buckley, the auditor who died during the campaign, had to be found. Thaddeus Buczko of Salem, a Polish-American, was the man. The two main referenda results led to the curbing of the Governors' Council and the establishment of four-year electoral terms for the six constitutional officers from the next election date (1966). Both of these measures were a signal victory for the cause of constitutional reform.

Over the next two years, there was a noticeable improvement in the political climate of the state. The 1965 Crime Commission report gave substance to many of the criticisms made during the previous few years but even by its appearance there were some signs that the demand for a more responsive political system and one that was relatively free from corruption were beginning to take effect. The politicians, who largely take their standards of morality from those prevailing with the public at any period of time, were made aware that voters were attuned to a wider range of issues than the simple bread-and-butter areas of the past, and that they demanded a higher standard of performance from legislators and administrators, one commensurate with the sophisticated life-style of the urban, and especially the suburban, inhabitants of the state. This is not to say that the "liberals" are now entrenched in power but that younger politicians are generally more responsive than the older ones and that even the latter often recognize the changing winds to which they must trim their sails.

There are constraints under which every American politician works even if he has a reputation for honesty and secures electoral victory as a result of it. The case of the "governor's brother" in John Volpe's second term illustrates this. When, in 1966, a State Senate committee investigating the method of selecting architects for the building of the University of Massachusetts Medical School found that there had been a "conflict of interest"

in that Peter Volpe had been the "decisive and essential factor" in
the choice of architects, John Volpe's reputation seemed to be in
danger. One of the firms involved had contributed to Volpe's
campaign fund, which was an additional compromising factor.
The report was written by a Democratic majority and disputed by
the Republican minority, also it may have been presumed by
many that a governor could consult his brother if the latter was
well qualified (and Peter Volpe had relevant qualifications),
therefore the incident did little permanent harm to the Volpe
cause. It did illustrate the need for a "Caesar's wife" approach on
the part of prominent public officials when a strong "reform"
trend is running.[64]

Public opinion had been sensitized to the issues such as the
foregoing by the publication of the final report of the Massachusetts Crime Commission in May 1965. Although some improvement in the political climate was noted by the Commission, as far as the recent past was concerned, they felt that "the
reality has been worse than we imagined."[65] As was expected,
money was the crucial issue to the degree that campaign contributions could not always be distinguished from bribes, and in
the Commission's view, "the moral standard used in raising money continues after the candidate is elected."[66] It was perhaps
naive of the Commission to believe that abuses in the raising of
campaign funds would be removed by legislation for this is a
problem which bites deeply into the whole fabric of American
politics and little progress is likely to be made in reforming it
until there is a decided shift in the cultural traits involved. Struc-
tural faults are more easily remedied and some, like the reorganization of the DPW, had already been carried out though, in the
views of the Commission, reform had not gone far enough.[67]

The Commission produced many recommendations aimed at
improving the standards of government in the state and some of
these, such as one suggesting the creation of a special division
in the attorney general's office to investigate suspected irregularities, would combat recurrences of chronic corruption in future.[68]
By the time of the 1966 election campaign, it was obvious that
reform would have to depend on measures like the strengthening
of the executive by the 1964 and 1966 referenda, allowing not
only the four-year term but the election of governor and lieutenant governor as a team and on increased powers for the governor in reorganizing executive departments.

By late 1965 and early 1966, the Crime Commission report tended to slip into the background, partly because of the amount of governmental energy and public interest that came to be expended over the new tax measures being pressed by John Volpe. In a nutshell, this was the sales tax which he felt had been virtually mandated by the result of the '64 election. The Democratic Party in the General Court argued that it was essentially a regressive tax and the governor then produced figures which claimed to show the opposite.[69] Luckily for Volpe, city and town governments, whether Democrat, Republican or noncommittal, were eager for relief from the soaring property tax and were easily persuaded that the sales tax was the most painless method of relief, partially because it was a tax that was shared by visitors and residents of the state alike.

The tax was to be a "limited" one, i.e. it exempted certain necessities of life but this did not mollify legislators such as the then Senate President Maurice Donahue who would have preferred an income-tax-based plan and added that, for him, it was a point of principle, "not . . . political intransigence."[70] In many ways, this was an occasion—a relatively rare one—where a clear class rift appeared between the two parties, the Democrats insisting that the tax would lead to a rise in the cost of living for blue-collar workers, the Republican governor emphasizing the need to protect property-owners from rising tax rates. In practice, since property taxes affect rents and all taxes influence the cost of living, the distinction was blurred but it suited the Democrats to give emphasis to it.

The Democrats in the General Court produced several counter-plans to raise the revenue that all felt was needed. These, including an income-tax-based plan created at the insistence of Speaker John Davoren, failed to gain the necessary approval of the legislature.[71] The trade unions opposed the tax and tried to counter the pressure that the governor was putting on legislators to pass his bill.[72] The 1965 legislative session ran into the 1966 one for the first time in the state's history, and it was evident that some compromise had to be reached. Despite last-ditch opposition by some Senate Democrats, the seventh tax package passed through both houses and was signed by the governor on March, 1966, the sales tax, still a central feature, taking effect from April 1st of that year.[73] Whether or not the sales tax was a famous victory for the governor may be long debated but extra revenue was certainly sorely needed. In particular, the educational improvements willed by the acceptance of the "Willis Report" made by the Massachusetts Education Commission in June 1965 had to be paid for. The measure was a progressive one but involved raising standards and providing extra financial help for all levels of public education. The sales tax was probably inevitable, since by the mid-1960s most of the states had adopted it. All the opponents could do was to delay its adoption which they had done for some considerable span of years.

The 1966 election involved high stakes for both parties for the first four year terms for constitutional office were to be contested and the Democrats obviously wished to end the anomaly of three Republicans heading the executive branch in what most observers considered to be a Democratic state. Added to this was the prize of one of the U.S. Senate seats since Leverett Saltonstall decided to retire at the close of the current term. When he announced this decision at the end of 1965, it was quickly followed by an announcement by Edward Brooke that he would be a candidate for the Republican nomination. Unlike Brooke, Volpe was taken off guard by news of Saltonstall's decision—evidently he expected the senior Senator to try for one more term and was deeply preoccupied with the sales tax question. He may have been impressed by a poll which showed the Attorney General as the most likely heir to Saltonstall, but whatever the reason it was soon evident that he would settle for another term as governor if he could secure reelection. Considering the relative lack of sympathy between him and the Democratic majorities in the General Court, his percentage of bills passed by the legislature (54%), though much lower than his predecessor's record, was a fair one. [74] But it was the sales tax issue which had given him a reputation as a tough executive, and he expected that the coming referendum, instigated by a repeal petition put together by organized labor and containing 40,000 signatures, would only bring him support from the many citizens hoping for relief from property taxes. The creation of an organization called the Alliance for Fiscal Responsibility in Massachusetts (AFFIRM) by a number of town and city officials reinforced this view.

With Volpe and Brooke certain for confirmation as gubernatorial and senatorial candidates respectively, the 1966 Republican Convention held in Boston in June 1966 revolved mainly around the question of who was to occupy the preferred places for the party's attempt to retain the post of lieutenant governor and attorney general. Elliot Richardson could virtually take his pick but his problem at that time was to decide which post, if he won the election, would advance his political career the more. If he retained the post of lieutenant governor and John Volpe was picked for the vice-presidential nomination in 1968, a Republican victory could catapult Volpe to Washington and the lieutenant governor would step into his shoes. On the other hand, the attorney general's position is one in which the incumbent can establish his own identity more effectively than can the lieutenant governor and this would also allow Richardson to be in a strong position for a gubernatorial nomination in 1970.[75] This was the one that he chose, and the Convention was left to make a choice between DPW Commissioner Francis W. Sargent and Representative Francis Hatch of Beverley as their nominee for lieutenant governor, with Sargent winning on the first ballot.[76] As it happened, there was an opponent to Brooke for the senatorial nomination in the shape of a right-wing Boston lawyer, G. Alan Mackay. His vote of 215 compared to Brooke's 1,485 was small but showed that some Goldwater sentiment still remained on the fringes of the party.[77]

The Democratic Convention was altogether more lively as is the norm. A whole generation of party stalwarts returned to the fray to secure nomination but not to establish any consensus in the way the party should be going. Feeling that Endicott Peabody had been shabbily treated helped the former Governor in his somewhat thankless task of fighting for the senatorial nomination. John Collins was also an aspirant for this opportunity and, when Peabody topped his 717 votes by 1,089, Collins turned bitterly on the Convention, accusing John Powers of seeking revenge for his 1959 mayoral defeat at Collins' hands by engineering the Peabody victory on this occasion. Collins' underdog position seemed inappropriate and inelegant at the Convention for he was well supported by the Boston delegates, yet it was in Boston that Powers had his base in his days as president of the State Senate.[78]

The somewhat stolid president of the Senate, Maurice Donahue, coveted the gubernatorial nomination but stood little chance against the returning Edward McCormack. Donahue's vote was a reasonable one, 722 to McCormack's 892, with former presidential aide Kenneth O'Donnell capturing only 129, and the Senator kept a former pledge to abide by the Convention decision by agreeing to work as McCormack's campaign manager for the primary and general elections. Other well-known names appeared for the favor of the Convention in the hope of becoming the new attorney general. Foster Furcolo was a contender, and there were two "reform" candidates from the younger membership of the party, but it was Frank Bellotti who beat one of these, Michael Dukakis, into second place. Bellotti apologized publicly for his overweening ambition in 1964 which led to his fatal challenge of Peabody, fatal, that is, to the party's retention of the governorship.[79] He was certainly not Edward Kennedy's choice but then the latter had deliberately refrained from being kingmaker at the Convention. One reason was evidently a reluctance to rekindle old feuds or, on the other hand, to "play favorites" by rewarding old friends of the Kennedys. Supporting Donahue or O'Donnell against McCormack would have done just this. The Senator contented himself by providing the following advice, suggesting that primary candidates should:

> . . . compete with one another not by engaging in personal attacks but by presenting positive programs for the benefit of the people and by making the issues the failures of the incumbent administration.[80]

In the subsequent primary, attention focussed on the Democratic senatorial nomination, for few felt that Kenneth O'Donnell would be a strong competitor to McCormack. In fact, the former presidential assistant ran McCormack quite close, perhaps helped by the support he received from Robert Kennedy, a factor which may have embarrassed Edward Kennedy and McCormack as well, for they showed little interest in stirring up the embers of the supposed feud between the two families. In the senatorial primary, Peabody and Collins were the main contenders, but the ballot also included the name of Thomas Boylston Adams, a member of that most distinguished of Massachusetts families. Adams' intervention was a sign of the times. Although he had no chance of winning, his candidature was a protest against President Johnson's Vietnam policy, now becoming a political issue of some magnitude even in state elections. Peabody and Collins were "hawkish" as, roughly speaking, was the state, in 1966. Adams secured less than ten percent of the primary vote and Peabody emerged the winner, even capturing Boston from Collins, although earlier public opinion polls had picked Collins as the likely winner.[81] In fact, Democratic Convention choices held up well in 1966. Bellotti, Thaddeus Buczko and Joseph McGuire (the lieutenant governor nominee) all beat off challengers, suggesting that Convention endorsement was now really worthwhile.

The gentlemanly facade of Republican unity was broken in 1966, not by a successful challenge to any of the constitutional offices but by one who ousted veteran Congressman Joseph Martin, once Speaker of the U.S. House of Representatives, from the Tenth District seat which he had held for forty-two years. Martin was nearing retirement (he died in 1968) but was expected to continue untl 1968 when a "succession" battle would have ensued, State Senator John Parker being the favorite. Now Martin was replaced by a thirty-five-year-old governor's councillor, Mrs. Margaret Heckler, from suburban Wellesley in a primary win which was an obvious surprise for the Republican leadership and must have caused considerable chagrin to Parker and others who had been chivalrously awaiting the word that Martin was about to retire.

No one doubted that the Democrats would make their usual good showing in the rank-and-file positions on the electoral ladder. In the summer of 1966 it looked as if the Republicans would lose about a third of both houses by default, i.e. they had no candidates chosen to run against the Democrat choices.[82] At county level, the Democrats were consolidating their hold—in Middlesex County it looked as if they would hold all the posts and they were making inroads into the former Republican stronghold of Essex—which meant that the state was drifting towards a one-party dominance at the junior levels.[83] This was offset by the ability of the Republicans to use the lack of unity in the Democratic Party to their advantage at the top of the ticket and, in 1966, this led to the four greatest prizes—U.S. senator, governor, lieutenant governor and attorney general—falling to them. Efforts to unify the Democratic ticket, with a poorly-attended Post Office Square rally headed by both Bobby and Teddy Kennedy as its focus, were not successful and many voters appeared to consider the major Democratic nominees as hangers-on to the Kennedy coattails.

The media tended to concentrate on the senatorial election

because of the possiblilty that Massachusetts would make history by being the first state to send a Negro to the Senate since the days of Reconstruction. Brooke's rival was as liberal in most respects as was the Republican, therefore there was little ideological contrast between them. Peabody's pro-civil rights attitudes (and those of his family) made it unlikely that he would pick up much of a "backlash" vote. Brooke could suffer from Republicans who might abstain because of the sentiments that he voiced in his 1966 book, for these criticized his own party for "poor programs" and "poor leadership" and for not being sympathetic to change.[84] Peabody stood on his record as governor and waged an intensive campaign as the seeming underdog of the two. The gubernatorial campaign was marred by a certain amount of petty bickering between McCormack and Volpe and only came alive on the issues when two face-to-face debates—at Worcester and Fall River—were staged.[85]

In the closing stages of the 1966 campaign, it was the election of a new attorney general that aroused most public interest. This is a post which was especially sensitive in the wake of the disclosures about corruption of the early '60s and debate raged between Bellotti and Richardson over the degree of control that the attorney general's office could exercise over potential corrupt practices.[86] The Republican Party organization expended a considerable sum in obtaining projections of the vote from a polling organization and, at one time, the sampling suggested that Bellotti and Richardson were running neck and neck.[87]

Then, a week before the election, Richardson charged Bellotti with an action when the latter was lieutenant governor by which he had "clearly demonstrated that he lacks the moral sensitivity to fill the office of attorney general."[88] It was a conflict-of-interest issue. Bellotti had received a twelve-thousand-dollar fee from the Nationwide Insurance Companies of Ohio for representation before the Massachusetts Insurance Department. Brooke, still attorney general at this time, ruled that it was a conflict of interest if Bellotti had represented the company while he was in office. Bellotti's reply was that the money was paid to his law firm but that he did not appear before the agency while he was lieutenant governor.[89] An impartial panel set up in 1967, when Richardson had replaced Brooke, reported that they were:

> . . . satisfied that there is no evidence that Francis X. Belo-
> lotti performed any acts during the years 1963-1964, being the

*term of his office as Lieutenant Governor, which were in viola-
tion of the conflict-of-interest sections of chapter 268A of the
General Laws.*[90]

In view of this, it is difficult to acquit Richardson of opportun-
ism in bringing up this issue so close to the election, i.e. at a time
when it would make the maximum effect on the voters and give
Bellotti the minimum time for rebuttal (although the effect may
well have been to attract a "sympathy vote" for Bellotti). Certainly, tempers run high and nerves are frayed at this juncture in a
close election and there may have been an error of judgement in
the Richardson camp over this issue but it is an error which does
not sit well with the Republican's former reputation for probity.

As far as the Democrats were concerned, the 1966 election and
its prelude (convention and primary) "sent down to defeat a whole
generation of Democrats at state level."[91] It is difficult to see
much political future in the 1970s for McCormack, Peabody,
Collins et al. Peabody lost every county except Suffolk to Brooke
and his majority there (26,000) was very low for a Democrat.
Although he won a few industrial centers (Chicopee, Holyoke,
Lawrence), most of the other cities and large towns went to
Brooke, including Peabody's "home town" of Cambridge. Volpe
even took Suffolk and lost only five cities and six towns to Mc-
Cormack.[92] Unlike Brooke, he took Somerville with its 6 to 1
Democratic registration, the only Republican running for high
office (apart from Eisenhower) to do this since 1930.[93] Sargent
came in on Volpe's coattails, but Kevin White's handsome majority lower down the ticked enhanced his position for the mayoral
election in Boston in 1967 and his attempt at the governorship in
1970.

One final point of contrast between Volpe and Brooke is worth
noting and that is the importance of the "Italian" vote in the
former's sweeping victory. Of the four heavily "Italian" centers
of eastern Massachusetts, Brooke won only one, whereas Volpe
took all of these normally heavily Democratic strongholds:

	Brooke	Peabody	Volpe	McCormack
Somerville	14,416	18,462	17,788	15,482
Watertown	8,828	6,943	10,250	5,734
Everett	7,917	8,427	11,126	6,781
Revere	7,960	9,409	10,365	7,248

The Republican victories at the top of the ticket can be construed as support for strong, effective government. This view is reinforced by the approval of the referenda measures which allowed the future election of governor and lieutenant governor as a team, gave the governor greater power to reorganize the executive and, by a 4 to 1 majority, upheld the sales tax.[94] The Democrats were now given four years to regroup and to complement their general predominance in the state with a similar degree of success in the executive leadership.

The four years between the elections of 1966 and 1970 were less eventful on the whole than the early 1960s. Public attention was focussed on a number of issues but these were generally fought out within the legislative-executive arena. The general pattern of policy-making continued to be reasonably "progressive" with increased funding of welfare, educational and other programs that could only improve the quality of life in the state. All of this needed money and the cry of "Taxachusetts" could occasionally be heard. The sales tax was soon seen as only a partial answer to the problem of raising revenue and, even by 1967, a $94 million rise in taxes was authorized in a bill signed by John Volpe, a measure made especially necessary by the state's assumption of local welfare costs.[95]

The greatest heat in these waning years of the 1960s was expended on what could be broadly described as constitutional crises. Two especially stand out. There was the necessity to redistrict the legislative and congressional seats, a course forced on all states by the series of Supreme Court cases that commenced with *Baker* v. *Carr* in 1962 and continued through a number of other cases in the next few years, notably *Reynolds* v. *Sims* (1964) and *Wesberry* v. *Sanders* (1964). The concept of "one man, one vote" (or, more accurately, "one man, one vote, one value") now gave a residual power to the federal courts to apportion seats themselves if state legislatures failed to do so, or even as a temporary measure to force candidates to run "at large," i.e. statewide.

It was in the shadow of this power that the Massachusetts Great and General Court spent three years over the process of apportioning both houses and the Congressional seats. The Massachusetts House and the Congressional redistricting went through in 1968 with, if not ease, no more bickering than one

could reasonably expect. Republicans and black representatives
in the Boston area were not happy with the House districts that
were established (the "black" Boston seats shrank from three to
two for example), while the Congressional districts produced, although now more or less equal, could still be honored by that
description named for Elbridge Gerry of Massachusetts in the
early years of the state's history. The Third District, in hot dispute
in both 1968 and 1970 elections, was the most altered and, instead
of hooking around the city of Worcester (but not including it),
its shape was transformed to give a wedge from a wide base on the
New Hampshire border to a narrower tip in the Boston suburbs
but with the weight of population at this latter end.[96]

The problem with state senatorial reapportionment lay with
the Democrat-dominated Senate committee, chaired by George V.
Kenneally, which produced a plan likely to increase the Democratic majority. The opposition to this was mainly centered in
the Republican Party, but it also included other groups such as
the Boston black leaders who saw a chance for a senatorial district which would give them a possible Negro senator in the name
of minority representation. Volpe vetoed this reapportionment
plan and the issue dragged on into the Sargent administration, a
final compromise not being made until the summer of 1970. By
this time, gubernatorial vetoes were ineffective if the Democrats
in both houses voted on party lines since the 27-13 Democratic/
Republican distribution of Senate seats had moved to 28-12 as
a result of the 1968 elections and the Democrats now had a two-
thirds majority in both houses.[97]

An even more bitter dispute sprawled over much of this period
and involved a number of pressure groups, including the League
of Women Voters and some "ad hoc" movements for constitutional reform such as the Committee for a Modern Legislature.
The drive to cut the size of the House of Representatives from
240 to 160 members seemed headed for the 1970 ballot after it
had reached the necessary seventy votes in a joint session of both
houses in June 1968 (eighty-five in all voted for it on this occasion). To appear as a referendum question, it again needed to be
supported at a joint session in the 1969-70 General Court by one-
fourth of the members. Democratic opposition to the proposed
referendum was especially bitter and the by then Speaker of the
House, David Bartley, a fiercely partisan leader, did his utmost
to kill the measure. The final legislative vote, taken in February

1970, was a knife-edge affair with, at one time, seventy-one votes
being cast for the inclusion of the referendum on the ballot. Persuasion bordering on coercion before the final recording of the
vote, led by David Bartley in particular, caused a switch by two
members of the joint session and the issue was dead for the time
being. Governor Sargent's bitter retort in a public statement,
"Your legislature has just proved that it represents its own selfish
interests, not the will of the people," was one that was widely
chorused in the state.[98]

Both sides expected that the public would overwhelmingly
have agreed to cut the size of the House. As the second largest
legislature in the United States (New Hampshire has the largest),
a prima facie case would seem to be made for the cut, providing
that the money saved was used to improve the inadequate provision that exists for staffing the legislature. Bartley claimed
that a larger house was "more representative" than a smaller one,
but was not prepared to allow the voters to decide on the validity
of this belief. Many legislators in recent years have argued that
there is a need to refurbish the image of the legislature, but given
the opportunity a degree of selfishness and "save himself, who
can" still permeates the structure.

David Bartley's emergence as a powerful Speaker was one of
the results of the changes in the hierarchy of both parties that
have occurred as a result of the movement of prominent officials
in the last few years. Kevin White's election as Mayor of Boston
in 1967 led to John Davoren's appointment by the legislature as
interim Secretary of State and his replacement as Speaker by
Robert Quinn. Quinn's tenure was comparatively brief for he
rounded up enough votes for an appointment similar to Davoren's when Elliot Richardson resigned as attorney general, consequent upon his entering the Nixon administration in January
1969. At this time, John Volpe became Secretary for Transportation in the Nixon Cabinet and Francis Sargent stepped up to
become acting governor. Thus by the 1970 election, there was a
mixture of old and new personalities in the ballot that could not
have been anticipated four years before.

But before 1970 came 1968. This should have been a relatively
quiet election year because of the lack of contests for the constitutional offices, but the general furor over the Vietnam War and
the presidential election spilled over into other contests, particularly those for the Congressional seats where a number of "peace"

candidates, usually pro-Eugene McCarthy, appeared. Because his was the only name on the ballot, the Massachusetts delegation to the Democratic National Convention were forced under the primary laws to support McCarthy on the first round of voting at Chicago, although Vice-Chairman Robert Quinn, casting the vote, obviously found the process distasteful.[99] Although the party broadly supported Humphrey, the dissident candidates attracted some support and were mostly endorsed by organizations —Citizens for Participation Politics and Voters' Choice—set up primarily to help the McCarthy cause. In some cases, they opposed men who were relatively liberal and this gave the primary voter a difficult choice. For example, the Reverend John Elder of the Harvard Divinity School opposed Torbert McDonald, long associated with the Kennedys, for the Seventh district nomination, and Charles V. Ryan faced incumbent Edward P. Boland, himself moderately pro-McCarthy, in the Second District.

The "peace" candidates failed to achieve a single victory and the state went overwhelmingly for Humphrey—by nearly 2 to 1— in November. George Wallace, who had secured a place on the ballot by amassing the necessary signatures, could only raise 3.7% of the vote. Yet the intrusion of the war/peace issue did not end there and, by 1970, it was virtually respectable to be against the Vietnam War, perhaps because there was now a Republican president and the Democratic majority felt free to attack his policies. Yet the Republican governor signed the bill challenging the right of the U.S. government to send Massachusetts men to fight in an "undeclared war". Perhaps Stuart Hughes, who had opposed Kennedy and Lodge in the 1962 senatorial election, was right when he described Massachusetts as the "most peace-minded" of U.S. states by the end of the decade.[100]

Attention in 1970 tended again to focus on Congressional elections despite the fact that constitutional offices were now at stake. This was because of the importance of the size of the vote secured by Edward Kennedy and because two of the Democratic Congressional districts were won by newcomers who were inevitably in the public eye. The "selling of a priest" removed Philbin from the Third District and substituted for him the figure of Catholic priest, the Reverend Robert Drinan, a "peace candidate" now succeeding and scoring something of a record as the first Catholic priest in Congress since the nineteenth century. Mrs. Louise Day Hicks' succession to John McCormack in the Ninth District also gave this formidable lady a new basis of power from which she could return to the mayoral or other frays in the 1970s. Yet it was Kevin White's failure to win the gubernatorial prize that rankled more than anything in the Democratic camp. Even the further encroachment of the Republican ranks in both legislative houses —to little more than a quarter of each—could not make up for it. Francis Sargent, with a new lieutenant governor, Donald Dwight, elected in tandem with him, was secure until 1974 and the hopes of all four of the contenders for the governorship—White, Maurice Donahue, Frank Bellotti, Kenneth O'Donnell—for a political future as executive head of the Commonwealth were dashed.

Nineteen seventy seems to have seen the end of a generation of political leaders in Massachusetts even more than did 1966. Kevin White is perhaps young enough to make use of his base as mayor of Boston, especially in view of his handsome victory in a rematch with Mrs. Hicks in 1971. However, Bellotti's successive defeats (1964, 1966, 1970) and Donahue's lack of any political base at all may remove these two entirely from the scene. It will rest with younger men like Michael Dukakis[101] (whom White took down to defeat as the candidate for lieutenant governor) and Attorney General Robert Quinn, as well as to Thaddeus Buczko and perhaps Speaker Bartley to provide leadership for the Democrats, although Dukakis is also temporarily handicapped by his lack of an office. Francis Sargent dominates the Republican side with younger legislators such as John Quinlan (although he is not a favorite of the governor's) as reinforcement for the time being. The Democrats will need a figure who can pull the party together behind him if they are to eradicate the obvious anomaly of Massachusetts politics in the 1970s—a Democratic state with a Republican governor as a semi-permanent state of affairs.

Conclusion
The Politics of Discernment

No matter which one of the fifty states had been the subject of
this study, similarities would have been evident in the pattern of
electoral struggle, voter pressures and reactions to the demands
that modern society places on the governing apparatus. Yet every
state tends to develop an approach to political problems that is
just a little different from those states adjoining it. Each state has
a history, an ethnic makeup, economic infrastructure and an ecol-
ogy that can be quite distinctive. Obviously, adjoining states will
evince certain similarities in many instances and these can be noted
in regional political trends best summed up in that cynical de-
struction of Maine's bellwether reputation in the 1936 presidential election, "As Maine goes, so goes Vermont" (though even
this proved untrue in 1970!). Regional characteristics may well
be on the decline, for one-partyism as a state tendency is beginning to disappear, but there is no reason to believe that the states
will lose their individual political identity.

Recent attempts to produce analytical frames for understanding political systems have laid a great deal of stress on the need to
define exactly how a discrete political system can be distinguished
from its neighbors. One way of doing this is to use the concept of
political culture as developed by Gabriel Almond and others.
Combined with this approach is the tendency to view the political system as a relatively closed-off artefact with influences per-
colating from outside and demands generating from one end of
the interior spectrum which are then processed until they reach
the output stage or die on the way. This pattern of "systems analysis" has been especially associated with the name of David
Easton. More recently still, these methods have been used to examine specific situations and to provide a heuristic means of
looking at them. It is argued, for example, that the individual
American state can be examined as a discrete culture stemming
from the ingredients mentioned in the first paragraph of this
chapter. Samuel C. Patterson has argued that:

Each level of the political system can be regarded as an object of orientation for elements of the political culture.[1]

There is, then, a strong influence of the makeup of political systems on the level of cultural differentiation that can be found. In the American federal system, therefore, there is no reason why a set of strong state cultural patterns should not coexist alongside the sort of distinct American culture that Almond and Verba describe in their well-known "Civic Culture." Patterson's suggestion that the sense of identity with a state reinforces the sense of identity with the nation seems a reasonable one and indicates the depth of attachment to the federal system that exists as a means of catering to diversity without eliminating a sense of national unity.[2] Another writer, Thomas R. Dye, excuses his attempt to provide an analysis of state (and local) politics by stressing that the states "provide an excellent opportunity for applying comparative analysis" due to the institutional and cultural factors that they hold in common: they share language, history, etc., and have written constitutions, separation of powers, and other "constants" that make it easier to compare the differences than when one compares systems that differ enormously in every characteristic.[3]

The most concise definition of political culture is probably still the following:

Political culture is the pattern of individual attitudes and orientations toward politics among the members of a political system.[4]

We have tried to show how this has developed in Massachusetts and, in particular, how the makeup of the state has affected the pattern of politics as it has crystallized in terms of elections, parties, administrations and the general relationship between the voter and the politician. Cultural patterns change slowly, but they are visible to observation since behavior is the very manifestation of culture.[5]

These changes are of the utmost importance, however, since they allow the political system at one point in time to resolve problems which seemed intractable at another and earlier one. The adoption of the sales tax and the gradual easing of the legal restrictions concerning the dissemination of information on, and equipment for, birth control are two good examples in Massachusetts of such resolution. The exact manner in which cultural patterns change is still something about which dispute exists, but it is possible that those aspects of cultural norms that are explicitly political do change more quickly than the general cultural patterns of society as a whole. Political culture relates to the solving of specific problems, of the distribution of resources, for example, and this may be more prone to rapid change than, say, the basic norms that affect family life (although an issue like birth control clearly relates to this area of experience).

There is little doubt that the political culture of the state is changing. It is still heavily dependent on ingredients that have given it the special patterns that one has tried to follow through the generations. Ethnicity is still a factor that appears as an ingredient in most major electoral situations and in probably more of the minor ones. It is still comparatively rare for a constituency which is heavily weighted towards one ethnic group to elect a state senator or representative from a group that would be seen as antipathetic. Roxbury produces the very few black members of the Massachusetts House, more often than not Brookline will produce Jewish candidates for the General Court, while Yankees appear from the suburban and rural areas where they still reflect the ethnicity of the local inhabitants. Similarly, one would expect the "Irish" district of Boston to be represented by men like the obviously "Irish" Senator George V. Kenneally. Yet the congruency is lessening: Michael Dukakis, of Greek descent, represented the predominantly Jewish Brookline in the House for eight years while John Quinlan, the Irish Republican, was elected to represent the Second Norfolk district, then heavily Yankee Protestant.

At the top of the ticket, ethnic considerations are becoming much less of an asset than they were once. Although Irish descent still seems to be the most marked ethnic characteristic of the state, it is twenty years since an Irish-American (Paul Dever) was elected as governor, assuming that Furcolo's half-Irish descent is ignored. Yankees and "Italians" have alternated in this office since the 1952 election. The latter fact indicates two things: the growing importance of the "Italian" vote with the resulting "hunger" of the Italo-Americans for a share of power, contrasting with the lingering respect for the Anglo-Saxon approach to government with its supposed emphasis on integrity and honesty. The ethnic "pull" may eventually disappear, the "melting-pot" may yet produce Americans who are ethnically as near homogeneous as is possible, but this will take time and, in the short run, the state will maintain the appearance, in ethnic terms, of a "layered culture," produced by successive immigrant waves, each of which matures and competes with the preceding ones for economic and political power.

Apart from the black community, relatively small in the state when compared with many others in the north and east of the country, the ethnics have all now broken the economic barriers and privations of their original ghetto quarters. Class differences, which have had their own reflection in the party dialogue, have been so bound up with the ethnic difference in Massachusetts that the isolation of the class element from the ethnic in the past was difficult. Yet what is usually termed the process of embourgeoisement and acculturation to a middle-class Anglo-Saxon ethos may be the most significant change that the Massachusetts political culture has experienced. Since attitudes are changing, political demands change too. The move is from a simple set of primarily economic demands to the more complex set now being presented. Elite groups in the polity must adapt to these changes or suffer eventual rejection at the hands of the electorate.

The recent campaign to cut the size of the legislature suggests that there is a dichotomy between the culture of the voting public and the political leadership or at least some of its members. In the sales tax issue, the bulk of Democratic legislators seem to have based their views on an older concept of the Democratic Party, one representing solely the interests of working-class immigrant groups. The tax, not being truly a progressive one, was to be rejected because, it was argued, it would not work to the interest of these groups. On the question of cutting the size of the House, the public is almost certain to ratify a cut if the question is put to them, partially perhaps because of a jealousy of the number of legislators living on the public purse, but mainly because of the general belief (reinforced by the experience of most states of the Union) that a smaller House would be as efficient, if not more so, than the present size. Political forecasting is always dangerous, but it would be reasonable to anticipate that a cut in the size of the House is likely to be delayed only and that, probably before the end of the 1970s, it will take place by the decision of a public referendum.

One feature of the cultural pattern prominent in Massachusetts politics is that old and new forms coexist side by side and, when expressed through organized groups, are prepared to do

business one with the other. The newer forms, which we have
been trying to contrast with the older, ethnic-created, private-
regarding concepts, are not too dissimilar from the classification
that Gabriel Almond has termed the "Civic Culture." In Almond's schema, the individual's orientation to politics is relatively
activist but in a limited way, for politics is only of intermittent
concern to him. When an issue arises which excites his political
interest though, the individual is prepared to expend a great deal
of energy in obtaining the desired output from the political system.[6] This is the spirit that seems to imbue the "reform" groups
on the input side of Massachusetts politics. Almond also links
the "Civic Culture" with a technological, well-educated society,
in that there is a fairly high correlation between the existence of
the two characteristics in comparative political terms.[7] This too
seems appropriate for Massachusetts with its advanced economy
and highly literate citizenry, factors that seem to have some influence on the growing desire for an efficient and modernized state
government.

The delineation of a particular political culture is tentative.
What seems fairly obvious is that the general framework, the
setting for the political systems that we think of as a root cultural
pattern is important because it establishes norms that are, in the
last analysis, a mix peculiar to that society. Easton refers to this
when he writes:

> *The political culture in a system will, of course, usually offer a*
> *rather unique combination of elements; in no two systems will*
> *it restrict or ease the conversion of the same kind of wants.*[8]

Words like Easton's "unique" and my own "peculiar" used in this
context are, of course, purely relative. There are similarities between the wants, demands, outputs, etc. in all American states
(and, to an extent, in all political systems). Yet the culture, history, and conditioning of each state does provide something that
is "unique" about the polity of that state.

As the techniques of political analysis become more sophisticated, it may be that one will be able to forecast the future
stresses in a political system by examining current cultural characteristics. It is not yet possible to do this at all accurately, but
certain rather elementary guesses could be made about the state
of Massachusetts without much difficulty. For example, one can
detect a new political ethos stemming from the educated and so-

phisticated middle class that makes up a fairly large proportion
of the voting population. As yet, the congruence between the
structure of state government and the demands of this group is
far from complete, although it has been more marked in the last
few years than hitherto in the post-1945 period (there is unlikely
to be a complete congruence in the foreseeable future for the state
is unlikely to become at all homogeneous in this sense). Instead
of turning to alternative structures as did the nineteenth century
immigrants, the "new ethicals," often working through pressure
groups, attempt to change the structure and practices of state
government to make it closer to their own "image" of what it
should be.

Change of this nature is a slow process when looked at year by
year, but its presence can clearly be detected in the political development of Massachusetts. The politician oriented solely towards specific racial groups has virtually disappeared at state
level and only persists as a representative of minorities in the limited constituencies with highly localized culture patterns as in the
low-income quarters of the major urban areas. The latter is likely
to become less typical of the legislator as time goes on, partially
because of general social change, partially because the politician
ambitious for advancement to higher levels of power must appeal to a wider range of aspirations than those of a generation or
two ago. Appeal to ethnic blocs is not as effective as it once was,
although this is not to say that group loyalty has disappeared.
Some sense of ethnic identification persists into the third and
fourth generation, and other group loyalties, such as class, appear from time to time, if in less marked fashion than in western
Europe.

A highly effective way of putting together a plurality of the
vote in a major electoral contest is to combine a significant ethnic identification with an appeal to what one has termed the "new
ethicals." It is this sort of critical combination that helped John
Volpe to his series of electoral victories (1960, 1964, 1966) and
one near-victory (1962). The Kennedy brothers have been another
obvious example of this phenomenon. However, one is now faced
with a refinement of this approach wherein the "ethnic pull" virtually disappears and the second ingredient becomes all-power-
ful. Edward Brooke, with a relatively small group directly identi-
fying with him, succeeds because of an appeal which cuts across
racial and class barriers. Successful politicians are such because

they appeal to a class of voters who seem to have sophistication, rather than alienation, as the prime label that one can attach to them.

If this study concludes on a reasonably optimistic note for the political future of the state, it is perhaps because the very real faults in the body politic that were discovered in the early 1960s seem to have blinded many to the overall progress that the state of Massachusetts is making in the programs provided and in the quality of state government. As long ago as 1830, Daniel Webster could take comfort that, for Massachusetts, "the past, at least, is secure."[9] Occasionally, this feeling has evidently percolated the modern mind, for it then seemed that the state was tempted to live on its past, to ignore the squalid realities of the present and the challenge that present problems posed.

We have tried to suggest the potential that exists in this relatively sophisticated and discerning society with a number of liberal and humane traditions. Massachusetts is now predominantly a Democratic state but many voters refuse to practice a slavish addiction to party and require candidates for the major offices, especially that of governor and U.S. senator, who meet the very high standards that these posts demand. The relatively open nature of American government at state level, the lack of a cohesive élite, even though dynastic power is relatively common, the reluctance of American society to curb the influence of money in politics are some of the factors which make what is often termed a "responsible party system"[10] and a fully responsive political system difficult to maintain at state level. Given the constraints, Massachusetts appears to be heading in the right direction, towards the good government goal that many of its citizens have propagated in the past and below which its standards have occasionally, perhaps often, fallen.

Tables

TABLE ONE
*The "Escalator" System in the Massachusetts
Republican Party, 1878–1931*

	Lt. Governorship	Governorship
John Davis Long	1879–1880	1880–1883
Oliver Ames	1883–1887	1887–1890
John Q.A. Brackett	1887–1890	1890–1891
Roger Wolcott	1893–1897	1897–1900
V. Murray Crane	1897–1900	1900–1903
John L. Bates	1900–1903	1903–1905
Curtis Guild Jr.	1903–1906	1906–1909
Eben S. Draper	1906–1909	1909–1911
Calvin Coolidge	1916–1919	1919–1921
Channing H. Cox	1919–1921	1921–1925
Alvan T. Fuller	1921–1925	1925–1929
Frank G. Allen	1925–1929	1929–1931

(Source: Manual of the General Court, 1963-64.)

TABLE TWO

*The Distribution of the Democratic Vote for the
Three Main Offices in the Election of 1928 in Massachusetts.*

County	A Governor	B President	C Gain.B over A	D Senator	E Gain.D over B	F Gain.D over A
Barnstable	22.8%	22.7%	−0.1%	27.7%	+5.0%	+4.9%
Berkshire	48.0%	50.2%	+2.2%	52.9%	+2.7%	+4.9%
Bristol	49.3%	51.8%	+2.5%	54.5%	+2.7%	+5.2%
Dukes	21.8%	24.0%	+2.2%	25.6%	+1.6%	+3.8%
Essex	45.3%	42.7%	−2.6%	51.4%	+8.7%	+6.1%
Franklin	27.4%	29.0%	+1.6%	33.5%	+4.5%	+6.1%
Hampden	49.4%	52.5%	+3.1%	54.4%	+1.9%	+5.0%
Hampshire	44.1%	47.4%	+3.3%	49.3%	+1.9%	+5.2%
Middlesex	44.8%	47.8%	+3.0%	51.3%	+3.5%	+6.5%
Nantucket	27.7%	31.3%	+3.6%	33.0%	+1.7%	+5.3%
Norfolk	38.2%	39.0%	+0.8%	43.4%	+4.4%	+5.2%
Plymouth	37.9%	37.6%	−0.3%	44.0%	+6.4%	+6.1%
Suffolk	66.1%	67.3%	+1.2%	70.9%	+3.6%	+4.8%
Worcester	46.1%	47.6%	+1.5%	50.3%	+2.7%	+4.2%
Total Vote	49.4%	50.5%	+1.1%	54.1%	+3.6%	+4.7%
Ten Towns and Cities						
Brookline	36.4%	37.4%	+1.0%	40.4%	+3.0%	+4.0%
Dover	28.5%	29.4%	+0.9%	33.0%	+3.6%	+4.5%
Lowell	61.2%	64.1%	+2.9%	64.4%	+0.3%	+3.2%
Fall River	60.2%	64.8%	+4.6%	65.8%	+1.0%	+5.6%
Chatham	10.0%	9.1%	−0.9%	13.7%	+4.6%	+3.7%
Worcester	47.7%	49.7%	+2.0%	51.5%	+1.8%	+3.8%
Southbridge	60.4%	59.2%	−0.9%	61.0%	+1.8%	+0.9%
Amherst	24.2%	27.0%	+3.8%	31.4%	+4.4%	+7.2%
Greenfield	33.2%	36.3%	+3.1%	39.8%	+3.5%	+6.6%
Pittsfield	49.3%	52.4%	+3.1%	53.9%	+1.5%	+4.6%

(Source: Primaries and Elections, 1928; Public Document No. 43, Commonwealth of Massachusetts.)

TABLE THREE
Party Designation of Successful Candidates for
Constitutional Office in Massachusetts, 1928-1970

Year	Governor	Lt. Governor	Att. General	Sec. of State	Treasurer	Auditor
1928	R	R	R	R	R	R
1930	D	R	R	R	D	D
1932	D	R	R	R	D	D
1934	D	D	D	R	D	D
1936	D	D	D	R	R	D
1938	R	R	D	R	R	R
1940	R	R	R	R	R	D
1942	R	R	R	R	D	D
1944	D	R	R	R	D	D
1946	R	R	R	R	R	D
1948	D	D	D	D	D	D
1950	D	D	D	D	D	D
1952	R	R	R	D	D	D
1954	R	R	R	D	D	D
1956	D	D	R	D	D	D
1958	D	D	D	D	D	D
1960	R	D	D	D	D	D
1962	D	D	R	D	D	D
1964	R	R	R	D	D	D
1966	R	R	R	D	D	D
1970	R	R	D	D	D	D

R= Republican elected   D= Democrat elected

Source: Public Document No. 43; Election Statistics 1928-1970.)

TABLE FOUR

The Gubernatorial Election in Massachusetts, 1934

County	Victor of Democratic Primary	Victor of November Election
Barnstable	Cole	Bacon
Berkshire	Cole	Bacon
Bristol	Curley	Curley
Dukes	Cole	Bacon
Essex	Curley	Curley
Franklin	Cole	Bacon
Hampden	Curley	Curley
Hampshire	Cole	Bacon
Middlesex	Curley	Curley
Nantucket	Curley	Bacon
Norfolk	Curley	Bacon
Plymouth	Curley	Bacon
Suffolk	Curley	Curley
Worcester	Curley	Curley

Ten Towns and Cities

Brookline	Curley	Bacon
Dover	Curley	Bacon
Lowell	Curley	Curley
Fall River	Curley	Curley
Chatham	Cole	Bacon
Worcester	Curley	Curley
Southbridge	Cole	Curley
Amherst	Curley	Bacon
Greenfield	Cole	Bacon
Pittsfield	Cole	Bacon

(Note: It should be emphasized that the total vote of each of these areas varies greatly. Among the counties in 1934, it ran (for Governor) from Dukes and Nantucket (total 3,110) to Suffolk (296,214) and Middlesex (353,246). For the ten towns and cities given here, it ranged from Dover (536) and Chatham (760) up to Worcester (65,343).)

(Source: Public Document No. 43, Election Statistics, 1934.)

TABLE FIVE

*A Comparison of the Two-Party Vote for the Presidential and
Senatorial Candidates in Massachusetts; Biennial Election, 1936*

| | % Vote for President | | % Vote for Senator | |
	Roosevelt	Landon	Curley	Lodge
Falmouth	36.3	63.7	27.8	72.2
Lanesborough	41.0	59.0	28.7	71.3
Windsor	35.5	64.5	27.6	72.4
Taunton	59.8	40.2	51.0	49.0
Ipswich	36.6	63.4	28.0	72.0
Topsfield	18.1	82.9	12.0	88.0
Northfield	22.4	77.6	16.0	84.0
Ludlow	26.8	73.2	43.2	56.8
Granby	35.5	64.5	24.6	75.4
Ayer	49.8	50.2	41.6	58.4
Littleton	22.0	78.0	17.1	82.9
Tyngsborough	46.1	53.9	31.7	68.3
Franklin	54.5	45.5	46.8	53.2
Bridgewater	42.2	57.8	55.6	64.4
Rochester	30.8	69.2	12.0	88.0
Clinton	65.6	34.4	57.6	42.4
Millville	82.1	17.9	71.5	28.5
Templeton	44.5	55.5	32.7	67.3
Boston	69.9	30.1	62.1	37.9
Cambridge	62.6	37.4	56.3	43.7
Fall River	72.0	28.0	53.2	46.8
Fitchburg	61.2	38.8	47.6	52.4
Holyoke	72.1	27.9	60.6	33.4
Lowell	67.3	32.7	58.2	41.8
Melrose	24.1	75.9	18.7	81.3
Pittsfield	57.6	42.4	47.2	52.8
Worcester	61.0	39.0	49.1	50.9
Springfield	56.1	43.9	46.1	55.9
Total Vote	55.1	44.9	45.8	54.2

(Source: Public Document No. 43, Election Statistics, 1936.)

TABLE SIX
Massachusetts Elections 1938
Some Selected Comparisons

(1) *Democratic Gubernatorial Primary % of Total Vote*

	Hurley	Curley	Kelley	Russell
Barnstable	49.0	29.3	9.6	8.3
Berkshire	54.5	23.4	10.6	7.4
Bristol	49.9	24.0	18.1	5.0
Dukes	54.0	16.9	15.9	6.9
Essex	38.8	31.7	20.0	6.2
Franklin	42.8	28.3	16.3	9.7
Hampden	28.5	31.9	32.6	4.1
Hampshire	30.9	32.2	28.0	5.3
Middlesex	33.1	41.6	15.5	7.4
Nantucket	71.2	5.0	4.0	7.9
Norfolk	33.9	35.2	22.8	5.7
Plymouth	38.5	36.2	17.8	5.3
Suffolk	22.6	50.4	19.4	5.2
Worcester	41.8	30.3	18.5	5.7
Total Vote	32.0	40.0	19.4	5.8

(Note: Blanks etc. omitted)

(2) *Republican Gubernatorial Primary % of Total Votes*

	Butler	McMasters	Saltonstall	Whitcomb
State Total	5.2	10.3	68.9	9.6

(3) *Biennial Elections % of Two-Party Vote*

	Governor		Attorney General	
	Democrat	Republican	Democrat	Republican
Barnstable	23.0	67.0	29.8	70.2
Berkshire	1.3	58.7	50.4	49.6
Bristol	48.3	51.7	56.5	43.5
Dukes	24.2	75.8	34.5	65.5
Essex	45.1	54.9	52.3	47.7
Franklin	29.0	71.0	34.3	65.7
Hampden	46.0	54.0	53.9	46.1
Hampshire	40.8	59.4	49.4	50.6
Middlesex	42.5	57.5	51.1	48.9
Nantucket	21.7	78.3	31.0	69.0
Norfolk	32.8	67.2	42.6	57.4
Plymouth	35.8	64.2	42.3	57.7
Suffolk	59.8	40.2	73.8	26.2
Worcester	45.5	54.5	52.0	48.0
Total Vote	45.7	54.3	54.3	45.7

(Source: Election Statistics, 1938, Public Document No. 43.)

TABLE SEVEN
Presidential Vote in Massachusetts, 1940

10 Cities	% of Two-Party Vote	
	Roosevelt	Willkie
Boston	63.3	36.7
Lowell	64.5	35.5
Lawrence	72.2	27.8
Fall River	70.8	29.2
New Bedford	71.1	28.9
Springfield	55.5	46.5
Holyoke	69.2	34.8
Worcester	59.5	40.5
Pittsfield	58.1	41.9
Cambridge	60.4	39.6
14 Small Towns		
Barnstable	28.4	71.6
Monterey	22.4	77.6
Easton	26.8	73.2
Chilmark	20.4	79.6
Georgetown	25.8	74.2
Rowley	25.7	74.3
Ashfield	18.0	82.0
Blandford	18.6	81.4
Tolland	16.6	83.4
Goshen	7.3	92.7
Boxborough	26.7	73.3
Weston	16.1	83.3
Duxbury	22.4	77.6
Bolton	18.5	81.5

(Source: Public Document No. 43, Election Statistics, 1940.)

TABLE EIGHT
Party-Membership in Massachusetts Legislature and
Congressional Delegation, 1920-1970

Election Year	Congress (House)		State Senate		House of Representatives		
	Rep.	Dem.	Rep.	Dem.	Rep.	Dem.	Ind.
1920	14	2	35	5	188	52	
1922	13	3	33	7	160	80	
1924	13	3	34	6	170	70	
1926	13	3	35	5	177	63	
1928	13	3	31	9	157	83	
1930	12	4	30	10	141	99	
1932	10	5	26	14	147	93	
1934	8	7	21	19	124	116	
1936	10	5	27	13	136	104	
1938	10	3	28	12	143	97	
1940	9	6	25	15	143	97	
1942	10	4	26	14	143	97	
1944	10	4	23	17	138	102	
1946	9	5	24	16	144	96	
1948	8	6	20	20	118	122	
1950	8	6	22	18	116	124	
1952	8	6	25	15	124	116	
1954	7	7	21	19	112	128	
1956	7	7	21	19	108	132	
1958	6	8	16	24	95	145	
1960	6	8	14	26	84	156	
1962	5	7	12	28	90	150	
1964	5	7	12	28	68	171	1
1966	5	7	14	26	69	170	1
1968	5	7	13	27	67	173	
1970	4	8	10	30	62	178	

(Source: Latham and Goodwin, *Massachusetts Politics,* updated from newspaper sources.)

TABLE NINE
City of Newton
Total Number of Votes Cast in Primary Elections
of Democratic Party, 1946-1966

Year	Vote (Gubernatorial Primary)	Total Population
1945	—	77,257
1946	832	—
1948	784	—
1950	1,306	81,994
1952	2,415	—
1954	1,270	—
1955	—	86,535
1956	4,370	—
1958	5,120	—
1960	7,043	92,384
1962	12,275	—
1964	10,469	—
1966	9,975	—

(Sources: Public Document No. 43, Election Statistics, 1946-66; Town and City
Monographs, No. 76—National and State Census figures.)

TABLE TEN
Revenue and Expenditure in Massachusetts (1960)

1. Sources of State Government Revenue

	All States %	Massachusetts %
Taxes on Sales and Gross Receipts	58.3	35.7
General	23.9	—
Motor Vehicle Excise	18.5	15.6
Other	15.9	20.1)
Income Taxes	18.8	36.7
Property Taxes	3.7	0.1
License Taxes	8.7	4.8
Other	10.8	22.7

2. Per Capita Expenditure by Function
   (State and Local Government Combined)

	All States %	Massachusetts %
Total	288.24	297.35
Education	104.00	78.09
Highways	52.38	47.55
Public Welfare	24.47	34.33
Health and Hospitals	21.09	28.55
Police	10.32	12.83
Local Fire Protection	5.53	11.59
Sewers and Sewage Disposal	6.13	3.83
Other Sanitation	3.47	4.47
General Control	11.74	13.28
Interest on General Debt	9.28	12.95
All Other	39.83	49.87

(Source: Carl J. Gilbert, "Fiscal Implications of Educational Improvement," Tufts Assembly, 1965.)

TABLE ELEVEN

A Comparison of the 1944 and 1946 Gubernatorial
Elections in Massachusetts

| Counties | Percentage of Two-Party Vote | | | | Democratic Losses |
| | 1944 | | 1946 | | |
	Dem. %	Rep. %	Dem. %	Rep. %	
Barnstable	33.2	66.8	20.7	79.3	12.5
Berkshire	57.3	42.7	49.9	50.1	7.4
Bristol	62.9	37.1	54.0	46.0	8.9
Dukes	37.3	62.7	28.2	71.8	9.1
Essex	55.4	44.6	46.1	53.9	9.3
Franklin	42.0	58.0	37.8	62.2	4.2
Hampden	59.0	41.0	53.5	46.5	5.5
Hampshire	53.0	47.0	44.9	55.1	8.1
Middlesex	49.9	50.1	40.8	59.2	9.1
Nantucket	40.0	60.0	30.0	70.0	10.0
Norfolk	39.3	60.7	30.9	69.1	8.4
Plymouth	44.4	55.6	34.5	65.5	9.9
Suffolk	59.8	40.2	51.6	48.4	8.2
Worcester	57.3	42.7	50.5	49.5	6.8
TOTAL	53.3	46.1	45.6	54.4	7.7

(Source: Public Document No. 43, Election Statistics, 1946.)

TABLE TWELVE
Massachusetts Election 1948
Distribution of the Two-Party Vote for Governor and Senator
Compared to the "Yes/No" Vote for the "Birth Control Amendment"

County	B.C. Amendment		Governor		Senator		% of R.C.'s in
	Yes	No	Rep.	Dem.	Rep.	Dem.	Total popn.
	%	%	%	%	%	%	
Barnstable	62.9	37.1	73.0	27.0	80.8	19.2	27.2
Berkshire	46.9	53.1	45.6	53.4	56.0	44.0	50.0
Bristol	36.2	63.8	35.1	64.9	54.2	54.8	56.1
Dukes	67.2	32.8	71.6	28.4	77.8	22.2	54.3
Essex	43.0	57.0	41.0	59.0	51.4	48.6	45.5
Franklin	61.3	38.7	57.0	43.0	67.6	32.4	34.0
Hampden	46.5	53.5	41.8	58.2	53.7	46.3	54.7
Hampshire	50.7	49.3	48.2	51.8	59.2	40.8	45.1
Middlesex	41.9	58.1	43.6	56.4	56.7	43.3	48.0
Nantucket	57.2	42.8	71.2	28.8	79.8	20.2	0.0
Norfolk	52.6	47.4	53.7	46.3	66.6	33.4	44.5
Plymouth	50.7	49.3	53.6	46.4	65.0	35.0	37.0
Suffolk	33.9	66.1	24.0	76.0	40.7	59.3	50.2
Worcester	43.3	56.6	43.0	57.0	53.9	46.1	49.7
TOTAL (State as a whole)	42.6	57.4	40.7	59.3	53.3	46.7	48.4

(Sources: Public Document No. 43, Election Statistics 1948 and Bureau of Research and Survey; Churches and Church Membership in U.S., Series C, No. 3.)

TABLE THIRTEEN
Massachusetts Elections, 1950
Republican Gubernatorial Primary
The Real "Friends and Neighbors" Vote

Candidates' Places of Residence	Percentage of Total Vote					
	Barnes	Coolidge	Denfeld	Miles	Needham	Rowe
Mansfield	<u>79.0</u>	7.8	4.1	1.7	3.1	0.5
Reading	0.4	<u>83.2</u>	0.4	0.2	0.5	0.1
Westborough	0.9	2.2	<u>94.8</u>	0.9	0.8	0.2
Newton	8.3	20.3	7.2	<u>11.4</u>	<u>49.7</u>	1.7
Cambridge	10.1	35.6	10.3	8.3	23.9	<u>8.8</u>
Total State Vote	16.0	34.1	18.0	9.8	15.1	4.8

Notes: (1) Blank votes are not included, hence the lines do not add up to 100 percent.
(2) Percentages underlined indicate the vote for the candidate in his own city or town. Both Miles and Needham were resident in Newton.

(Source: Public Document No. 43, Election Statistics, 1950.)

TABLE FOURTEEN
Voter Attitudes in Pittsfield, Mass., 1952

1. *Question* As you know, in the recent presidential election, Pittsfield, Massachusetts and the country voted Republican.

   (A)   As you see it, what were the most important reasons why Pittsfield went Republican?
   N = 198

	%
People wanted a change of administration, dissatisfied with Democrats, Democrats in long enough	65
Korean War	14
Corruption	13
Choice of candidates—Ike best, all Republicans best	10
(All other answers under 10%)	

   (B)   To your way of thinking, what were the most important reasons why Massachusetts went Republican?
   N = 198

	%
People wanted a change of administration	56
Massachusetts people sick of Dever	21
People worried about the Korean War	11
Corruption	11
Promise of lower taxes	10
Eisenhower's popularity, people liked him	10
(All other answers under 10%)	

2. *Face Data*: Political Affiliation. N = 198
   Republican   26%
   Democratic   24%
   Independent   43%
   No answer   4%
   None   3%

(Source: Pittsfield Project 1952, Elmo Roper Center, Williams College, Williamstown, Mass., November, 1952.)

TABLE FIFTEEN
Massachusetts Elections 1954
Distribution of the Two-Party Vote in the
Gubernatorial and Senatorial Contests

Counties	(A) Governor		(B) Senator		Democratic Gain % B over A
	Rep. %	Dem. %	Rep. %	Dem. %	
Barnstable	80.8	19.2	81.5	18.5	−0.7
Berkshire	56.4	43.6	53.9	46.1	2.5
Bristol	49.8	50.2	48.8	51.2	1.0
Dukes	64.7	35.3	75.9	24.1	−11.2
Essex	53.0	47.0	50.5	49.5	2.5
Franklin	67.5	32.5	65.4	34.6	2.1
Hampden	50.5	49.5	44.8	55.2	5.7
Hampshire	59.2	40.8	55.2	44.8	4.0
Middlesex	52.8	47.2	52.6	47.4	0.2
Nantucket	76.8	23.2	79.6	20.4	−2.8
Norfolk	63.8	36.2	62.5	37.5	1.3
Plymouth	64.6	35.4	62.6	37.4	2.0
Suffolk	35.7	64.3	35.8	64.2	−0.1
Worcester	52.5	47.5	52.1	47.9	0.4
State Total	52.0	48.0	50.8	49.2	1.2
Cities (Specimen)					
Pittsfield	53.0	47.0	49.5	50.5	2.5
Fall River	39.9	60.1	38.2	61.8	1.7
New Bedford	46.2	53.8	44.8	55.2	1.4
Lynn	45.1	54.9	42.6	57.4	2.5
Holyoke	44.8	55.2	39.8	60.2	5.0
Cambridge	39.3	60.7	39.7	60.3	−0.4
Brockton	54.8	45.2	51.3	48.7	3.5
Worcester	51.1	48.9	50.9	49.1	0.2
"Home Towns"					
Millis (Herter)	65.4	34.6	65.4	34.6	0.0
Dover (Saltonstall)	86.9	13.1	88.5	11.5	−1.6
Malden (Murphy)	41.2	58.8	44.3	55.7	−3.1
Longmeadow (Furcolo)	88.1	11.9	78.6	21.4	9.5

(Source: Public Document No. 43, Election Statistics 1954.)

TABLE SIXTEEN
Massachusetts Elections, 1956
"Split-Ticket Voting"

County	President		Governor		Attorney General	
	Rep. %	Dem. %	Rep. %	Dem. %	Rep. %	Dem. %
Barnstable	83.4	16.6	74.6	25.4	77.4	22.6
Berkshire	62.0	38.0	52.3	47.7	56.1	43.9
Bristol	58.0	42.0	44.8	55.2	46.9	53.1
Dukes	82.9	17.1	76.7	23.3	78.2 ·	21.8
Essex	60.2	39.8	49.5	50.5	51.2	48.8
Franklin	72.3	27.7	62.6	37.4	65.8	34.2
Hampden	56.2	43.8	39.2	60.8	49.9	50.1
Hampshire	62.2	37.8	47.7	52.3	56.4	43.6
Middlesex	52.9	47.1	49.2	50.8	52.8	47.2
Nantucket	83.3	16.7	74.7	25.3	74.1	25.9
Norfolk	66.6	43.4	56.1	43.9	58.9	41.1
Plymouth	71.9	28.1	59.9	40.1	61.7	38.3
Suffolk	46.0	54.0	31.6	68.4	35.6	64.4
Worcester	60.2	39.8	47.9	52.1	51.0	49.0
TOTAL	59.5	40.5	47.0	53.0	50.9	49.1

(Source: Public Document No. 43, Election Statistics 1956.)

TABLE SEVENTEEN
John Kennedy's First Electoral Victory:
The 1946 Democratic Primary in the
Eleventh Congressional District of Massachusetts

	John F. Cotter of Boston %	Michael De Luca of Boston %	Robt. D. Fruscio of Boston %	Cath. E. Falvey of Somerville %
Boston, Wards				
1, 2, 3, 22	18.5	1.3	0.8	2.8
Cambridge	3.0	0.6	0.1	1.6
Somerville, Wards 1, 2, 3	3.9	0.7	0.4	19.1
Totals	12.2	1.0	0.5	4.5

	John F. Kennedy of Boston	Joseph Lee of Boston	Michael J. Neville of Cambridge	Francis X. Rooney of Somerville
Boston, Wards				
1, 2, 3, 22	40.0	5.1	7.5	0.8
Cambridge	40.3	0.9	47.3	0.4
Somerville, Wards 1, 2, 3	43.4	0.9	20.0	2.9
Totals	40.5	3.4	20.7	1.5

	Joseph Russo of Boston	Joseph Russo of Boston	Blanks	Totals	Total Vote
Boston, Wards					
1, 2, 3, 22	15.8	2.1	5.1	100.0	32,025
Cambridge	1.9	0.4	3.5	100.0	16,068
Somerville, Wards 1, 2, 3	4.3	0.8	3.7	100.0	6,661
Totals	10.3	1.5	4.5	100.0	54,754

(Source: Public Document No. 43, Election Statistics 1946.)

TABLE EIGHTEEN

*A Comparison of the Size of the Democratic Vote for
Senator (John Kennedy) and Governor (Paul Dever) in 1952*

County	Percentage of the Two-Party Vote	
	Kennedy	Dever
Barnstable	32.3%	22.6%
Berkshire	44.1	41.0
Bristol	58.7	49.4
Dukes	32.2	24.6
Essex	49.9	48.6
Franklin	35.8	34.2
Hampden	50.3	47.6
Hampshire	43.2	41.7
Middlesex	49.5	49.4
Nantucket	29.2	27.8
Norfolk	40.6	38.7
Plymouth	39.1	36.5
Suffolk	66.7	67.9
Worcester	50.8	48.1
Total	51.5	49.7
New Bedford	70.3	50.3

(Source: Public Document No. 43, Election Statistics 1952.)

TABLE NINETEEN

John Kennedy and the "Catholic Vote" in Massachusetts
Senate Election, 1958 and Presidential Election, 1960

County	Kennedy % of Two-Party Vote		% of Catholics in Total Popn. (1950)
	1958	1960	
Barnstable	55.1	37.3	27.2
Berkshire	74.4	60.1	50.0
Bristol	79.4	66.9	56.1
Dukes	55.7	39.1	54.3
Essex	73.1	57.0	45.5
Franklin	62.3	43.9	34.0
Hampden	73.1	62.7	54.7
Hampshire	72.5	57.0	45.1
Middlesex	72.7	59.1	48.0
Nantucket	57.6	36.4	0.0
Norfolk	67.2	52.7	44.5
Plymouth	63.3	48.4	37.0
Suffolk	84.9	74.7	50.2
Worcester	72.8	60.6	49.7
Total (State as whole)	73.6	60.4	48.4

(Sources: Public Document No. 43, Election Statistics 1958 and 1960. Bureau of Research and Survey; Churches and Church Membership in U.S., Series C, No. 3.)

TABLE TWENTY

*Comparative Percentage of the Two-Party Vote Received by
John and Edward Kennedy in their first Senatorial Contests*

Counties	1952 John Kennedy	1962 Edward Kennedy	Increase
Barnstable	32.3%	33.8%	1.5%
Berkshire	44.1	53.5	9.4
Bristol	58.7	65.6	6.9
Dukes	32.2	39.6	7.4
Essex	49.9	54.6	4.7
Franklin	35.8	41.4	5.6
Hampden	50.3	57.6	7.3
Hampshire	43.2	53.2	10.0
Middlesex	49.5	54.7	5.2
Nantucket	29.2	36.6	7.4
Norfolk	40.6	48.5	7.9
Plymouth	39.1	47.0	7.9
Suffolk	66.7	72.3	5.6
Worcester	50.8	59.0	8.2
Total	51.5	57.0	5.5

(Source: Public Document No. 43, Election Statistics, 1952 and 1962.)

TABLE TWENTY-ONE
Massachusetts Democratic Primary, 1964
Main Candidates for the Gubernatorial Nomination

County	Percentage of Total Vote	
	Peabody	Bellotti
Barnstable	57.6%	39.2%
Berkshire	61.2	33.1
Bristol	47.4	46.4
Dukes	70.6	24.8
Essex	40.1	53.0
Franklin	53.7	44.6
Hampden	46.5	48.8
Hampshire	50.3	46.0
Middlesex	43.8	47.2
Nantucket	66.7	27.5
Norfolk	43.8	52.1
Plymouth	44.9	51.3
Suffolk	45.2	47.5
Worcester	45.4	49.3
Total Vote	44.8	48.4
Specimen Cities and Towns		
Brookline	61.6	33.1
Fall River	46.0	46.9
Southbridge	42.6	52.1
Dover	61.2	36.7
Pittsfield	60.2	33.5
Milton	51.3	44.9
Lawrence	37.2	53.8
Somerville	40.6	48.4
Watertown	46.2	45.2
Revere	34.8	57.7
Everett	31.0	62.4
Chicopee	46.1	50.3

Note: Figures for the two minor candidates, Pasquale Caggiano and John Droney, are omitted.

(Source: Public Document No. 43, Election Statistics 1964.)

NOTES

Chapter One

1. Duane Lockard, *New England State Politics* (Princeton University Press, 1959), p. 4 n.

2. Louis B. Wright, *The Colonial Civilisation of North America, 1607-1763* (Eyre and Spottiswoode, 1949), p. 88.

3. Samuel Eliot Morison, *The Maritime History of Massachusetts, 1783-1860* (Houghton Mifflin Co., 1941), p. 23.

4. See, for example, Charles Francis Adams quoted in L. H. Butterfield ed., *The Adams Papers* (Atheneum, New York, 1904), p. lxiii.

5. Lawrence Henry Gipson, "The American Revolution as an Aftermath of the Great War for the Empire," *Political Science Quarterly*, 55, No. 1 (March, 1950), reprinted in *The Causes of the American Revolution* edited by John C. Wahlke (D. C. Heath and Co.: Boston, 1950), p. 93.

6. R. P. McCormick, *The Second American Party System* (University of North Carolina Press, 1966), p. 40.

7. H. L. Coles, *The War of 1812* (University of Chicago Press, 1965), p. 269.

8. McCormick, pp. 43-44.

9. 1960 Census of Population, Vol. 1, Part 23; Massachusetts (U.S. Department of Commerce, Bureau of the Census, 1963), Table 1, pp. 23-26.

10. Monograph for Franklin County (Massachusetts Department of Commerce, 1963), IV.

11. John C. Miller, *The Federalist Era* (Harper and Row, 1963) pp. 101-102.

12. Morison, p. 234.

13. Margaret C. Parker, Lowell; *A Study of Industrial Development* (Macmillan, 1940), p. 63. Louis Taylor Merrill, "Mill Town on the Merrimack," *New England Quarterly*, Vol. 19 (1946), pp. 19-31. John Coolidge, *Mill and Mansion* (Columbia University, 1942), pp. 10-16.

14. Donald B. Cole, *Immigrant City* (University of North Carolina Press, 1963), p. 26.

15. Morison, p. 21.

16. Oscar Handlin, *Boston's Immigrants* (Harvard University Press, 1959 ed.), p. 37.

17. Cecil Woodham-Smith, *The Great Hunger; Ireland, 1845-1849* (Hamish Hamilton:

London, 1962), p. 246.

18. Woodham-Smith, p. 247.

19. Handlin, p. 52.

20. Ibid., p. 117.

21. H. L. Trefousse, *Ben Butler* (Twayne Publishers: New York, 1957), p. 41.

22. D. L. Marsh and W. H. Clark, *The Story of Massachusetts* (American Historical Society, 1938), Vol. 2, p. 146.

23. Ibid., p. 144.

24. Svend Petersen, *A Statistical History of American Presidential Elections* (Frederick Ungar, 1963), p. 136.

25. Geoffrey Blodgett, *The Gentle Reformers: Massachusetts Democrats in the Cleveland Era* (Harvard University Press, 1966), p. 4.

26. Trefousse, p. 247.

27. William D. Mallan, "Butlerism in Massachusetts," *New England Quarterly*, Vol. 33 (1960), pp. 186-206.

28. Gordon S. Wood, "The Massachusetts Mugwumps," *New England Quarterly*, Vol. 33 (1960), pp. 435-451. Also Blodgett, passim.

29. Michael E. Hennessey, *Four Decades of Massachusetts Politics, 1890-1936* (The Norwood Press, 1935), pp. 44-65.

30. Richard M. Abrams, *Conservatism in a Progressive Era; Massachusetts Politics, 1900-1912* (Harvard University Press, 1964), Chapter 1.

31. Henry Adams, *The Education of Henry Adams* (Houghton Mifflin Co., 1918), p. 419.

32. W. Dean Burnham, *Presidential Ballots, 1836-1892* (Oxford University Press, 1955), p. 191.

Chapter Two

1. Nathan Glazer and Daniel Patrick Moynihan, *Beyond the Melting Pot* (MIT Press, 1963), p. 291.

2. See Edward C. Banfield and James Q. Wilson, *City Politics* (Harvard and MIT Press, 1963), pp. 38-41, and Richard Hofstadter, *The Age of Reform* (Alfred A. Knopf, 1955), p. 9.

3. John A. Garraty, *Henry Cabot Lodge* (Alfred A. Knopf, 1933), p. 91.

4. Henry G. Pearson, *Son of New England* (privately printed, Boston, Massachusetts, 1932), pp. 31-32 and 44.

5. Garraty, p. 74.

6. Garraty, pp. 231-2.

7. Ibid., p. 281.

8. Nicholas Murray Butler, *Across the Busy Years* (Charles Scribner's Sons, 1939), p. 288.

9. Cole, p. 89 and pp. 149-150.

10. Hennessey, p. 76.

11. Quoted in Garraty, p. 232.

12. Cole, p. 95.

13. Kenneth Wilson Under-

wood, *Protestant and Catholic* (The Beacon Press: Boston, 1957), pp. 256-288.

14. 1960 Census of Population, pp. 23-6, 23-8, 23-27.

15. The economic element in the machine is evident if one notes that it originally existed where ethnic rivalries were not strong as in the early Democratic machine in New York, run by and partially for Americans of older stock. See, for example, M. R. Warner, *Tammany Hall* (Doubleday, Doran and Co. 1928), passim.

16. Robert K. Merton, *Social Theory and Social Structure* (Free Press, 1957), pp. 81-82.

17. Cleveland Amory, *The Proper Bostonians* (E. P. Dutton and Co.: New York, 1955), p. 47.

18. James Bryce, *The American Commonwealth* (Macmillan, 1891), Vol. 1, p. 598. Steffens is quoted in Don Martindale, *American Society* (D. Van Nostrand Co., 1960), pp. 190-191.

19. W. B. Munro, *The Government of American Cities* (Macmillan, 1931), p. 216.

20. Walter Firey, *Land Use in Central Boston* (Harvard University Press, 1947), p. 181.

21. Leslie G. Ainley, *Boston Mahatma* (Bruce Humphries, 1949), p.41.

22. Lincoln Steffens, *The Autobiography of Lincoln Steffens* (Harrap and Co., 1931), p. 618.

23. Francis Russell, *The Great Interlude* (McGraw-Hill, 1964), p. 171.

24. Russell, p. 169.

25. John Henry Cutler, *Honey Fitz* (Bobbs-Merrill Co., 1962), p. 122.

26. Thomas R. Mason, "Reform Politics in Boston" (Ph.D. diss., Harvard, 1963), pp. 314-332. Storrow did well in wards like Ten and Eleven with comparatively low percentages of foreign-stock voters (36.7 and 33.7 respectively) and Fitzgerald in wards like Three and Fourteen where these percentages were high (74.9 and 91.4 respectively).

27. Ibid., p. 312.

28. Ibid., p. 236.

29. Joseph N. Dineen, *The Purple Shamrock* (W. H. Norton and Co.: New York, 1949), p. 45.

30. J. Joseph Huthmacher, *Massachusetts People and Politics 1919-1933* (Harvard University Press, 1959), p. 261.

31. Dorothy G. Wayman, *David J. Walsh, Citizen Patriot* (The Bruce Publishing Co.: Milwaukee, 1952), p. 219. Also Huthmacher, p. 263.

32. From a Citizens' Committee circular, 1940 (Shattuck papers, Littauer Center, Harvard University).

33. Abrams, p. 257.

34. Richard B. Sherman,

"Charles Sumner Bird and the Progressive Party in Massachusetts," *New England Quarterly,* Vol. 33 (1960), pp. 328-329.

35. John Allen Hague, "The Massachusetts Constitutional Convention, 1917-1919," *New England Quarterly,* Vol. 27 (1954), pp. 147-167. Also A. D. Von Nostrand, "The Lomasney Legend," *New England Quarterly* (December 1948), p. 455.

36. Garraty, p. 328; Cutler, pp. 209-211.

37. From an article in the *Worcester Telegram,* January 12, 1919, quoted in Wayman, pp. 101-102.

38. Richard L. Lyons, "The Boston Police Strike of 1919," *New England Quarterly,* Vol. 20 (1947), pp. 147-168. Calvin Coolidge, *Autobiography* (Chatto and Windus ed., 1929), Ch. IV. Coolidge says of the police strike, "That furnished the occasion and I took advantage of the opportunity."

39. Coolidge, *Autobiography,* p. 148. M. R. Werner and John Starr, *The Teapot Dome Scandal* (Viking Press, 1959; Cassell: London, 1961), p. 25.

40. William Allen White, *A Puritan in Babylon* (Macmillan, 1938), p. 258.

41. Interview with Channing L. Cox conducted by Robert C. Wood and Bradbury Seasholes, 1961 (typescript).

42. Huthmacher, pp. 57 and 278.

43. Ibid., pp. 146-147.

44. *Boston Evening Transcript,* September 14, 1926, quoting the *Springfield Republican* (Shattuck collection clipping). Huthmacher, p. 125.

45. Channing Cox interview, p. 31.

46. V. O. Key, Jr., "A Theory of Critical Elections," *The Journal of Politics,* Vol. 17 (February, 1955).

47. *Boston Evening Transcript,* November 7, 1928.

48. Ruth C. Silva, *Rum, Religion and Votes: 1928 Re-examined* (Pennsylvania State University Press, 1962), pp. 43-49.

49. Huthmacher, p. 183.

50. Counties are not significant governmental divisions in Massachusetts and vary enormously in area (Suffolk's total vote is always about two hundred times that of Nantucket) but they can be useful in suggesting the dispersal of the vote over the state.

51. *Boston Post,* October 9, 1928.

52. *Boston Evening Transcript,* November 7, 1928.

Chapter Three

1. See David Easton, *A Framework for Political Analysis* (Prentice-Hall, 1965),

pp. 69-73 and *A Systems Analysis of Political Life* (John Wiley, 1965), pp. 21-23.

2. Charles E. Artman, "Industrial Prospects," *New England's Prospects; 1933* (American Geographical Society, 1933), p. 56.

3. New England Council, *Transactions in the New England Economy* (Boston, 1954), p. 15.

4. From figures compiled by Charles Hoskins and reproduced by Edward A. Filene, "Unemployment in New England," in *New England's Prospects*, p. 76.

5. Parker, p. 105.

6. Hoskins' figures in *New England's Prospects,* p. 85.

7. Parker, p. 126.

8. *Boston Traveler,* August 29, 1962.

9. The Constitution of the Commonwealth of Massachusetts, Article LV.

10. See, for example, V. O. Key, Jr., *American State Politics* (Alfred A. Knopf, 1956), pp. 162-164 and note. Also Murray B. Levin and George Blackwood, *The Compleat Politician* (Bobbs- Merrill Co. 1962), pp. 42-43.

11. W. Lloyd Warner and Leo Srole, *The Social System of American Ethnic Groups* (Yale University Press, 1945), pp. 96-97.

12. Michael E. Hennessey, *Four Decades of Massachu-* *setts Politics, 1890-1936* (The Norwood Press, 1935), pp. 425-427. Huthmacher, pp. 204-205.

13. *Worcester Telegram-Gazette,* August 31, 1930.

14. James Michael Curley, *I'd Do It Again* (Prentice-Hall, 1957), pp. 231-232.

15. Harold Gorvine, "The New Deal in Massachusetts" (Ph.D. diss., Harvard University, 1962), p. 15. This unpublished thesis is a highly detailed account of Massachusetts politics in the mid-30s.

16. Easton, *A Systems Analysis of Political Life,* p. 257.

17. Talcott Parsons, "'Voting' and the Equilibrium of the American Political System," in Burdick and Brodbeck, *American Voting Behavior* (Free Press, 1959), pp. 92-93.

18. See, for example, David Mayhew, *Party Loyalty Among Congressmen* (Harvard University Press, 1966), passim.

19. James Roosevelt and Sidney Shallott, *Affectionately FDR* (Harrap, 1960), p. 202. Also see Curley, pp. 248-252 and Dineen, pp. 204-210.

20. Gorvine, p. 160.

21. Dineen, p. 216.

22. Francis Russell, "The Last of the Bosses," *American Heritage* (June, 1959), p. 87.

23. G. R. Serino, "Italians in the Public Life of Boston," (M.A. thesis, Harvard Uni-

versity, 1950), p. 202.

24. *Boston Post*, October 25, 1936. Quoted in Serino, p. 203.

25. So-called "League of Nations" politics did not prove a great success in 1934 but some of the ethnic groups were showing signs of swinging with the times—the Franco-Americans, formerly heavily Republican, now swung more Democratic. Fitchburg's Ward 2B, heavily Franco-American, voted in Hurley over Dionne by 3 to 1. See Gorvine, pp. 336-350.

26. Gorvine, pp. 458-465.

27. Compare, for example, Wendell D. Howie, *The Reign of James the First* (privately printed, 1936) with Citizens Security Committee, *This Man Curley* (privately printed, 1936) for two diametrically opposed views of the man.

28. Quoted in Gorvine, p. 392.

29. Henry A. Zeiger, *The Remarkable Henry Cabot Lodge* (Popular Library: New York, 1964), p. 53. This appears to have been a "campaign biography" inspired by Lodge's emergence as a possible presidential candidate in early 1964.

30. Curley, pp. 296-299.

31. Lawrence Dame, *New England Comes Back* (Random House: New York, 1940), pp. 17-18, 160-172.

32. Russell, *The Great Interlude,* p. 208.

33. Cutler, pp. 274-275.

34. *Boston Globe,* October 23, 1948.

35. Walter Firey, *Land Use in Central Boston* (Harvard University Press, 1947), p. 188.

36. Serino, p. 10.

37. Public Document No. 43, Election Statistics 1936.

38. "Washington Conversation", a television interview with Leverett Saltonstall, April 1, 1962 (CBS transcript), p. 4.

39. William Foote Whyte, *Street Corner Society* (University of Chicago, 1947, 1955), p. 89.

40. Samuel Lubell, *The Future of American Politics* (Doubleday Anchor ed., 1956), pp. 57-58.

41. Lawrence H. Fuchs, *The Political Behavior of American Jews* (Free Press, 1956), p. 137. Each ward mentioned had at least a 65% majority of the predominant ethnic group.

42. Ibid., p. 136.

43. See Public Document No. 43, Election Statistics 1940, p. 3.

44. *Boston Globe,* November 3 and 4, 1942.

45. Ibid., November 2, 1942.

46. See Frederick L. Collins, "New England's Saltonstall," *The Saturday Evening Post* (October 24, 1942), pp. 14, 46, 48, 50; *Time Magazine*

(April 10, 1944), pp. 19-22, an article entitled "Yankee Face."

47. From an interview given to Professor Robert C. Wood early in 1961 (typescript copy).

48. Leverett Saltonstall, "A Governor looks at Government," *The American Mercury* (November, 1943), p. 525.

49. John Gunther, *Inside U.S.A.* (Harper, 1947), p. 482.

50. *Boston Traveler,* November 8, 1944.

51. Ibid.

52. Gunther, p. 479.

53. *Boston Traveler,* November 6, 1944. Also Gunther, p. 508.

54. Curley, p. 317.

55. *Boston Traveler,* November 9, 1944.

56. Public Document No. 43, Election Statistics 1940, p. 287; 1944, p. 261.

57. Serino, p. 78. Also see *Boston Traveler,* November 9, 1944. The emergence of Italy as a "co-belligerent" in 1944 does not seem to have modified Italian suspicion of Roosevelt.

58. Lubell, p. 225.

59. Gunther, p. 509.

60. *Boston Traveler,* November 6, 1944.

61. Ibid.

62. League of Women Voters of Massachusetts, *Massachusetts State Government* (Harvard University Press, 1956), p. 332.

63. *Boston Herald,* November 1, 1954.

64. Huthmacher, p. 260.

65. Paul David, Malcolm Moos and Ralph Goldman, editors, *Presidential Nominating Politics in 1952* (John Hopkins Press, 1954), Vol. 2, p. 71.

Chapter Four

1. Austin Ranney, "Parties in State Politics," Jacob and Vines, *Politics in the American States* (Little, Brown and Co., 1965), pp. 64-67.

2. V. O. Key, Jr., *American State Politics,* pp. 28-41.

3. V. O. Key, Jr., *American State Politics,* p. 50. For an optimistic account of the possibility of a new Republican "majority coalition," see Kevin P. Phillips, *The Emerging Republican Majority* (Arlington House, 1969), passim. Also see Richard M. Scammon and Ben J. Wattenberg, *The Real Majority* (Coward-McCann 1970) for a view which is more balanced about the Democratic chances for victory in the 1972 presidential election.

4. From November 1918 to November 1964, the State Treasurer was limited to three successive terms. The referendum of 1964 allowed all constitutional offices a four-year term without any limit on the number of terms; this took ef-

fect as from the 1966 election.

5. Robert A. Dahl, *A Preface to Democratic Theory* (University of Chicago, 1963), p. 145.

6. Edgar Litt, *The Political Cultures of Massachusetts* (MIT Press, 1965), pp. 180-185.

7. Duane Lockard, *New England State Politics* (Princeton University Press, 1959), p. 162.

8. Earl Latham and George Goodwin, Jr., *Massachusetts Politics* (Tufts Civic Education Center, 1960), p. 75.

9. *Christian Science Monitor,* April 16, 1966.

10. Ibid., March 30, 1966.

11. Latham and Goodwin, pp. 74-75.

12. See, for example, Gabriel A. Almond and G. Bingham Powell, Jr., *Comparative Politics* (Little, Brown and Co. 1966), p. 259 and passim.

13. Lockard, p. 79.

14. *Time Magazine* (April 10, 1944), p. 19.

15. Robert C. Estall, *New England: A Study in Industrial Adjustment* (G. Bell and Sons 1966), p. 16.

16. Ibid., pp. 114, 119-120.

17. National Planning Association, *The Economic State of New England* (Yale University Press, 1954), p. 341.

18. Ibid., p. 315.

19. New England Council, p. 15.

20. Estall, pp. 86-103.

21. Board of Economic Advisers to the Governor, First Annual Report to the Governor and General Court (Commonwealth of Massachusetts, December, 1964), pp. 4-8.

22. 1960 Census of Population, Vol. 1, Part 23, pp. 23-361, 366 (Table 120).

23. Robert E. Lane, *Political Life* (Free Press, New York, 1959), p. 334.

24. Julian L. Woodward and Elmo Roper, "Political Activity of American Citizens," *APSA Review,* 44 (December, 1950), reprinted in Eulan, Eldersveld and Janowitz, eds., *Political Behavior* (Free Press, 1956), p. 136.

25. C. Wright Mills, *White Collar* (Oxford University Press, 1951; Galaxy ed., 1956), p. 354.

26. Anthony Downs, *An Economic Theory of Democracy* (Harper and Row, 1957), p. 274.

27. See for example, James Q. Wilson and Edward C. Banfield, "Public-Regardingness as a Value Premise in Voting Behavior," *American Political Science Review* (December, 1964), Vol. 58, No. 4., p. 876. Wilson and Banfield suggest that income and ethnicity are important and that middle-class Anglo-Saxons are more likely to be "public-regarding" than any other group.

28. Edgar Litt, "The Politics of a Cultural Minority," in M. K. Jennings and L. K. Zeigler, eds., *The Electoral Process* (Prentice-Hall, 1966) p. 118.

29. See for example, William H. White, *The Organization Man* (Simon and Schuster, 1956; Pelican Books, 1960), pp. 276-277.

30. Lubell, pp. 62-63. Campbell, Converse, Miller and Stokes, *The American Voter* (John Wiley, 1964 ed.), p. 260. Robert C. Wood, *Suburbia* (Houghton Mifflin Co., 1958), Chapter 5.

31. Campbell et al, pp. 244-249.

32. Interview material. Both of those interviewed were residents of Newton and active politically in the "city."

33. Thomas J. Hargadon, "Activists' Political Perception of the Party" (M.Sc. thesis, MIT, 1964), passim.

34. Massachusetts Crime Commission Report, Vol. 1 (Commonwealth of Massachusetts, May 17, 1965), pp. 3-4.

35. Ibid., pp. 64-65.

36. Latham and Goodwin, p. 53. Public Document No. 43, Election Statistics 1964, p. 5. Also interview material. Chapter 55 of the General Laws of the state requires disclosure of all campaign expenditure but few politicians believe the disclosures to be completely accurate. After the 1970 election, Governor Sargent declared over $1.8 million as his provisional total of expenditure in securing reelection.

37. Massachusetts Crime Commission Report, Vol. 1, p. 9.

38. Charles L. Whipple, "Dirty Money in Boston," *Atlantic Monthly* (March, 1961), p. 43.

39. Anthony Lewis, "Corruption in Massachusetts," *New York Times*, June 19, 1961; Reprinted by the New England Citizens Crime Commission, Joy Street, Boston). Massachusetts Crime Commission, Vol. 1, p. 60.

40. Edward Sheehan, "Rogues and Reformers in a State on Trial," *Saturday Evening Post,* June 5, 1965, pp. 34-35, 86-87.

41. Ibid., p. 87.

42. Elliot L. Richardson, "Poisoned Politics," *Atlantic Monthly* (October, 1961), p. 77.

43. Richardson, p. 78.

44. Ronald Wraith and Edgar Simpkins, *Corruption in Developing Countries* (George Allen and Unwin, 1963; W. W. Norton & Co. N.Y., 1964), Conclusion.

45. Sheehan, p. 90.

46. V. O. Key, Jr., *Politics, Parties and Pressure Groups* (Thomas J. Crowell Co., 5th ed., 1964), p. 105.

47. From a duplicated cir-

cular entitled "The Four Year Term and the Initiative Petition" (League of Women Voters of Massachusetts, June 16, 1956).

48. *Christian Science Monitor,* September 8, 1966.

49. *Christian Science Monitor,* September 20 and 21, 1966.

50. From Chandler Stevens' campaign literature, 1964 election.

51. Kenneth Prewitt, "Political Ambitions, Volunteerism and Electoral Accountability," *American Political Science Review,* Vol. 64, No. 1 (March, 1970), p. 15.

Chapter Five

1. Clara Penniman, "The Politics of Taxation," in Jacob and Vines, *Politics in the American States* (Little, Brown and Co., 1965), p. 296 (Table 1).

2. Stephen Rubinstein, "Issues and Problems A, Finance," in Edward C. Banfield and Martha Derthick, *A Report on the Politics of Boston* (Joint Center for Urban Studies of MIT and Harvard University, 1960), p. VI-3. Based on data taken from David P. Rollands, *Property Taxes in Atlanta and Other Large Cities* (Atlanta, 1957).

3. Rubinstein, p. VI-6.

4. "The Governor's Program," a duplicated "kit" produced in 1965, p.1, quoting the 1938 report.

5. Phillips, p. 186.

6. Addresses and Messages to the General Court, Proclamations, Official Addresses and Statements of His Excellency Governor Maurice J. Tobin, 1945 and 1946 (Commonwealth of Massachusetts, 1947), p. 7.

7. James S. Bruner and Sheldon J. Korchin, "The Boss and the Vote," *Public Opinion Quarterly* (Spring, 1946), pp. 1-23.

e 8. Gunther, p. 507.

9. *Boston Herald,* August 3 and 5, 1946.

10. League of Women Voters, pp. 101, 103, 259.

11. *Boston Post,* September 9, 1946.

12. *Boston Globe,* October 22, 1946 (C. R. Owens).

13. *Boston Herald,* November 1, 1946. The list of signatories to this advertisement consists mainly of English and Scots names suggesting that it was aimed at the Anglo-Canadians (surprisingly) and not the French-Canadian immigrants who were "working class."

14. *Boston Herald,* November 6, 1946. The "sweep" in the state was more apparent than real since the Democrats won a Congressional seat (Fourth District) and their losses in the legislature were relatively slight.

15. Addresses and Messages to the General Court, Proclamations, Public Addresses, Official Statements and Correspondence of General Interest of His Excellency Governor Robert F. Bradford, 1947 and 1948 (Commonwealth of Massachusetts, 1949), p. 10 (Inaugural Address, January 2, 1947) and pp. 40-41 (Budget Message, January 22, 1947).

16. *Boston Globe*, October 22, 1948.

17. Ibid., October 25, 1948.

18. *Boston Traveler,* July 12 and 14, 1948. *Boston Post,* September 14 and 19, 1948.

19. *Boston Post*, September 11, 1948.

20. Public Document No. 43, Election Statistics 1948, pp. 142 and 216.

21. John Henry Cutler, *Honey Fitz* (Bobbs-Merrill Co., 1962), p. 317.

22. *Boston Globe,* October 28, 1948. *Boston Sunday Globe,* October 31, 1948. One Globe reporter, Doris Fleeson, did feel that Dewey and Bradford "may really be in trouble" due to a drop in their lead as shown in the polls.

23. *Boston Herald,* November 4, 1948.

24. Opponents to the amendment included Governor Bradford, Attorney General Clarence Barnes, James Michael Curley and the Roman Catholic establishment. See, for example, John Fenton, *The Catholic Vote* (Hauser Press, 1960), Chapter 11.

25. Clinton Rossiter, *Parties and Politics in America* (Cornell University Press, 1960), pp. 148-149.

26. Robert C. Wood, "The Metropolitan Governor" (Ph.D. thesis, Harvard University, 1949), p. 103.

27. William V. Shannon, in Robert S. Allen, *Our Sovereign State* (Vanguard Press, 1949), pp. 24-25.

28. Wood, "The Metropolitan Governor," pp. 138-139.

29. Latham and Goodwin, pp. 16-18. The "gerrymander" was named for Elbridge Gerry, Governor 1810-1812.

30. McCormack and Democratic leaders in the General Court had commissioned a survey which showed that Tobin's 1944 majority, if reflected in the House districts, would have given a Democratic majority there. Interview material.

31. Shannon, in Allen, p. 59.

32. *Boston Herald,* November 5, 1948.

33. See Addresses and Messages to the General Court, Proclamations, Public Addresses, Official Statements of General Interest of His Excellency Governor Paul A. Dever (Commonwealth of Massachusetts, 1952), p. 62.

34. *Boston Herald,* September 7, 1950.

35. Lockard, pp. 141-143.

36. See, for example, the editorial "Dever and Prosperity," *Boston Post,* October 27, 1952. In 1958, it was disclosed that Fox had secured two loans at this time to help the *Post,* one from Bernard Goldfine via Paul Dever and another from Joseph Kennedy. Fox, in testimony before the Special U.S. House Sub-Committee on Legislative Oversight, insisted that the loans had no connection with his decision to support Dever, John Kennedy and the Democratic ticket! *New York Times,* June 17, 18, 28, 1958.

37. James Reichley, *States in Crisis* (University of North Carolina Press, 1964), p. 151. *Boston Post,* October 5, 1952.

38. *Boston Traveler,* September 3, 9-15, 1952.

39. Dever's vote in the primary was 310,505 while Cronin's (as Secretary) was 346,633 and Buckley's (as Treasurer), 362,184. Public Document No 43, 1952, pp. 140, 149, 158.

40. From a duplicated sheet entitled "Massachusetts Republican District Council Organization" in the possession of Mr. Tyler.

41. League of Women Voters, pp. 324-325; Latham and Goodwin, pp. 43-45. The pre-primary convention law was repeated once more in 1972.

42. *Boston Herald,* November 6, 1952.

43. See especially David, Moos and Goldman, pp. 84 and 98.

44. Ibid., pp. 85-86. Eleven French-Canadians, seven Irish, three Italians, four Jews, etc.

45. Ibid., pp. 92-95.

46. Campbell et al. *Elections and the Political Order* (John Wiley and Sons, 1966), p. 71.

47. Laurence H. Fuchs, "Presidential Politics in Boston; the Irish Response to Stevenson," *New England Quarterly* (December, 1957), p. 438.

48. Ibid., p. 445.

49. Pittsfield Project 1952, Elmo Roper Center, Williams College, Mass., October-November 1952, pp. 34 and 38. (Table Fourteen).

50. See for example W. E. Mullins in the *Boston Herald,* November 7, 1952, who claims that only Ohio and Colorado exceeded Massachusetts in split-ticket voting.

51. *Boston Traveler,* June 2, 1954.

52. Reichley, p. 153. *Boston Traveler,* June 7, 1954.

53. Public Document No. 43, Election Statistics, 1954, p. 119.

54. Kevin O'Connell, "The Party and the People—A Case Study in the Politics of Democracy—The Massachusetts Democratic Campaign for Governor, 1954" (Harvard B.A.

thesis, 1955), passim.

55. *Boston Traveler,* June 14 and 22, 1954.

56. Quoted by W. J. McCarthy in the *Boston Herald,* November 4, 1954.

57. Addresses and Messages to the General Court, Proclamations, Public Addresses, Official Statements and Correspondence of General Interest of His Excellency Governor Christian A. Herter (Commonwealth of Massachusetts, 1956), p. 6.

58. Ibid., pp. 13-14.

59. Ibid., p. 684.

60. *Boston Herald,* June 17, 1956.

61. *Boston Herald,* June 10, 1956.

62. Ibid.

63. Public Document No. 43, Election Statistics 1956, pp. 238 and 247.

64. *Boston Herald,* June 10, 1956.

65. *Boston Globe,* September 20, 1956.

66. Fuchs, *Presidential Politics,* pp. 442-443. Pittsfield Project Survey No. 10, October, 1956. 55% of the sample thought that Eisenhower "would handle our foreign affairs well" and 56% thought that he "would keep this country at peace."

67. Public Document No. 43; Election Statistics, 1952, pp. 316-317, 1956, pp. 312-313.

68. Ibid.; 1948, p. 287; 1952, p. 315; 1956, p. 311.

69. *Boston Herald,* November 8, 1956. W. E. Mullins called it "probably the greatest incidence of ticket splitting in local election history". See Table Sixteen.

70. *Boston Sunday Herald,* November 4, 1956.

71. *Boston Sunday Globe,* November 11, 1956.

72. By May 1962, 52% of a sample of Massachusetts voters believed that corruption in Massachusetts was worse than in other states. See *Massachusetts Voters Talk,* prepared by Opinion Research Corporation, New Jersey (Mass. Federation of Taxpayers Associations, 1962), p. 47.

73. John Foster (pseudonym), *Let George Do it* (Harcourt, Brace and Co., 1957), passim.

74. Special Commission on the Audit of State Needs, Needs in Massachusetts Higher Education (Commonwealth of Massachusetts, 1958), p. 35.

75. Address and Messages to the General Court, Public Speeches and other Papers of General Interest of his Excellency Governor Foster Furcolo (Commonwealth of Massachusetts, 1961), pp. 68-87.

76. John Mallan and George Blackwood, "The Tax that Beat a Governor," in A. Westin, ed., *The Uses of Power* (Harcourt, Brace and World

1962) pp. 310-312.

77. Ibid., p. 318.

78. *New York Times,* September 1, 1958.

79. Public Document No. 43, Election Statistics, p. 158.

80. Ibid., p. 70. Also James L. Collier, *The Chub Peabody Story* (Popular Library: New York, 1964), p.89.

81. Public Document No. 43 and the *Boston Globe,* November 5, 1958.

82. *Boston Globe,* November 5, 1958.

83. Relevant issues of Public Document No. 43. David Farrell stated in the *Boston Herald,* June 8, 1960, "The state's senatorial districts have been reorganised to favor the perpetuation of the Democratic Party in power in the State Senate."

84. *Boston Globe,* September 11, 1960.

85. Addresses and Messages to the General Court, Public Speeches and Other Papers of General Interest of His Excellency Governor Foster Furcolo for the years 1957, 1958, 1959 and 1960 (Commonwealth of Massachusetts, 1961), p. 216.

86. *New York Times,* October 18, 1959.

87. Lockard, Chapter 5, passim.

88. Ibid., pp. 151-158. Malcolm Jewell, *The State Legislature* (Random House, 1962),

Chapter 3, passim.

Chapter Six

1. Arthur W. Schlesinger, Jr., *A Thousand Days* (Houghton Mifflin Co., 1965), p. 91.

2. See James MacGregor Burns, *John Kennedy* (Avon Book ed., 1961), p. 30.

3. Quoted by Robert F. Kennedy in his introduction to John F. Kennedy, *A Nation of Immigrants* (Popular Library ed., 1964), p. 10.

4. Burns, p. 49.

5. William Manchester, *Portrait of a President* (McFadden-Bartell ed., 1964, 1967), p. 57.

6. Richard J. Whalen, *The Founding Father* (New American Library, 1964), p. 34. Joe McCarthy, *The Remarkable Kennedys* (Dial Press: N.Y., 1960), pp. 77 and 84.

7. Burns, p. 73.

8. *Boston Sunday Herald,* March 26, 1967 (article by Joseph Dever). See also *Congressional Quarterly Guide* (Spring, 1966), p. 73.

9. Cutler, p. 308.

10. *Boston Traveler,* June 15, 1946.

11. *Boston Globe,* June 19, 1946.

12. As far as his "image" was concerned, John Kennedy's dislike of hats appears to have

been genuine but the public avoidance of cigar smoking was a ploy for he enjoyed them in private (See illustration in Tom Wicker, *Kennedy Without Tears,* (Wm. Morrow and Co., 1964), p. 33).

13. Theodore C. Sorensen, *Kennedy* (Hodder and Stoughton ed., 1965), pp. 334 and 338.

14. Burns, p. 79.

15. *Boston Herald,* September 22, 1950.

16. Sorensen, pp. 57-58. Whalen, p. 419.

17. Zeiger, *The Remarkable Henry Cabot Lodge* (Popular Library: New York, 1964), p. 112.

18. Whalen, pp. 430-431. *New York Times,* June 17, 1958.

19. *New York Times,* June 28, 1958.

20. "Congress and the Nation, 1945-64," *Congressional Quarterly* (June, 1965), pp. 1701-1703.

21. *New York Times,* June 28, 1958.

22. Pittsfield Project 1952, August and October Surveys (Elmo Roper Center, Williams College, Mass.) Kennedy received 43.7% of the total vote in Pittsfield in the November election, Lodge received 49.6%.

23. Richard Rovere, *Senator Joe McCarthy* (Methuen and Co., 1960), pp. 16-17; Burns, Chapter 8; Sorensen, pp. 45-49.

24. Excerpt from a B.B.C. radio program, "J. F. Kennedy—Inquest on a Reputation," broadcast on April 16, 1967 (typed transcript).

25. Kennedy's biographers make it plain that the ambition to be president was present in embryo from his early days in the Senate. Sorensen, pp. 95-96; Schlesinger, pp. 98-99.

26. Burns, pp. 169-173. Sorensen, pp. 78-80. Also from an interview with a member of the state committee and subsidiary interview material.

28. Burns, pp. 146-147.

29. Sorensen, p. 77.

30. "How Kennedy Did It," Thomas Winship in the *Boston Sunday Globe,* November 9, 1958.

31. Philip E. Converse, "Religion and Politics; the 1960 Election," in Campbell et al. *Elections and the Political Order,* pp. 96-124.

32. Interview material.

33. From a 1965 interview.

34. Schlesinger, p. 92.

35. *New York Times,* December 17, 1961.

36. Whalen, pp. 474-475.

37. Murray Levin, *Kennedy Campaigning* (Beacon Press: Boston, 1966), p. 11.

38. *New York Times,* March 17, 1962.

39. *Boston Globe,* May 23, 1962

40. *Boston Globe,* May 24, 1962. Also interview material.

41. *Boston Globe,* June 8, 1962.

42. *Boston Globe,* June 9, 1962.

43. Ibid. Also see John H. Foster, "Political Parties and Personal Organisation: A Study of Democratic Intra-Party Factionalism in Massachusetts," (B.A. thesis, Williams College, May 1964).

44. Levin, *Kennedy Campaigning,* Chapter 6. Also see Benjamin DeMott, "Party Apolitics," *American Scholar,* Vol. 31 (1961-62), pp. 595-602.

45. Public Document No. 43. Election Statistics 1962, pp. 152-155.

46. This was the first time that the brother of a president had served in the Senate. When Robert Kennedy was elected to the Senate in the 1964 election, it made Joseph Kennedy the only man in American History to have fathered three U.S. senators. Wm. Shannon, *The Heir Apparent* (Macmillan: New York, 1967), p. 74.

47. From "More Democrats for Massachusetts: A Report of the Research and Development Committee" made to Gerard F. Doherty, Chairman, Democratic State Committee, 11 Beacon St., Boston, Mass. (duplicated, October 1963). Also background information from interviews with members of the committee.

48. Interview material.

49. *Boston Traveler,* June 20, 1946.

49. *Congressional Quarterly Guide* (Fall, 1966), pp. 72-73. The *Boston Globe* was active in opposing Morrissey's appointment. See for example, *Boston Sunday Globe,* October 17, 1965.

50. *Boston Globe,* May 15, 1965.

51. *Christian Science Monitor, December 20, 1965.*

52. *Boston Globe,* July 17, 1968. The delegation was, of course, committed to Eugene McCarthy on the first ballot as a result of the presidential primary.

53. While Kevin White was hospitalized in the closing stages of the 1970 campaign, Edward Kennedy did intervene by accompanying the gubernatorial candidate's wife around the state in support of her husband's candidacy. *Christian Science Monitor,* November 2, 1970.

54. Unofficial returns suggested that the Senator had acquired 62% of the vote and this was the figure that received nation-wide and world-wide publicity. In fact, the more accurate tabulations of a week or two later showed that he had only 58.8% of the total vote. David Harrison, who had been a member of the Massachusetts House of Representatives,

was defeated in November 1970.

Chapter Seven

1. See the following: Murray B. Levin, *The Alienated Voter* (Holt, Rhinehart and Winston, 1960), Murray B. Levin and George Blackwood, *The Compleat Politician* (Bobbs-Merrill Co. Ltd., 1962). Murray B. Levin and Murray Eden, "Political Strategy for the Alienated Voter," *Public Opinion Quarterly* (Spring, 1962), pp. 47-63. Murray B. Levin, *Kennedy Campaigning* (Beacon Press: Boston, 1966).

2. One of the photographs used was "cropped" to eliminate the "third man"; on the original this turns out to be Senator John Kennedy!

3. Levin, *The Alienated Voter,* pp. 61-62.

4. Levin, *The Compleat Politician,* p. 164.

5. *Boston Herald-Traveler,* October 2, 1967. *Newsweek* (November 6, 1967).

6. Allen Schick, "Massachusetts Politics: Political Reform and 'Alienation,'" in Robert Robbins, ed., *State Government and Political Responsibility 1963* (Tufts University, 1963).

7. Lipset, *Political Man,* pp. 216-217 (based on materi-al drawn from V. O. Key, Jr.). Also see Berelson, Lazarsfeld and McPhee, *Voting* (University of Chicago Press, 1954), p. 314, for another treatment of "apathy" in voting behavior.

8. Quoted in Banfield and Derthick, *Report on the Politics of Boston* p. 111-13 (Joint Center for Urban Studies of MIT and Harvard University, 1960).

9. See, for example, Robert Lane, *Political Life* (Free Press, 1959), pp. 166-169.

10. Steven Lukes, "Alienation and Anomie," in Laslett and Runciman, eds., *Philosophy Politics and Society* (Basil Blackwell: Oxford, England, 1967), p. 135. Lukes suggests that ". . . modern versions of these concepts vary widely in the range of their empirical reference."

11. Levin, *The Compleat Politician,* pp. 92-97. Under state law, the Secretary is responsible for the design of the ballot paper and his name was picked out in bolder type than his opponents. This was probably the work of an over-enthusiastic subordinate, since it seems unlikely that Ward would deliberately leave himself open to criticism in this way.

12. *Boston Herald,* November 1, 1966.

13. *Boston Globe,* June 18, 1960. Furcolo received 1,189 of the 1,608 delegate votes to

331 for O'Connor.

14. *Boston Sunday Globe,* June 19, 1960.

15. *Boston Globe,* September 14, 1960.

16. *Boston Traveler,* November 8, 1960. Volpe took six of Boston's twenty-two wards and ran ahead of the usual Republican vote in many others. It was later estimated that 100,000 Democrats of Italian ancestry switched their vote to Volpe. See James L. Collier, *The Chub Peabody Story* (Popular Library, 1964), p. 105.

17 All figures taken from Public Document No. 43, Election Statistics 1960.

18. *Boston Traveler,* November 11, 1960.

19. *Boston Globe,* November 10, 1960. There is a belief that the many Italian voters, who would have voted for Furcolo against Saltonstall, abstained. (Interview material.)

20. Frank Colcord, "The Politics of Metropolitan Transportation" (Ph. D. thesis, MIT, 1964), passim.

21. Ibid., p. 157. Also Addresses and Messages to the General Court, Proclamations, Public Addresses, Official Statements and Correspondence of General Interest of His Excellency Governor John A. Volpe for the years 1961 and 1962. Compiled and edited by Leslie G. Ainley (Commonwealth of Massachusetts, n.d.), pp. 365-372.

22. Volpe's Addresses and Messages, pp. 126-128.

23. Massachusetts Voters Talk, p. 3.

24. *Boston American,* March 31, 1969, quoted by Greene, pp. 86-87.

25. *Boston Evening Globe,* October 17, 1960, quoted by Greene, p. 85.

26. *New York Times,* June 21, 1961. Also see Litt, *The Political Cultures of Massachusetts* (MIT Press, 1965), pp. 157-158. Iannello was reelected while serving a jail term.

27. *Boston Herald,* October 27, 1962.

28. *Boston Globe,* May 23, 1962.

29. *Boston Sunday Globe,* June 17, 1962.

30. See especially Benjamin DeMott, "Party Apolitics," *American Scholar,* Vol. 31 (1961-62).

31. *Boston Globe,* June 6, 1962.

32. *Boston Traveler,* September 21, 1962.

33. See especially Collier, chapters 2-5.

34. DeMott, p. 598.

35. *Boston Traveler,* September 20, 1962 (Cornelius Dalton).

36. *Boston Globe,* November 2, 1962 (Robert Healy).

37. *Boston Globe,* Novem-

ber 1, 1962.

38. *Boston Globe,* November 7, 1962.

39. *Boston Globe,* November 7, 1962.

40. *Time Magazine* (February 17, 1967).

41. Governor Endicott Peabody, "A Partnership for Progress 1963-65" (Commonwealth of Massachusetts, n.d.), p. 4.

42. Quoted in Colcord, p. 295.

43. Colcord, pp. 338-347. Also see a Message of His Excellency Governor Endicott Peabody delivered in a Joint Convention of the Two Houses, Relative to the Transportation Problems of the Commonwealth, April 21, 1964 (Senate Paper No. 820), especially p. 13.

44. There were evidently more than 100 indictments of this type handed down by grand juries during the four years that Brooke was Attorney General. *Time Magazine* (February 17, 1967).

45. *Boston Sunday Globe,* July 11, 1965.

46. *U.S. News and World Report* (February 1, 1965), p. 70.

47. *Boston Traveler,* June 11, 1964.

48. Sheehan, "Rogues and Reformers in a State on Trial," *Saturday Evening Post,* June 5, 1965, p. 30.

49. *Boston Traveler,* June 4, 1964.

50. A typical Bellotti ad. was the following on the eve of the poll: "Tomorrow the politicians will vote for Peabody. The people will vote for Bellotti for governor." *Boston Globe,* September 7, 1964.

51. "Image, organization and reform" defeated him according to Robert Healy in the *Boston Globe,* September 15, 1964.

52. *Boston Globe,* September 3 and 4, 1964.

53. *Boston Globe,* September 10 and 11, 1964.

54. *Boston Sunday Globe,* September 15, 1964.

55. Thomas C. Gallagher in the *Boston Herald,* October 22, 1964.

56. *Boston Sunday Herald,* October 18, 1964.

57. Public Document No. 43, Election Statistics 1964.

58. *Boston Evening Globe,* November 4, 1964.

59. *Boston Traveler,* November 6, 1964.

60. Voting and Civil Rights in Springfield, an analysis of a post-election survey conducted by students at Mount Holyoke and Amherst Colleges in Springfield, November, 1964, directed by Richard L. Hendrickson (Amherst-Mount Holyoke Political Studies Center, January, 1965), p. 16.

61. The Democratic presidential vote was 74.7%, a record for the state and about 25% ahead of that received by Bellotti.

62. Brooke won virtually every town and city in the state, even including Boston. The only victories for his rival that one can find in the P.D. 43 are two towns in Worcester County, Blackstone and Millville.

63. *Boston Sunday Globe,* November 8, 1964.

64. See *Boston Globe,* October 7, 1966; *Boston Traveler,* April 26, 1966, *Boston Sunday Herald,* May 29, 1966. McCormack used the issue in his 1966 campaign. See *Christian Science Monitor,* October 11, 1966.

65. Massachusetts Crime Commission Report, Volume I, p. 2.

66. Ibid., p. 9.

67. Ibid., pp. 31 and 37.

68. Massachusetts Crime Commission Report, Vol. 1, pp. 67-71.

69. From "The Governor's Program", the duplicated "kit" cited earlier. It was produced by Governor Volpe's staff in 1965, setting out the arguments for the sales tax and countering the objections levelled against it.

70. *Boston Sunday Herald,* October 31, 1965.

71. *Christian Science Monitor,* September 17, 1965.

72. Ibid., October 1–26, 1965.

73. Ibid., November 19 and December 1, 1965. The tax was fixed at 3%, with exemptions that included food, clothing, rent and utilities. Several minor taxes were included in the "package" including a 5% tax on hotel/motel rooms and increases in cigarette and liquor tax.

74. See articles by the late Edgar Mills in the *Christian Science Monitor,* July 11 and September 17, 1966. The successful bills included some in the fields of housing, water pollution and recreation but little of the highway safety program that the governor had tried to press on the legislature.

75. *Boston Sunday Globe,* June 19, 1966. The question was to be an academic one since both men found themselves members of the Nixon Administration in 1969.

76. *Boston Sunday Herald,* June 26, 1966. Sargent resigned his position prior to the Convention to enter the contest.

77. Ibid.

78. *Christian Science Monitor,* June 11, 1966. *Boston Sunday Herald,* June 12, 1966.

79. *Boston Sunday Globe,* June 12, 1966.

80. *Boston Sunday Globe,* June 17, 1966.

81. James G. Colbert, *Brookline Chronicle-Citizen,* September 1, 1966 (citing a *Boston Globe* poll).

82. *Christian Science Mon- 25 and September 24, 1966. By the latter date, 90 seats in the House and 13 in the Senate were still uncon- tested by the Republicans.*

83. *Boston Globe,* Septem- ber 12, 1961.

84. Edward W. Brooke, *The Challenge of Change; Crisis in our Two-Party Sys- tem* (Little, Brown and Co., 1966), esp. p. 26.

85. *Boston Herald,* Octo- ber 18 and 23, 1966. *Boston Globe,* October 24, 1966.

86. *Boston Globe,* October 26, 1966.

87. Figures secured from the Opinion Research Corpo- ration and quoted in the *Christian Science Monitor,* November 11, 1966. Those pertaining to the Brooke-Pea- body contest were later used in John F. Becker and Eugene Heaton, Jr., "The Election of Senator Edward W. Brooke," *Public Opinion Quarterly* (Fall 1967), pp. 346-358.

88. *Christian Science Mon- itor,* November 3, 1966.

89. Ibid., and issue for No- vember 4, 1966.

90. Ibid., March 20, 1967.

91. *Boston Herald,* Novem- ber 10, 1966.

92. Public Document No.

43, Election Statistics 1966, pp. 230-241. The percentage of the two-party votes for the unsuccessful Democrats were: Peabody, 39%; McCormack, 37.1%; McGuire, 44.8%; Bellot- ti 47.7%.

93. *Boston Globe,* Novem- ber 9, 1966.

94. The sales tax was made permanent in 1967.

95. *Christian Science Mon- itor,* December 21, 1967.

96. Sixty percent of the primary vote for the Demo- crats was centered in the New- ton/Watertown/Waltham area. *Christian Science Monitor,* September 7, 1968.

97. Evidence of Republican decline was also noted in the loss of the Sixth Congressio- nal District to the Democrats in a special election in late 1969, giving the Democrats now an 8-4 lead. *Christian Science Monitor,* October 2, 1969.

98. *Christian Science Mon- itor,* September 27, 1970.

99. This is based on one's impression of the telecast from the notorious Chicago Con- vention and informal talks with political figures in Boston in the summer of 1968. It should be noted that McCar- thy only took about 51% of the primary vote because of heavy "write-in" figures for Edward Kennedy, Humphrey and Johnson.

100. *Christian Science Monitor,* June 8, 1970.

101. During the period that Mayor White spent in the hospital shortly before the 1970 general election, Dukakis took on the main burden of electioneering for the Democratic team for these two main executive positions.

Conclusion

1. Samuel C. Patterson, "The Political Cultures of The American States," *The Journal of Politics,* Vol. 1, No. 30 (February 1968), p. 189.

2. Ibid., p. 191.

3. Thomas R. Dye, *Politics in States and Communities* (Prentice-Hall, 1969), p. 8.

4. Gabriel A. Almond and G. Bingham Powell, Jr., *Comparative Politics* (Little, Brown and Co., 1966), p. 50.

5. See for example, Robin M. Williams, Jr., *American Society, A Sociological Interpretation* (Alfred A. Knopf, 1961), p. 25.

6. Almond and Verba, *The Civic Culture* (Little Brown and Co. edn., 1965), p. 30.

7. Ibid., pp. 312-313 and Chapter 11, passim.

8. David Easton, *A Systems Analysis of Political Life* (John Wiley, 1965), pp. 102-103.

9. From Daniel Webster's Second Speech on Foot's Resolution of January 26th, 1830, quoted in Howe, p. XV.

10. See, for example, "Towards a More Responsible Two-Party System, A Report of the Committee on Political Parties," American Political Science Association, Supplement to the *American Political Science Review,* Vol. 44 (September, 1950). For a contemporary critique of this concept, see also Evron M. Kirkpatrick, "Towards a More Responsible Two-Party System: Political Science, Policy Science, or Pseudo-Science?" in *American Political Science Review,* Vol. 65 (December, 1971), pp. 965-990.

Index